# ORIGINALS!

## BLACK WOMEN BREAKING BARRIERS

**JESSIE CARNEY SMITH, PH.D.**

# ABOUT THE AUTHOR

Photo: Vando Rogers

Distinguished in the library profession and a recognized educator, author, and scholar, **Jessie Carney Smith** is Librarian Emerita of Fisk University in Nashville, Tennessee. Previously, she was dean of the library and held the Camille Cosby Distinguished Chair in the Humanities at Fisk. She completed her undergraduate degree at North Carolina A&T State University, continued her studies at Cornell University, holds master's degrees from Michigan State University and Vanderbilt University, and received her Ph.D. from the University of Illinois.

Dr. Smith's work with Visible Ink Press resulted in three previous editions of *Black Firsts*; two editions of *Black Heroes*; *The Handy African American History Book*; and, with her colleague Linda T. Wynn, *Freedom Facts and Firsts: 400 Years of the American Civil Rights Experience*. Other works that she wrote or edited include *Black Women of the Harlem Renaissance Era* (with colleague Dr. Lean'tin L. Bracks); *Encyclopedia of African American Business* (two volumes, two editions); *Encyclopedia of African American Popular Culture* (three volumes); *Notable Black American Women* (Books I, II. and III); *Notable Black American Men* (Books I and II); *Epic Lives: One Hundred Black Women Who Made a Difference*; *Powerful Black Women*; *Ethnic Genealogy*; and *Black Academic Libraries and Research Collections*.

Widely celebrated for her work, Dr. Smith's recognitions include the National Women's Book Association Award; the Candace Award for excellence in education; *Sage* magazine's Anna J. Cooper Award for research on African American women; the Academic/Research Librarian of the Year Award from the Association of College and Research Libraries; the Distinguished Alumni Award from Peabody College of Vanderbilt University; the Distinguished Alumni Award from the University of Illinois, School of Library and Information Science; the Research Career Award from Fisk University; and the Belle Ringer Image Award from Bennett College for Women. She has been cited by the American Library Association for her contributions to that organization and long tenure at Fisk.

# ORIGINALS!

## BLACK WOMEN BREAKING BARRIERS

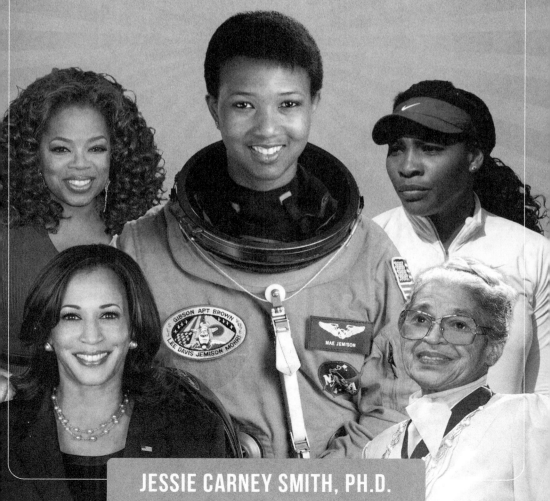

JESSIE CARNEY SMITH, PH.D.

Visible Ink Press®
43311 Joy Rd., #414
Canton, MI 48187-2075

Visible Ink Press is a registered trademark of Visible Ink Press LLC.

Most Visible Ink Press books are available at special quantity discounts when purchased in bulk by corporations, organizations, or groups. Customized printings, special imprints, messages, and excerpts can be produced to meet your needs. For more information, contact Special Markets Director, Visible Ink Press, www.visibleink.com, or 734-667-3211.

Managing Editor: Kevin S. Hile
Cover Art: Graphikitchen, LLC
Typesetting: Cinelli Design
Proofreaders: Larry Baker, Christa Gainor
Indexer: Shoshana Hurwitz

Cover images: stock.adobe.com.

Paperback ISBN: 978-1-57859-759-8
Ebook ISBN: 978-1-57859-771-0
Hardbound ISBN: 978-1-57859-734-5

Cataloging-in-Publication Data is on file at the Library of Congress.

Printed in the United States of America.

10 9 8 7 6 5 4 3 2 1

# TABLE OF CONTENTS

# ALSO FROM VISIBLE INK PRESS

*African American Almanac: 400 Years of Triumph, Courage and Excellence*
By Lean'tin Bracks, Ph.D.
ISBN: 978-1-57859-323-1

*The American Women's Almanac: 500 Years of Making History*
By Deborah G. Felder
ISBN: 978-1-57859-636-2

*Black Firsts: 500 Years of Trailblazing Achievements and Ground-Breaking Events*
By Jessie Carnie Smith, Ph.D.
ISBN: ISBN: 978-1-57859-688-1

*Black Heroes*
By Jessie Carnie Smith, Ph.D.
ISBN: 978-1-57859-136-7

*Freedom Facts and Firsts: 400 Years of the African American Civil Rights Experience*
By Jessie Carnie Smith, Ph.D., and Linda T. Wynn
ISBN: 978-1-57859-192-3

*The Handy African American History Answer Book*
By Jessie Carnie Smith, Ph.D.
ISBN: 978-1-57859-452-8

*The Handy American History Answer Book*
By David L. Hudson, Jr.
ISBN: 978-1-57859-471-9

*The Handy Christianity Answer Book*
By Stephen A. Werner, Ph.D.
ISBN: 978-1-57859-686-7

*The Handy Islam Answer Book*
By John Renard, Ph.D.
ISBN: 978-1-57859-510-5

*Native American Almanac: More Than 50,000 Years of the Cultures and Histories of Indigenous Peoples*
By Yvonne Wakim Dennis, Arlene Hirschfelder, and Shannon Rothenberger Flynn
ISBN: 978-1-57859-507-5

*Native American Landmarks and Festivals: A Traveler's Guide to Indigenous United States and Canada*
By Yvonne Wakim Dennis and Arlene Hirschfelder
ISBN: 978-1-57859-641-6

*Trailblazing Women! Amazing Americans Who Made History*
By Deborah G. Felder
ISBN: 978-1-57859-729-1

*Please visit us at www.visibleinkpress.com.*

# PHOTO SOURCES

Administrative Office of the United States Courts: p. 231.

Alpha Kappa Alpha: p. 315 (top).

Associated Booking Corporation: p. 30 (top).

*The Austin American:* p. 187.

Bassano Ltd.: p. 12 (top).

Bibliothèque National de France: p. 13.

*Bilboard:* p. 30 (bottom).

BlackPast.org: p. 183.

Brazile & Associates LLC: p. 263 (bottom).

Brightline: p. 74.

Career Girls: p. 44.

Carolina Digital Library and Archives: p. 288.

Brian Cavan: p. 84.

CDC Public Health Image Library: p. 108.

*The Champion Magazine:* p. 166.

*Chicago Sun Times:* p. 31 (bottom).

City of Compton: p. 274.

City of Minneapolis Archives: p. 249.

City of San Francisco: p. 278.

Kizzmekia Corbett: p. 312.

*The Crisis:* p. 93.

Virginia DeBolt: p. 40.

DenverStoryTrek.org: p. 300.

District of Columbia, Office of the Secretary: p. 233.

Dutch National Archives: p. 318.

Flickr.com/commons: p. 6.

Mark Flores: p. 71.

Florida Memory Project: p. 219.

Florida Supreme Court: p. 271.

Irvine Garland Penn: p. 7 (top).

Adrian Hood: p. 208.

Valerie Brisco Hooks: p. 322.

Jewish Women's Archive: p. 292.

King Kong Photo & www.celebrity-photos.com: pp. 25, 31 (top).

KTBS News: p. 153.

J. D. Lasica: p. 105.

Library of Congress: pp. 4, 11, 15, 17, 22, 24, 26, 27, 90, 91, 214, 21, 221, 276 (top), 286.

*Los Angeles Daily News:* p. 19.

Los Angeles Public Library: p. 58.

Lyndon B. Johnson Presidential Library: p. 242 (top).

Fraser MacPherson: p. 28 (bottom).

Marion County, Oregon: p. 236.

Jack Mitchell: p. 39.

MGM Television: p. 28 (top).

Marsha Miller: p. 266 (bottom).

Mingle Media TV: p. 203.

Larry D. Moore: p. 142.

NASA: pp. 109, 112, 124, 303 (top and bottom), 304, 307, 310.

National Archives at College Park: p. 167.

National Archives Catalog: p. 16.

National Oceanographic and Atmospheric Administration: p. 262.

New York Public Library: pp. 9, 12 (bottom).

*New York Times:* pp. 7 (bottom), 14.

*New York World-Telegram and Sun:* pp. 215, 317.

Oberlin College Archives: p. 87 (top).

Office of the Surgeon General of the United States: pp. 194, 246.

*PBS NewsHour:* p. 143.

Peabody Awards: p. 139.

Penn Libraries: p. 97.

Bernard Pollack: p. 266 (top).

PopTech.org: p. 276 (bottom).

George Rinhart/Corbis: p. 165.

Rklear (Wikicommons): p. 232.

Russell Roederer: p. 154.

Schlesinger Library on the History of Women in America: pp. 92, 94, 98, 135.

May Wright Sewall: p. 87 (bottom).

*Scott's Official History of the American Negro in the World War*: p. 184.

Lorie Shaull: p. 325.

Shutterstock: pp. 32, 33, 37, 41 (top and bottom), 42, 43 (top and bottom), 45, 46, 47 (top and bottom), 49, 50, 51 (top, middle, bottom), 52, 53 (top and bottom), 54 (top and bottom), 55, 56, 72, 82, 171, 174, 176, 178, 240, 267, 273, 277, 280, 323, 324, 326 (top and bottom), 329, 332, 333, 334, 335 (top and bottom), 336, 337, 338, 339.

John Mathew Smith & www. celebrity-photos.com: p. 122.

Smithsonian American Art Museum: p. 21.

Smithsonian Institution, National Museum of American History: p. 60 (bottom).

Southern California Library for Social Studies and Research: p. 134.

Swann Galleries: p. 149.

Temple University Libraries, Charles L. Blockson Afro-American Collection: p. 315 (bottom).

Tennessee State University Special Collections: p. 103.

Nydia Tisdale: p. 242 (bottom).

TonyTheTiger (Wikicommons): p. 327.

University of Houston Libraries: p. 114.

University of Pennsylvania: p. 133.

U.S. Air Force: pp. 156, 293, 306, 331.

U.S. Army: p. 155 (bottom), 159 (bottom).

U.S. Army Office of Public Affairs: p. 155 (top).

U.S. Congress: pp. 216 (top and bottom), 222, 225 (bottom), 227, 243 (top and bottom), 245 (bottom), 256 (bottom), 256 (top), 272.

U.S. Department of Agriculture: p. 224.

U.S. Department of Defense: p. 159 (top).

U.S. Department of Energy: p. 245 (top).

U.S. Department of Health and Human Services: p. 238.

U.S. Department of Housing and Urban Development: p. 225 (top).

U.S. Department of Labor: p. 328.

U.S. Department of State: p. 263 (top).

U.S. District and Bankruptcy Court, Southern District of Texas: p. 248.

U.S. Embassy, New Zealand: p. 244.

U.S. Government Printing Office: p. 75.

U.S. House of Representatives: pp. 239, 275, 279.

U.S. National Library of Medicine: pp. 302, 305, 309.

U.S. National Park Service: p. 60 (top).

U.S. Navy: pp. 158, 161.

The Visibility Project: p. 81.

Voces de la Frontera: p. 226.

Jim Wallace: p. 118.

White House Staff Photographers Collection: p. 110.

*Who's Who among the Colored Baptists of the U.S.*: p. 8.

William Morris Agency: p. 20.

World Economic Forum: p. 123.

Public domain: pp. 5, 10, 20, 88, 89, 270, 283, 297, 298, 319.

# ACKNOWLEDGMENTS

Pioneering work on black women who made a difference has resulted in recognitions too numerous to mention. Those who have worked with me over the years as we researched the lives and accomplishments of black people for inclusion in the four editions of my book *Black Firsts* share my enthusiasm for producing a different work than readers are accustomed to seeing. That enthusiasm transcends the boundaries of *Black Firsts* and gives greater attention to many women who were achievers and whose work called for a separate publication to give them the recognition that they deserve. *Originals! Black Women Breaking Barriers* is the result.

As we drew women who we call "Originals" from *Black Firsts,* we acknowledge those who inadvertently made this new work possible. I especially appreciate the contributions of Dr. Helen R. Houston, my friend and retired English professor from Tennessee State University; and Cheryl J. Hamberg, another friend and former staff member of the Fisk University library. As they remained vigilant to the topic and the importance of first black achievers, other members of our library staff who provided information are Bryanna Farris, DeLisa Minor Harris, Brandon Owens, and Rachel Delaney (who moved on to another library).

I am indebted to members of my family for the information that they shared. They are nieces Dr. Duane P. Lambeth and Karen Carney Filmore; nephew Frank T. "Frankie" Lambeth Jr; and last but never least, my son, Frederick "Ricky" Smith.

Thanks to the Visible Ink team for a long and pleasant working relationship. Publisher Roger Jänecke, thanks for yielding to my persuasion to focus this new work on women; and editor Kevin Hile, thanks for your superb editorial skill. Thanks also to proofreaders Larry Baker and Christa Gainor and to indexer Shoshana Hurwitz, as well as typesetter Marco Divita and designers John Gouin and Allesandro Cinelli.

To all of those acknowledged here, please know that you helped me to bring out a different work on black women whose names and contributions are again enshrined in history.

# INTRODUCTION

This inaugural work is a spinoff of my popular book *Black Firsts*, which was initially published in 1994 and covers many years of trailblazing, groundbreaking, pioneering, and historical events of black men and women in America. Titled *Originals!: Black Women Breaking Barriers*, we limit the entries to black women in America, and we view them as groundbreaking, pioneering, and so on just as we did in the parent work. This is the culmination of my long-established desire to make available a single work on black women and a chance to focus on another direction—that is, "firsts." It is another way of saying that there is a continuing need to give our women the focus that they deserve.

We direct this work to the younger set—teenagers and young adults who have an interest in black women, black women firsts, or who may be stimulated to develop that interest. Still, we encourage people of various races, ages, genders, and backgrounds to enjoy the work. The entries cover the earliest date that we could document, and we end primarily with 2020. A few pioneering entrants for 2021 are included. As much as we were tempted to include more entrants for 2021, we were restricted to meeting short deadlines, making the work available for quick reading, and providing a teachable moment for librarians, educators, and parents. To keep within the limited space available, we shortened most of the original selections.

Our "Originals" include black women who came to America with their families and were enslaved. They came in chains along with their cultural agendas. This transcended generations, and they refused to discard their musical and artistic talents from the slave plantation and beyond. Enriched with slave songs or spirituals, dance, and use of musical instruments, their talents entertained families and slave contacts. Perhaps the most fertile period of artistic expression came at a time known as the Harlem Renaissance, the years between 1920 and the mid-1930s. In the works that these women produced during this period and beyond, they aimed to remove old negative stereotypes and highlight the positive side of black culture. They were talented in art, dance, music, and other forms of cultural expression, and they recorded their talents in the books and essays that they wrote. From that point forward, we know these women by their works.

In this volume, we celebrate the life and times of some of our achievers, including artists Augusta Savage and Edmonia "Wildfire" Lewis; dancers like Janet Collins, Katherine Dunham, and Misty Copeland; and actors, directors and playwrights Anita Bush, Florence Mills, and Anna Deavere Smith. Our musical women include Elizabeth Taylor Greenfield ("the black swan"), Marian Anderson, Bessie Smith, Billie Holiday, Rosetta Tharpe, Gertrude "Ma" Rainey, and Ella Fitzgerald. Women artists in film, radio, and television include Fredi Washington, Halle Berry, Viola Davis, Catherine "Cathy" Hughes, Shonda Lynn Rhimes, and Oprah Winfrey. Our barrier-breakers who expressed themselves with the mighty pen include Phyllis Wheatley, Zora Neale Hurston, Maya Angelou, Octavia Butler, Alice Walker, and Toni Morrison. Officials honored some of them for their work and made them Pulitzer Prize and Nobel Prize winners.

When black women crossed America's shores, they came with entrepreneurial skills. Although unable to know whether they would be able to demonstrate these skills, for many years they lost the opportunity. From exquisite embroidering and fashionable dressmaking, which early black women practiced, they demonstrated entrepreneurial skills later on by opening businesses like beauty shops. Madame C. J. Walker and Annie Turnbow Malone remain the most popular icons of the early beauty industry. Both became millionaires.

Feminist and bank founder Maggie Lena Walker exemplifies the success of other black women who became important business leaders in the black community and beyond. The power of black women business leaders strengthened and expanded over the years as they became automobile dealers and plant managers, opened restaurants, and moved into leadership positions in major companies. Ann Fudge, Ursula Burns, and Rosalind "Roz" Brewer are examples of women who headed Fortune 500 companies or led divisions of other prominent companies.

Whether they came to America as slaves or were freeborn Americans, this nation consistently denied black women their human rights. They responded by becoming warriors for racial justice, abolitionists, participants in the Underground Railroad, and prominent civil rights activists. Tenacious leader Harriet Tubman led about three hundred enslaved people to freedom, and her work enshrined her in the annals of American history.

Our women were pioneers in the modern Civil Rights Movement. They led the courts to dismantle laws that enforced segregation in interstate transportation, as seen in the work of Irene Morgan (Kirkaldy). Both black and white high school and college students joined the Sit-In Movement. The result of the work of black women activists led to the removal of many racial barriers to freedom throughout the nation. The legendary Rosa Parks, who was active in the massive 1955 Montgomery Bus Boycott, stands out as a monument to the freedom of black American people, despite the limitations resulting from that protest. Black women's civil rights leadership helped to bring about changes in practically every area known. Their leadership enabled them to establish, direct, and participate in women's organizations, serve on corporate boards, and become mayors of cities. They continue to spread their trailblazing and groundbreaking achievements throughout the nation.

During slavery, segregationists aimed to prevent blacks from learning to read or write (although many did so), thus underscoring the need to educate the black community. Black women were always believers in education and seized opportunities to overcome obstacles to training their families and themselves. In time, black women became teachers, school principals, school founders, college presidents, medical school leaders and educators, and law school founders and administrators. Virginia Estelle Randolph became an outstanding educator known as a Jeanes teacher; she concentrated on improving education in small, rural schools in the South. Among our early school founders were Lucy Laney, founder of Haines Normal and Industrial Institute; Charlotte Hawkins Brown, founder of Palmer Memorial Institute; and Mary McLeod Bethune, who founded what became Bethune-Cookman University. As the need to educate our women became a critical issue, educators founded colleges exclusively for black women, such as Hartshorne Memorial College and Mary Holmes Seminary.

Although established to educate black men and women, Bennett College for Women and Spelman College are the only existing institution whose mission is to educate black women. Among the prominent black women educators in higher education are Johnnetta Betsch Cole, Anna Cherrie Epps, Ruth J. Simmons, and Dorothy Cowser Yancy. We also recognize the women cited here as role models for the young, emerging educators.

Newspapers spread the voice of black American women, especially in the early years of the black press. They were protest-oriented and focused on slavery, lynching, brutality against entire black families, and other examples of racial injustice. Early journalist Ida B. Wells (Barnett) and later editors and journalists like Gertrude Emily Hicks Bustill Mossell, Charlotta A. Spears Bass, and Elizabeth B. Murphy Moss (Phillips) ensured that the voices of our women would remain in the news. Black women founded and/or edited newspapers and headed nationally circulated black newspapers. Later, they occupied prominent roles in the broadcast media, anchored and co-anchored television news programs, and served as reporters for nationally televised sports programs.

This nation's racial segregation practices have covered practically every aspect of life, and the military embraced that practice. We acknowledge Harriet Tubman for her work as conductor on the Underground Railroad. History has given little attention to her work as nurse, cook, and laundress for Union troops in South Carolina during the Civil War. We cite the efforts of Cathay Williams, the first and only known female member of the Buffalo Soldiers—the first all-black unit for men in the regular army that was created in 1867. After the military ceased racial exclusionary practices, our women joined the various units in existence or those soon established. Later, they held high military ranks such as brigadier general, four-star-general, and four-star admiral. One woman was the first black to lead the Long Gray Line at West Point. Our women commanded warships, and some gave to this country their full measure of devotion.

Our women are leaders of their own organizations as well as those that were once racially exclusive. These include national organizations for educators, scientists, entrepreneurs, and others. Perhaps the subject area in which most black women firsts fall is politics, including at the local, state, and federal levels. We rejoiced when they became mayors, judges, legislators, and heads of federal departments. We proudly recognized them when they became attorney general of the United States, secretary of state, and members of congress, which put them in powerful positions to help shape policies for a race that this nation should have never ignored. Black women and their daughters proudly hailed Michelle Robinson Obama when she became the first black first lady of the United States. When we saw our first black vice president of the United States—a woman—we witnessed a magnificent achievement that had been far too long in coming. Kamala Harris immediately became a prime role model for young girls of different races.

Male religious leaders denied women access to the pulpit for many years, yet some sources indicate that unlicensed female preachers existed. There are references to early faith healers and traveling evangelists. Abolitionist Sojourner Truth was one of our early black women religious leaders. One religious leader founded a large Shaker family. In 2009, we saw our first ordained rabbi in Jewish history. Women never failed to protest against their mistreatment in the ministry, and in the 1900s many joined the feminist movement and embraced a trend called woman's theology, a term that writer and Pulitzer Prize-winner Alice Walker called "Womanist" theory.

Our enslaved female ancestors were concerned about the unsanitary conditions in which society forced them to live. When ill, they treated themselves and their families with herbs, barks, and other items then common in the household and in their communities. In time, women became involved in the medical community and were formally educated or treated in black medical facilities and black medical schools. Finally, previously segregated mainstream medical facilities admitted them. Two of our black colleges established medical schools early on. Black women also became veterinarians, and some were educated at Tuskegee University, and to this day about 70 percent of black veterinarians in the United States are alumni of Tuskegee.

In science and space, we note the accomplishments of our first black woman astronaut. We highlight the work of three black women pioneers known as "hidden figures." Black women were also inventors and received patents for their creations. We acknowledge the pioneering work of Kizzmekia "Kizzy" Corbett, the female lead scientist in COVID-19 vaccine research, and we credit her with helping to save lives worldwide.

Barrier-breaking black women have made outstanding contributions to sports—an area long dominated by men. Due in large measure to Title IX of the Civil Rights Act, our women are engaged in sports activities such as basketball, baseball, tennis, golf, track and field, and swimming. They are players, coaches, referees, organizers, and members of important sports boards. They have distinguished themselves in college sports for women, on professional teams, and by winning medals in the Olympics. Well before the 2020 Olympics held in Tokyo in 2021, Simone Biles brought distinguished performance to gymnastics and became the world's greatest gymnast. In the Tokyo Olympics, Allyson Felix became the most decorated track and field athlete in Olympic history.

Our research identified black women firsts in numerous categories. They became accomplished aviators, and winners of prestigious awards. They have won titles such as Miss America, and had ships named for them. Our women continue to gain recognition in existing and new areas, attesting to the fact that they are historymakers, innovators, groundbreakers, explorers, pioneers, trailblazers, barrier-breakers, and visionary leaders.

# Arts & Entertainment

Despite the experiences of women in America who endured discrimination because of race, gender, or age, those of the black race set their own cultural agenda when they entered the United States and extended it to the present time. They came to America in chains, but the chains never prevented them from exercising their musical and artistic talent, or from giving full expression to their creativity on the slave plantation and beyond. Their cultural expressions shaped the slave communities where they lived, the white community, which they served, and much later the broader community.

The birth of slave songs or spirituals, dance, and use of musical instruments can be traced to this time. The hidden messages that the slave songs presented were meant to console and entertain their families and slave contacts, as a shield against the inhumanity of the enslaved, and to instruct their people to get ready for a change—an escape. For example, enslaved people told of a planned escape by using the words "Jordan River" when they sang, which meant that the route would be by means of the nearby river.

As time passed from that distressing period, African American women never lost their desire to express their cultural strivings and talent in the arts and humanities. Perhaps the most fertile period of artistic expression came during a time known as the Harlem Renaissance, which fermented much earlier but found expression around 1920 and extended into the mid-1930s. It was a literary and cultural movement of black Americans to celebrate their culture and racial identity. They sought to remove old racial stereotypes and highlight their positive side. Black women before, during, and after this era were talented in art, dance, and music. They were writers whose works went down in history and are still studied and analyzed.

As the Harlem Renaissance moved toward an end, there were organized efforts of the federal government to encourage and support black artistic talent of men and women artists, dramatists, and writers. These programs were the Works Progress Administration and the Federal Theatre Project.

Among those talented in art and sculpture were Elizabeth Catlett, Edmonia "Wildfire" Lewis, and Augusta Savage. Black women demonstrated another form of cultural expression that expanded into an artistic form that struck a chord among audiences. These artists include dancers Janet Collins, Katherine Dunham, and more recently Misty Copeland. Black women excelled as actresses, directors, and playwrights in drama and theater, as seen in the works of early achievers Anita Bush and Florence Mills and later followed by Ruby Dee and Anna Deavere Smith.

Many Americans label blacks as musical people. Without a doubt, women of the race continue to make an unparalleled mark on this art form. They are celebrated singers like nineteenth-century concert singer Elizabeth Taylor Greenfield (called "the Black Swan"), followed by an array of singers, composers, and choral directors, and those with other musical talents. These included Marian Anderson, Billie Holiday, Lillian Evanti, Florence Beatrice Price, Rosetta Tharpe, Bessie Smith, Gertrude "Ma" Rainey, Ella Fitzgerald, Ethel Waters, and Queen Latifah.

Black women artists excelled in film, radio, and television. Film stars, directors, and writers Fredi Washington, Euzhan Palcy, Whoopi Goldberg, Halle Berry, and Viola Davis are a few examples. Dorothy Brunson, Bernadine Washington, and Catherine "Cathy" Liggins Hughes are among the radio station owners and managers. Television stars, writers, and hosts like Della Reese, Cicely Tyson, Diahann Carroll, Shonda Lynn Rhimes, Tamron Hall, Robin Roberts, and Oprah Winfrey helped to portray black women in positive and meaningful roles.

Perhaps nothing can exceed the rich results of black women's mighty pen. There were nonfiction writers dating back to 1835, when Susan Paul emerged, followed much later by Zora Neale Hurston and Maya Angelou. Nonfiction writers Harriet E. Adams Wilson (first black woman to publish a novel), Ann Petry, and science-fiction writer

Octavia Butler took their place in history. Other poets include Lucy Terry Prince, our first American poet. African-born Phillis Wheatley emerged as the first person in America to publish a book of poetry, and one whose name is widely known throughout the country. Other black women poets include Gwendolyn Brooks, the previously noted Maya Angelou, Pulitzer Prize winners Gwendolyn Brooks and Alice Walker, and Nobel Prize winner Toni Morrison.

This review of black American women who were first to achieve in the arts and humanities is at most a snapshot of their pioneering work to showcase the contributions of their efforts.

## HISTORIC SLAVE WOMAN POET                     1746

*LUCY TERRY (PRINCE) (1730?–1821)*, a slave and orator, was the first black American poet. "Bars Fight," written this year (her only known poem), was inspired by an Indian ambush of haymakers in the Bars, a small plateau near Deerfield, Massachusetts. It was published in 1855, in Josiah Gilbert Holland's *History of Western Massachusetts*. Terry was kidnapped as an infant in Africa and brought to Rhode Island. In 1756 Terry married Abijah Prince and obtained her freedom.

## 1835            TREND-SETTING BIOGRAPHER

*SUSAN PAUL (1809–1841)* wrote *Memoir of James Jackson, the Attentive and Obedient Scholar, Who Died in Boston, October 31, 1833, Aged Six Years and Eleven Months*, the first black American biography. She was also the first black American to write an evangelical juvenilia. The work was based on Paul's daily experiences as a teacher with a child named Jackson. Paul was one of the black women in Boston who joined the Boston Female Anti-Slavery Society, founded in 1832, and was one of the first black women to become well known in the anti-slavery movement.

## PIONEERING EVANGELIST WRITES             1836
## AUTOBIOGRAPHY

The first autobiography by an American black woman was *The Life and Religious Experiences of Jarena Lee, a Coloured Lady* by religious leader *JARENA LEE (1783–1864)*. Lee was a nineteenth-century evangelist

# PHILLIS WHEATLEY

## (1753?–1784)

## Pioneering Poet

Phillis Wheatley, born on the west coast of Africa, published the first book of poetry by a black person in America (and the second published by a woman), *Poems on Various Subjects, Religious and Moral*, which was published in London, England, in 1773. A Boston merchant, John Wheatley, had bought Phillis as a child of about seven or eight and allowed her to learn to read and write. Wheatley's first published poem, "On the Death of the Reverend George Whitefield," appeared in 1770 in a Boston broadside. In 1773 she traveled abroad with the Wheatleys' son, partially in the hope of restoring her health with exposure to sea air, and she attracted considerable attention in England as a poet. It was at about this time that she was freed.

and itinerant preacher who called herself "the first female preacher of the First African Methodist Episcopal Church." She published two autobiographies; the second, *Religious Experiences and Journal of Jarena Lee*, was published in 1849. Little is known about her life after that time.

## 1841                     TRAILBLAZING ESSAYIST

**ANN PLATO (1820?–?)** published *Essays; Including Biographies and Miscellaneous Pieces, in Prose and Poetry*, becoming the first black woman to publish a book of essays. The biographies provide a capsule of what life for young, middle-class black women of New England was like at that time, and the 20 poems are typical of early nineteenth-century works. A devout Congregationalist, she wrote about her experiences as a church member in the poem "Advice to Young Ladies."

## TRAILBLAZING BLACK SWAN            1853

Elizabeth Greenfield

*ELIZABETH (TAYLOR) GREENFIELD (1819?–1876)*, the nation's first black concert singer, became the first black singer to give a command performance before royalty when she appeared before Queen Victoria on May 10, 1853. She was called "the Black Swan" because of her sweet tones and wide vocal compass. Greenfield toured the United States and Canada extensively during her career and became the best-known black concert artist of her time. In the 1860s, she organized and directed the Black Swan Opera Troupe.

## 1857            ENSLAVED WOMAN WRITER

The earliest known manuscript of an unpublished novel by a black enslaved woman, *The Bondswoman's Narrative*, by **HANNAH CRAFTS (1830–?)**, was written around this time. (Analysis of the document places its authorship between 1853 and 1860.) The manuscript is probably the earliest known novel by a black woman anywhere, enslaved or free. It may be one of a few novels by a black enslaved person in America as well. The manuscript surfaced in 1995 and resurfaced in 2001 at auction. Black scholar Henry Louis Gates (1950–) purchased the manuscript and edited it, and Warner Books published it in 2002.

## FIRST PUBLISHED SHORT            1859
## STORY WRITER

In 1859 *FRANCES E(LLEN) W(ATKINS) HARPER (1825–1911)* wrote "The Two Offers," the first short story published by a black woman in the United States. It appeared in the *Anglo-African* magazine in 1859. Harper was born in Baltimore, Maryland, of free parents. By age 14, she was already established as a writer and scholar. She became a noted speaker in the abolition movement, including as a permanent lecturer for the Maine Anti-Slavery Society. After the Civil War, her

Frances E. W. Harper

lectures addressed such issues as the suffrage and temperance movements as well as women's rights. Harper is often referred to as an abolitionist poet; she was also the most popular black poet of her time. Her first volume appeared in 1845. *Poems on Miscellaneous Subjects* launched her career, and her novel *Iola Leroy* (1892) had three editions printed.

## 1859     HISTORY-MAKING NOVELIST

**HARRIET E. ADAMS WILSON (1825–1900)** was the first free black woman to publish a novel. *Our Nig; or, Sketches from the Life of a Free Black, in a Two Story White House North, Showing That Slavery's Shadows Fall Even There* was published on August 18 in Boston. The book was also the first novel published in the United States by a black man or woman. *Our Nig* presents social, racial, and economic brutality suffered by a free mulatto woman in the antebellum North. Although several copies of the work are extant, in the early 1980s, scholar Henry Louis Gates rediscovered the book and removed it from obscurity.

## WILDFIRE IN ROME     1870

**(MARY) EDMONIA "WILDFIRE" LEWIS (1845–1890?)** was the first black American sculptor to study abroad in 1870, and in 1871 she was the first black artist to exhibit in Rome. She was born of black and Native American heritage. Lewis received commissions for her neoclassical sculpture from all over the United States. She received national recognition at Philadelphia's Centennial Exhibition in 1876.

## 1876     GROUNDBREAKING BLACK MUSICAL COMEDY TROUPE

The **HYERS SISTERS COMIC OPERA COMPANY** was organized, becoming the first permanent black musical-comedy troupe. The sisters' father led his daughters to success from the post–Civil War period until the 1890s. The sisters, Anna Madah Hyers (1856?–1930s) and Emma Louise Hyers (1858?–1899?), received their early musical training from their parents, and later they studied voice and piano with a German professor and a former Italian opera singer. On April 22, 1867, the sisters made their professional debut at the local Metropolitan Theater. They left the stage to continue to study and prepare for a national tour. Their first major recital came on August 12, 1871, in Salt Lake City, Utah, and had successful concerts in principal cities all over the country. By the mid-1870s, their father changed the concert company into a musical-comedy company, the Comic Opera Company. They toured the country under the Redpath Lyceum Bureau. The first and only black repertory company, for more than a decade they were the nation's most celebrated troupe.

## BAPTIST SOCIETY'S PIONEERING WRITER                    1890

**AMELIA E. JOHNSON (1858–1922)** published *Clarence and Corinne; or God's Way*, the first book by a woman and the first by a black American published by the American Baptist Publication Society. The novel was also the first Sunday School book published by a black American. She was responsible for such publications as *Joy* (1887), which included other poems and stories, and *Ivy*, designed to promote African American history and to encourage young black Americans to read.

Amelia E. Johnson

## 1902        CHANGE-MAKING MOTHER OF THE BLUES

Ma Rainey

**MA RAINEY (GERTRUDE PRIDGETT) (1886–1939)**, of the Rabbit Foot Minstrels, was the first black to sing the blues in a professional show. She specialized in blues and became known as the "Mother of the Blues." After marrying Will Rainey, the couple traveled with the Rabbit Foot Minstrels and performed as "Ma" and "Pa" Rainey, touring the South with several companies. She sang in a raw and gritty style and became a flashy dresser who loved jewelry and glitter. Rainey met fellow blues singer Bessie

Smith and greatly influenced Smith's musical career. Rainey extended her audience through the recordings that she made with Paramount Record Company beginning in December 1923 and through performances on the Theatre Owners Booking Association (TOBA) circuit.

## TEXAS WRITER PROTESTS STEREOTYPES

### 1905

The first book written by a black woman and published in Texas was *Moral and Mental Capsule for the Economic and Domestic Life of the Negro, as a Solution to the Race Problem*, by **JOSIE BRIGGS HALL (1869–1935)**, of Waxahachie, a writer and teacher. In her book of essays and poems, Hall made a plea for the reversal of racial stereotypes and urged young women to raise the standard of womanhood.

Josie Briggs Hall

## 1915    DRAMATIC COMPANY FOUNDER

**ANITA BUSH (1883–1974)** organized the Anita Bush Players and became the first black woman to run a professional black stock dramatic company in the United States. The players opened at New York City's Lincoln Theater with *The Girl at the Fort*. They transferred to the larger Lafayette Theatre, where they became the Lafayette Players. She joined Williams and Walker Company when she was 16 and toured England with them in the smash hit *In Dahomey*. She formed her own dance group about 1909 and toured with the four or five other women members until she was injured in a serious accident in 1913. After the Anita Bush Players ended their short life, Bush continued to perform.

## PIONEERING "BUTLER KIDS"    1916

In this year, **LAURETTA GREEN BUTLER (1881–1952)** opened the first black professional dance studio in Los Angeles. She later performed with some of the country's best black orchestras. She gave up her musical career and opened a professional dance studio for children—the first such venture in the country. Butler presented her first

Kiddie Minstrel Review in 1917, establishing herself as the foremost producer of children's acts. The studio was renamed the Kiddie Review around 1923, eliminating blackface makeup. The "Butler Kids," as her students became known, were in constant demand. Black as well as white children were trained in the studio, including some members of *The Little Rascals* TV series and *Our Gang* movies. Butler Studio closed in the late 1940s.

## 1916        PIONEERING PLAYWRIGHT

Angelina W. Grimké

*Rachel*, a play by **ANGELINA W. GRIMKÉ (1880– 1958)**, was the first known play written by a black American and presented on stage by black actors in the twentieth century. It portrayed a respectable black family destroyed by prejudice. The play was first produced by the Drama Committee of the NAACP at Myrtilla Miner Normal School, in Washington, D.C.

## TIRELESS GOSPEL SONG COMPOSER    1919

**LUCIE (LUCY) CAMPBELL (WILLIAMS) (1885–1963)** published "Something Within" and became the first black woman composer to have a gospel song published. She wrote more than 80 songs, and a number of them became classics in the field of gospel. These included "Jesus Gave Me Water," "There Is a Fountain," and "In the Upper Room with Jesus"; her songs for liturgical use included "This Is the Day the Lord Has Made." Campbell, along with Charles A. Tindley (1851–1933) and Thomas Andrew Dorsey (1899–1993), is considered a gospel music pioneer. A self-taught musician, she played the piano and organ at the Metropolitan Baptist Church in Memphis.

## 1919       PLAYWRIGHT PUBLISHES FEMINIST DRAMA

**MARY P. BURRILL (1881–1946)** published her play *They That Sit in Darkness*. This was possibly the first black feminist drama ever published. One of her two known published plays, it appeared in *Birth Control Review* in September 1919, in a special issue on "The Negroes' Need for Birth Control, as Seen by Themselves."

## RECORD-MAKING RECORDING ARTIST    1920

On February 14, *MAMIE SMITH (1883–1946)* was the first black woman to make a record. She recorded "You Can't Keep a Good Man Down," "This Thing Called Love," and "It's Right Here for You." The first blues song ever recorded, "Crazy Blues" sold 790,000 copies in the first year. Its success led Okeh Records to establish the "Original Race Records" series under black musical director Clarence Williams (1893–1965).

Mamie Smith

## 1921         FINDS A PLACE IN JAZZ BANDS

*LILLIAN "LIL" HARDIN ARMSTRONG (1898–1971)* joined "King" Oliver's Creole Jazz Band as pianist and is believed to have been the first woman to enter the jazz field. She was the first woman to play piano with jazz bands and led many of the finest black bands from the 1920s on, including the Dreamland Syncopators (also known as Lil's Hot Shots). "Miss Lil," as she was called, married Louis Armstrong in 1924 and was a positive influence on his career.

## SILENT FILM STARS AND COWBOYS        1921

Anita Bush, Lawrence Chenault, Bill Pickett, Steve Reynolds, and 30 black cowboys appeared in the first all-black Western movie, *The CRIMSON SKULL* (also known as *The Scarlet Claw*). The 30mm, silent, black-and-white movie was filmed on location in the all-black town of Boley, Oklahoma.

# 1922  THE CHARLESTON INTRODUCED ON BROADWAY

Singer and dancer **MAUDE RUTHERFORD (1897?–2001)** is said to have introduced the Charleston on Broadway. She appeared on Broadway in the all-black revue *Liza*, with lyrics and music by Maceo Pinkard, and led the chorus girls in the dance called the Charleston. Some critics claim, however, that the Charleston was brought to Broadway in 1923, in the show *Runnin' Wild*. Rutherford also worked with Josephine Baker, Fats Waller, and Pearl Bailey, and was billed as the Slim Princess. She was a favorite at Harlem's Cotton Club. Her theater credits included *Dixie to Broadway* (1924), *Chocolate Scandals* (1927), and *Keep Shufflin'* (1928).

## BLUES-SINGING STAR OF LANDMARK WORKS   1923

"Downhearted Blues/Gulf Coast Blues" was the first record by a black to sell more than a million copies. Singer **BESSIE SMITH (1894–1937)** became one of the most important women in the history of American music, both as a stage performer and recording star. Between 1923 and 1933, she gave us such works as "Backwater Blues" and "Do Your Duty," which became twentieth-century landmarks. Smith first performed on the city streets of Chattanooga. She eventually performed with Ma Rainey, the first professional to sing blues, in the Rabbit Foot Minstrels. Smith's only movie appearance was in the first film short featuring black musicians, *Saint Louis Blues*, later retitled *Best of the Blues*, in 1929.

Bessie Smith

# 1925  HARLEM RENAISSANCE DANCER

The first black woman to headline at a Broadway venue was **FLORENCE MILLS (1896–1927)**. She became the preeminent woman

Florence Mills

jazz dancer during the Harlem Renaissance. By age eight, she was a stage phenomenon, having been guided by the accomplished performer Aida Overton Walker. Mills sang "Miss Hannah from Savannah" in the musical comedy *Sons of Ham*, which led to her work with a vaudeville company. Mills joined Noble Sissle and Eubie Blake's production of *Shuffle Along*. Her success in the musical led Lew Leslie to hire her to perform at the Plantation Club on Broadway. When the musical comedy *From Dixie to Broadway* opened in New York in October 1924, Mills sang "I'm a Little Blackbird Looking for a Bluebird" and was a show-stopper. Mills's heavy workload contributed to her declining health and eventual death. During her grand funeral in Harlem, it has been said that a flock of blackbirds flew over her funeral procession as it made its way up Seventh Avenue to Woodland Cemetery in the Bronx.

## ACCLAIMED DIRECTOR OF                  1926
## *HALLELUJAH* AND *PORGY AND BESS*

**EVA A. JESSYE (1895–1992)**, composer, musician, choral director, educator, writer, and actress, became the first black woman to achieve acclaim as director of a professional choral group. Jessye directed the choir in Hollywood's first black musical, *Hallelujah*, in 1929. In 1935 Jessye became choral director for the premiere of George Gershwin's *Porgy and Bess*.

Eva A. Jessye

## 1926   PIONEERING ROMANCE MOVIE STARS

**CAROLYNNE SNOWDEN (1900–1985)** and Stepin Fetchit (Lincoln Theodore Monroe Andrew Perry) (1902–1985) played in the first onscreen black romance in the movie *In Old Kentucky*.

## OPERA SINGER AND COMPOSER        1927

**LILLIAN EVANTI (1890–1967)** was the first black American to sing opera with an organized European opera company, performing *Lakmé* in Nice, France. Novelist Jessie Redmon Fauset suggested the stage name Evanti, a contraction of her maiden name and her married name (Evans and Tibbs). She was a founder of the Negro Opera Company in Washington. Presidents Harry S. Truman and Dwight D. Eisenhower invited her to sing at the White House during and after World War II.

Lillian Evanti

## 1927        HARMON AWARD WINNER

Artist **LAURA WHEELER WARING (1887–1948)** was the first black woman to receive the Harmon Award for her painting. She painted prominent persons in the struggle for black culture. In 1946 she began a series of religious paintings that included *Jacob's Ladder, The Coming of the Lord*, and *Heaven, Heaven*.

## SOUND FILM STARS        1928

The first black sound film was **MELANCHOLY DAME**, a comedy two-reeler, starring Evelyn Preer, Roberta Hyson, Edward Thompson, and Spencer Williamson.

## 1929        "BLACK TEMPTRESS" IN TALKING PICTURES

**NINA MAE McKINNEY (1912–1967)** was cast in the starring role as Chick in King Vidor's film *Hallelujah*—the first all-black musical—and in March became the first "black temptress" in talking pictures. In that role, she also became the first recognized black woman actor in a Hollywood film. When she was 16, the self-taught dancer was spotted in the chorus line of Lew Leslie's *Blackbirds* (1929) and was hired for the role in *Hallelujah*. With her dance of seduction, the Swanee Shuffle, she became the first leading lady to create a tradition of style that Lena Horne and Dorothy Dandridge would express. Although she signed a five-year contract with MGM when she was only 17, Hollywood had no place for beautiful, sexy, mulatto women; the movie industry cast her in minor roles in obscure films, while the American film public ignored her. McKinney moved to Europe in December 1929 where she was billed as the black Greta Garbo. She sang in cellars and cafés and later starred with Paul Robeson in *Congo Road* (1930) and *Sanders of the River* (1935). She returned to the United States in 1940 and sang and toured the country with her own band. Eleven years after her death, McKinney was inducted into the Black Filmmakers Hall of Fame.

Nina Mae McKinney

## ALL-BLACK CASTS AND FULL-LENGTH FILMS                    1929

The first two full-length films with all-black casts were **HEARTS IN DIXIE**, starring Nina Mae McKinney, Victoria Spivey, and Daniel Haynes; and **HALLELUJAH**, starring Mildred Washington, Clarence Muse, and Stepin Fetchit.

## 1930          BLUES-SINGING HISTORY MAKER

The first woman to lead an all-male band was **BLANCHE CALLO-WAY (1902–1978)**, one of the most successful bandleaders of the 1930s. She moved from Baltimore to Miami, where she became the first woman disc jockey on American radio. For a while, she and her brother, Cab, had their own act. Calloway toured with the 12 Clouds of Joy as a singer, dancer, and conductor.

## NOVELIST FOREMOTHER EMERGES          1930

**NELLA MARIAN LARSEN (1891–1964)** was the first black woman recipient of a Guggenheim Fellowship in creative writing. Her novels, *Quicksand* and *Passing,* were highly acclaimed. Both deal with the tragic mulatto theme. She treated black women characters in urban settings and was the foremother to African American novelists to follow her. Larsen was one of the first black women novelists to grapple with female sexuality and sexual politics.

## 1933    SYMPHONY-PERFORMING SOLOIST

Margaret Bonds

**MARGARET (ALLISON) BONDS (1913–1972)** became the first black American guest soloist with the Chicago Symphony Orchestra, performing Leontyne Price's Piano Concerto in F Minor at the 1933 World's Fair. Her arrangements of spirituals for solo voice and chorus are well known. Her arrangement of "He's Got the Whole World in His Hands," commissioned and recorded in the 1960s by Price, is among Bonds's best-known pieces.

## PASSIONATE COMPOSER                    1933

**FLORENCE BEATRICE SMITH PRICE (1887–1953)** was the first black woman to have a symphony performed by a major orchestra. The Chicago Symphony, under Frederick Stock, first played her Symphony in E Minor at the Chicago World's Fair. She was the first black woman to achieve distinction as a composer. Price won her first Harmon prize for composition in 1925. She wrote a number of works, many of which were published.

## 1933    SINGER SHUFFLES ALONG

When **CATERINA JARBORO (1898?–1986)** sang *Aida* at New York City's Hippodrome Theater, she became the first black to sing with an all-white company. She was also the first black to sing with the Chicago Opera Company. She began her career in Broadway musicals, including *Shuffle Along* (1921) and *Running Wild* (1923). In 1926 she went to Paris to continue her education and to become a classical singer. She studied with Nino Campinno in Italy and in 1930 made her debut at the Puccini Opera House in Milan. She returned to the United States in 1932 and received a number of singing engagements.

## LIFTS VOICE THROUGH SCULPTURE    1934

**AUGUSTA (CHRISTINE FELLS) SAVAGE (1892–1962)**, a sculptor and educator, was the first black member of the National Association of Women Painters and Sculptors. One of her major commissions was the creation of sculpture for the New York World's Fair 1939–40, *Lift Every Voice and Sing*, a sculptural group symbolizing blacks' contributions to music, which became Savage's best known and most widely recognized work. In 1937 she became the first director of the Harlem Community Art Center and organized programs in education, art, and recreation. Savage was also an organizer of the Harlem Artists Guild.

Augusta Savage

## 1934     WHITE HOUSE SINGING ACTRESS

When ***ETTA MOTEN BARNETT (1901–2004)*** sang at a White House dinner in January before President Franklin D. Roosevelt and his guests, she became the first black movie actress to entertain there. In the 1930s, she was one of the first black actresses to be cast in a romantic role in film. After moving to New York, Barnett began to appear in Broadway musicals, yet sometimes only her voice was used. Her singing voice was used in several films, but it was not until *The Gold Diggers of 1933* that she appeared on screen. In 1934 she sang "Carioca" in *Flying Down to Rio*, starring Ginger Rogers and Fred Astaire, and for the first time received screen credit. Barnett made her concert debut in New York's Town Hall, and from 1942 to 1945 she toured as Bess with the show *Porgy and Bess*, singing opposite Todd Duncan as Porgy. Her singing career tapered off in the early 1960s.

## OPERA SINGER                              1937

***LA JULIA RHEA (1898–1992)*** was the first black to sing with the Chicago Civic Opera Company during the regular season. She opened December 26, 1937, in the title role of Verdi's *Aida*.

## 1937     PIONEERING PERFORMER/ACTIVIST

***FREDI WASHINGTON (1903–1994)***, actress, dancer, and civil rights activist, founded the Negro Actors Guild of America and became its first executive secretary. She landed a spot in the chorus line in the 1921 production of the musical *Shuffle Along*. Her role in the 1926

# ZORA NEALE HURSTON
## (1891–1960)

### Groundbreaking Folklorist

Zora Neale Hurston published *Mules and Men* (1935), which is based on her field studies in Louisiana. This became the first such collection of folklore compiled and published by a black American woman. It is also the first by a woman indigenous to the culture from which the stories emerge. Born in Eatonville, Florida, Hurston left home to work with a traveling Gilbert and Sullivan theatrical troupe. She left the troupe when it arrived in Baltimore and graduated from high school in 1918. She enrolled in Howard University, taking courses intermittently. Hurston moved to New York and became absorbed in the Harlem Renaissance; she befriended and worked alongside such writers as Jean Toomer, Langston Hughes, and Wallace Thurman. She also collaborated with Hughes and others in publishing the short-lived literary magazine *Fire!* Hurston graduated from Barnard College and continued graduate study at Columbia University under renowned anthropologist Franz Boas. She returned to Eatonville and collected black folklore. Her book *Mules and Men* includes the folklore that she collected in Florida and Alabama as well as her hoodoo essay written for the *Journal of American Folklore*. Hurston's other works include *Jonah's Gourd Vine*; *Their Eyes Were Watching God*; Tell My Horse; Moses, Man of the Mountain; Dust Tracks on a Road; and *Seraph on the Sewanee*. Hurston's career began to slide in the 1950s, forcing her to take a series of menial jobs in Florida's small towns. After suffering a stroke in 1959, she was confined to Saint Lucie County Welfare Home in Fort Pierce, Florida, and she died in poverty. In August 1973, novelist Alice Walker placed a

continued on next page

stone marker at the approximate site of her grave in Fort Pierce. A Zora Neale Hurston festival, which is held annually, and the Hurson National Museum of Fine Arts, both in Eatonville, celebrate the author's life and work. Hurston's play *Polk County* resurfaced in 1997 at the Library of Congress, where she had deposited copies of ten of her unpublished and unproduced plays for copyright protection between 1925 and 1944.

Broadway play *Black Boy* typecast her as the tragic mulatto and led her to leave stage and screen. In the late 1920s, Washington toured Europe and returned to the United States to star in a series of films. By the 1930s, she had become one of the country's great black dramatic actresses, appearing in strong roles in such movies as *The Emperor Jones*, *The Old Man of the Mountain*, and *Imitation of Life*. She returned to the Broadway stage in the late 1930s, where she played opposite Ethel Waters in *Mamba's Daughters*.

## LEADING SYNDICATED CARTOONIST        1937

**ZELDA JACKSON "JACKIE" ORMES (1911–1985)** became the first nationally syndicated black woman cartoonist. In this year, she began her cartoon "Torchy Brown in 'Dixie to Harlem,'" which ran in the *Pittsburgh Courier*. She also created the strips "Patty Jo 'n' Ginger" and "Candy." She became a general assignment reporter for the *Chicago Defender*. Her work was syndicated in black newspapers nationwide, and until the 1990s she was the only nationally syndicated black woman cartoonist.

## 1937                    THE SUBLIME "LADY DAY"

When jazz great **BILLIE "LADY DAY" HOLIDAY (1915–1959)** teamed up with the Artie Shaw Band and toured the country, this was the first time a black woman and a white band shared the same stage. She was born Elenora Fagan in Baltimore. Later, she became a regular in Harlem clubs and also toured with Count Basie's orchestra and became soloist with Artie Shaw's white band. Jazz saxophonist Lester Young nicknamed her "Lady Day" when she was with Count Basie's band. She assumed the name "Billie" from movie star Billie Dove. Holiday

Billie Holiday

was known for wearing gardenias in her hair, and she performed with her eyes nearly closed. Her protest song "Strange Fruit" was a ballad about lynching; the fruit represented black men hanging from trees. At the peak of her career in the late 1930s and early 1940s, she began to struggle with drug and alcohol addiction.

## GOSPEL-SINGING RECORDING STAR        1938

**"SISTER" ROSETTA THARPE (ROSETTA NUBIN) (1915–1973)** was the first black to take gospel music into a secular setting, when she sang on a Cab Calloway show from the Cotton Club. She signed with Decca and became the first gospel singer to record for a major company. Tharpe began touring as a professional when she was six. She took the lead in bringing gospel music to the mainstream. Tharpe was the first major gospel singer to tour extensively in Europe, and in 1943 she was the first to sing gospel at the Apollo Theater in New York City.

## 1939    SINGER PERFORMS BEFORE ROYALTY

Singer **MARIAN ANDERSON (1897–1993)** became the first black to sing before a reigning British monarch at the White House. King George VI and Queen Elizabeth of England were the first reigning British monarchs to visit the United States, and President Franklin Roosevelt and First Lady Eleanor Roosevelt planned an "Evening of American Music" in which Anderson sang Schubert's "Ave Maria."

## PIONEERING SINGING-STAR ON        1939
## TELEVISION

**ETHEL WATERS (1896–1977)** became the first black singer to appear on television and the first black American to star in her own television show, *The Ethel Waters Show*. This was an experimental, one-night event for the new medium of television. She returned to television 11 years later as the star of *Beulah*.

# 1939                                   BROADWAY SINGER

Ethel Waters

**ETHEL WATERS (1896–1977),** as Hagar in *Mamba's Daughters*, became the first black woman to perform the leading role in a dramatic play on Broadway. Waters appeared in nightclubs and vaudeville, and in 1927 she made her Broadway debut in *Africana*. When she toured in *As Thousands Cheer* (1934), she became the first black person to costar with white players below the Mason-Dixon line. Her greatest role came in 1940, when she appeared on stage in *Cabin in the Sky*; she appeared in the movie version in 1943. From 1957 to 1976, she toured with evangelist Billy Graham and achieved wide recognition for the gospel hymn "His Eye Is on the Sparrow." In 1950 Waters was the first black to star in a scheduled comedy program on television. She appeared in *Beulah* on ABC on October 3, taking over the role played by Hattie McDaniel (1895–1952) on the radio.

## GOSPEL-SINGING SISTERS                    1940

"Surely God Is Able," written by Memphis Baptist minister W. Herbert Brewster Sr. (1897–1987), and recorded by the Ward Singers, is said to be the first gospel recording by a black singing group to sell more than one million copies. Principal singers in the group were organizer **GERTRUDE WARD (1901–1981)** and **CLARA MAE WARD (1924–1973)**. In 1957 the group was the first to perform at the Newport Jazz Festival. They were also the first to appear in nightclubs in 1961 and the first to sing at Radio City Music Hall in New York City in 1963.

# 1940                             ACADEMY AWARD WINNER

Hattie McDaniel

In 1940 **HATTIE McDANIEL (1895–1952)**, singer, vaudeville performer, and actress, was the first black to win an Academy Award for her supporting role of Mammy in *Gone with the Wind*. McDaniel made her radio debut in 1915 and is said to be the first black American woman to sing on radio. Often called "Hi-Hat Hattie," she made her movie debut in *The Golden West* in 1932 and appeared in more than 300 films during the next two decades. Her career was built on the "Mammy" image, a role she played with dignity. She appeared on radio with Eddie Cantor and the *Amos 'n' Andy* shows.

# BLACKS IN HORROR FILM                                      1940

*SON OF INGAGI* was the first black-cast horror film. Originally titled *House of Horror,* the 70-minute film was in black and white with sound. The black cast included Laura Bowman, Spencer Williams (who wrote the story), Daisy Bufford, Alfred Grant, Earl J. Morris, Arthur Ray, Jesse Graves, and The Four Toppers.

# 1941                     BLACK OPERA COMPANY

*MARY LUCINDA CARDWELL DAWSON (1894–1962)* founded the first permanent black opera company, the National Negro Opera Company, in Pittsburgh. The company functioned through 1962.

# SCULPTOR                                          1943

*SELMA HORTENSE BURKE (1900–1995)*, sculptor, educator, and school founder, was the first black sculptor to design a U.S. coin. She won a competition to design the portrait of President Franklin D. Roosevelt that appeared on the dime. In 1983 the Selma Burke Gallery opened at Winston-Salem State University. This marked the first time a gallery was named for a black American woman artist. In 1990 the gallery was moved to Johnson C. Smith University in Charlotte.

Selma Burke

# 1943       HISTORY-MAKING JAZZ PIANIST

Jazz pianist *DOROTHY DONEGAN (1922–1998)* became the first black musician to play in Chicago's prestigious Orchestral Hall. Donegan made her professional debut in 1943 at Orchestra Hall. During the 1940s and 1950s, she played at top clubs in New York, Chicago, and Los Angeles, but with the advent of rock music in the 1960s, she had difficulty finding work. By the 1970s, however, she was playing at festivals in the United States and abroad.

## SOCIAL PROTEST DANCER                    1943

**PEARL PRIMUS (1919–1994)** was the first dancer to present the African American experience within a framework of social protest, in such dances as *Strange Fruit, Hard Times Blues*, and *The Negro Speaks of Rivers*. She began to create and perform the dances around 1943. Born in Trinidad, Primus moved to the United States, formed her own dance company, and later became a nightclub performer. Primus toured with her company, concentrating their appearances in the South. Sometime later, she opened a dance school in New York. She studied dance in Africa and became the first director of the African Performing Arts Center in Monrovia, Liberia. Primus brought African dance to the United States and to schoolchildren and dance companies. Three of her social protest dances were revived in 1988 and presented at Duke University for the American Dance Festival. The Alvin Ailey American Dance Theater presented her piece *Impinyuza* at New York's City Center in 1990.

## 1944          NAUMBERG AWARD WINNER

The first black American to receive the Walter Naumberg Award was **CAROL BRICE (1918–1985)**. She was a child prodigy who traveled with her school's glee club. She also toured as a soloist with the Palmer Institute Singers in North Carolina when she was 14. She made her Town Hall debut in 1945 and had stage roles in such musical works as *Show Boat; Gentlemen, Be Seated*; and *Porgy and Bess*.

## PIONEERING OPERA SINGER              1945

**CAMILLA (ELLA) WILLIAMS (1919–2012)** was the first black woman to sing with the New York City Opera when she performed the title role in Puccini's *Madama Butterfly*. The next year, she became the first black to sign a full contract with a major opera company in the United States. In 1954 she was the first black singer to appear on the stage of the Vienna State Opera.

Camilla Williams

# 1945                                    MUSIC CRITIC

**NORA (DOUGLAS) HOLT (1885?–1974)** became the first black American member of the Music Critics Circle of New York. She became a music critic for the *Chicago Defender*. From 1919 until 1921, she published the magazine *Music and Poetry*. Holt helped to establish the National Association of Negro Musicians.

# SENSATIONAL NOVELIST                            1946

**ANN PETRY (1908–1997)** became the first black woman to write a best-selling novel. *The Street* quickly became a sensation; over one million copies were sold. She was also one of the first black woman writers to address the problems that black women face. After publishing several of her stories, in 1946 she published her novel *The Street*. She also published other works, including two other novels—*Country Place* and *The Narrows*.

# 1948             BLACK STARS IN LIVING COLOR

**NO TIME FOR ROMANCE** was the first all-black-cast film in Cinecolor. Vivian Cosby wrote the original story, which recounts the struggle of a young musician of superior talent who is successful in his efforts to reach the top. The film's cast included 46 black actors and actresses.

# TREND-SHATTERING AWARD WINNER     1949

In this year **JUANITA HALL (1901–1968)**, singer, actress, and choral director, became the first black American to win a Tony Award for her performance as Bloody Mary in the 1949 Broadway production of *South Pacific*. In 1928 she appeared in the chorus of the Ziegfeld production of *Show Boat*. Hall became a soloist and assistant director of the noted Hall Johnson Choir. For more than 20 years, she devoted her life to the performing arts, working as a choral conductor, actress, and singer on stage and screen.

# 1950            QUEEN OF GOSPEL SONG

Mahalia Jackson

Joe Bostic (1908–1988), the "Dean of Gospel Disc Jockeys," produced the Negro Gospel and Religious Music Festival at Carnegie Hall in New York, the first all-gospel concert. The show featured **MAHALIA JACKSON (1911–1972)**, whose recording of "Move On Up a Little Higher" (1946) was the second gospel recording to sell more than a million copies in a year. Through her recording, she became the first to bring gospel singing to the general public. Acclaimed as America's greatest gospel singer, Jackson was the first gospel singer to appear on *The Ed Sullivan Show* and became the first gospel artist to sing at the Newport Jazz Festival in 1958. She was known as the "Queen of the Gospel Song." The New Orleans native moved to Chicago at age 16 and met Thomas A. Dorsey, her musical advisor and accompanist.

# HISTORY-MAKING TELEVISION HOST     1950

When DuMont Network launched *The Hazel Scott Show* on July 3, **HAZEL SCOTT (1920–1981)** became the first black host of a television show presented in musical format. The show was first broadcast as a local program but became a network show in 1950. Most television hosts at that time were men; Scott, however, broke new ground. While the show looked promising, especially for the image of black American women, Scott was accused of being either a Communist or Communist sympathizer, and her contract was not renewed. Her program went off the airways on September 29.

# 1950            BROADWAY OPERA SINGER

**ZELMA WATSON GEORGE (1903–1994)**, singer, social worker, actress, and educator, was the first black woman to play a leading role in an American opera on Broadway. She was cast in a revival of composer Gian-Carlo Menotti's opera *The Medium*. In 1960 George was approved as an alternate to the U.S. delegation to the Fifteenth General Assembly of the United Nations and was in great demand as a speaker and lecturer.

# GWENDOLYN BROOKS

## (1917–2000)

### Pulitzer Prize–winning Poet

*Gwendolyn Brooks*, poet and novelist, was the first black to win a Pulitzer Prize in 1950. She won for poetry with *Annie Allen*. She became established as a major American poet, and in 1976, she was the first black woman inducted into the National Institute of Arts and Letters. A sensitive interpreter of Northern ghetto life, she began to write poetry at age seven; her first poems were published in the *Chicago Defender*. Beginning in 1969, she promoted the idea that blacks must develop their own culture. She changed her writing style to become accessible to the ordinary black reader. She was the poet laureate of Illinois for 16 years and was named poetry consultant to the Library of Congress in 1985. In 1945 she published *A Street in Bronzeville*, the book that launched her career. Her autobiographical novel, *Maude Martha*, was published in 1953, followed by the first of four books of poetry for children in 1956, then *The Bean Eaters* (1960), *In the Mecca* (1968), *The Riot* (1969), and other works.

## GROUNDBREAKING CONCERT ARTIST    1951

*MURIEL RAHN (1911?–1961)* and William Warfield (1920–2002) appeared on *The Ed Sullivan Show*, marking the first appearance of black concert artists on a television show. Rahn joined the casts of at least two Broadway musicals, *Black Birds of 1929* and *Hot Chocolates* (1929–30). She became a star in the original production of *Carmen Jones* and costarred in *The Barrier*. She was also in the opera *Salome*, where she performed in "The Dance of Seven Veils."

## 1951                                      MET PRIMA BALLERINA

Janet Collins

**JANET COLLINS (1917–2003)** was the first black prima ballerina at the Metropolitan Opera Company. She made her debut in *Aida* on November 13 and had the lead in *Carmen, La Gioconda,* and *Sampson and Delilah.* Collins studied dance under Katherine Dunham, who was known for her landmark modern dance company, the Dunham Dance Company. Collins moved to New York in search of a career in dance and made her debut in 1949. In 1950 she appeared in Cole Porter's *Out of the World,* in which she danced the role of "Night." She taught at the School of American Ballet, performed in concerts and on television, but became known chiefly for her choreography and her dance instruction.

## HISTORY-MAKING OPERA SINGER          1953

**DOROTHY MAYNOR (1910–1996)**, opera singer, choral director, and school founder, became the first black to sing at a presidential inauguration when she sang "The Star-Spangled Banner" at Dwight D. Eisenhower's swearing-in. In 1965 she founded the Harlem School of the Arts.

## 1953   OPERA SINGER PERFORMS IN EUROPE

**MATTIWILDA DOBBS (1925–2015)**, who sang at all of the major opera houses in Europe, was the first black woman to sing a principal role at La Scala, in Milan, Italy, where she played Elvira in Rossini's *L'Italiana in Algieri.* On November 9, 1956, she became the third black to sing at New York City's Metropolitan Opera, and as Gilda in *Rigoletto,* she was the first black to sing a romantic lead there.

## ARCHITECTURAL FIRM FOUNDER          1954

In this year **NORMA MERRICK SKLAREK (1926–2012)** became the first black woman registered architect in New York State. In 1962 she became the first black woman licensed in California. She was also the first black woman fellow of the American Institute of Architects in

1980. In 1955 she joined the architectural firm of Skidmore, Owings & Merrill and in 1960 moved to Gruen and Associates in Los Angeles, where she remained for 20 years. In 1966 Sklarek became the first woman director of architecture with 20 architects on staff. That same year she was the first woman honored with a fellowship in the American Institute of Architects. In 1985 she founded her own architectural firm, Siegel Sklarek Diamond.

# 1955      MET SINGER AND THE DAR

Marian Anderson

In 1955 **MARIAN ANDERSON (1897–1993)**, one of the twentieth century's most celebrated singers, was the first black to sing a principal role with the Metropolitan Opera. She made her debut as Ulrica in Verdi's *Un Ballo in Maschera*. In October 1930 Anderson received critical acclaim for her concert at the Bach Saal in Berlin and from there embarked on an extensive tour of Europe. She made national news in 1939 when the Daughters of the American Revolution refused to allow her to appear at their Constitution Hall. Anderson performed to a huge crowd at the Lincoln Memorial instead and continued to tour until her farewell trip in the 1964–65 season.

# COOKING SHOW AND JIM CROW     1955?

**MAUDE EUDORA McCLENNAN BOXLEY (1882–1970)** was the first black woman to host a Southern television cooking show, demonstrating cooking techniques. Aired on WLAC, Channel 5, in Nashville, Tennessee, the show was known as *The Eudora Boxley Cook Show*. It aired during the Jim Crow era, when blacks were rarely seen on television, especially with their own show.

# 1955      ACADEMY AWARD NOMINEE

**DOROTHY DANDRIDGE (1922–1965)** was the first black woman nominated for an Academy Award in a leading role for her portrayal of Carmen in *Carmen Jones*. Dandridge appeared in a number of films, often typecast in the stereotypical roles commonly given to black actresses—in her case, she was cast as the "tragic mulatto." In 1951 she

was the first black to perform in the Empire Room of New York's Waldorf Astoria. She conquered international audiences, integrated many previously "whites only" night spots, and, when performing at hotels, broke attendance records. *Island in the Sun*, a 1957 film in which she appeared opposite white actor John Justin, marked the first time the theme of interracial love was explored in the movies. In 1959 Dandridge appeared in the film version of the black opera *Porgy and Bess* and won a Golden Globe Award as best actress in a musical.

Dorothy Dandridge

## AWARD-WINNING PLAYWRIGHT                  1956

Writer, actress, and director ***ALICE CHILDRESS (1920–1994)*** became the first black woman to win an Obie Award, for her off-Broadway play *Trouble in Mind*. The play dealt with stereotypes of black actors in white plays. Due to disagreements over its theme and interpretation, the play was never produced on Broadway. Childress began her career as an actress in New York in 1940. She worked with the American Negro Theater and also performed on Broadway and on television.

## 1959    SKAT-SINGING "FIRST LADY OF JAZZ"

***ELLA FITZGERALD (1917–1996)*** was the first black woman to win a Grammy. In 1935 she was hired by Chick Webb's band to sing at a dance at Yale University. Fitzgerald recorded the well-known "A-Tisket, A-Tasket" in 1938, and it became the band's first hit. Following Webb's death, Fitzgerald kept the band together for several years. She developed her famous skat singing style while on a tour with Dizzy Gillespie. Known as the "First Lady of Jazz," Fitzgerald became one of the most celebrated singers of the century. She recorded more than 250 albums and won 13 Grammys. She also won the Kennedy Center Honor, the National Medal of the Arts, and the American Black Achievement Award.

Ella Fitzgerald

# FROM GOSPEL TO CABARET                     1959

**BESSIE GRIFFIN (1922–1989)** was the first gospel singer to move to cabaret. She sang a leading role in *Portraits in Bronze* at New Orleans's Cabaret Concert Theatre. The show was called the first gospel musical in history. After that, other gospel singers began to appear in coffee-houses and nightclubs.

# 1959          PLAYWRIGHT AND ACTIVIST

**LORRAINE HANSBERRY (1930–1965)** was the first black woman to premiere a play on Broadway; it opened at the Barrymore Theatre on March 11. Hansberry took the title of her play, *A Raisin in the Sun*, from Langston Hughes's poem "Harlem." In 1959 she was the first to win the New York Critics Award for that play. *Les Blancs*, her unfinished play, was produced in 1970 but received mixed reviews and had a short run. Robert Nemiroff selected scenes from Hansberry's writings that NBC commissioned and produced as a book, *To Be Young, Gifted and Black*. He adapted the work into a play produced in 1969 and aired on television in 1972. In 1973 the musical *Raisin*, a revival of her play, won the Tony Award for best musical. In addition to plays, her works include poems, articles, and books.

# *RAISIN* WINS AWARD                        1959

Playwright and activist **LORRAINE HANSBERRY (1930–1965)** was the first to win the New York Drama Critics Award, for *A Raisin in the Sun*, in May 1959. The play, whose title she took from Langston Hughes's poem "Harlem," premiered on March 11 this year. It was the first on Broadway written by a black woman and the first serious black drama to impact the dominant culture.

# 1960      BARRIER-BREAKING COMEDIENNE

**JACKIE "MOMS" MABLEY (1894–1975)** was the first black comedienne to have a best-selling record. For many years she was the only black comedienne in the country, and she was the first to become widely recognized. Mabley portrayed a cantankerous, raucous old woman who dressed shabbily and had a toothless smile. She had a gravelly voice, often told off-color jokes, and levied insults on men. In

Jackie "Moms" Mabley

real life, however, she was a compassionate woman. Mabley traveled on the vaudeville circuit and often appeared with "Pigmeat" Marcum, Bill "Bojangles" Robinson, and Cootie Williams. She was a regular at the Apollo in Harlem in 1939, made several recordings, and appeared in Broadway shows, on television, and had bit parts in films.

## MOTOWN'S HIT ON POP CHARTS                    1961

**THE MARVELETTES** released "Please Mr. Postman" on September 4 this year. It hit the top spot on the Rhythm and Blues charts on November 13. By December 3 it was the number-one Rhythm and Blues single and Motown's first record to hit number one on the pop charts. By December 11 it was the number-one pop single.

The Marvelettes included (clockwise from top left) Gladys Horton, Katherine Anderson, Georgeanna Tillman, and Wanda Young.

## 1962                       ROMANTIC LEAD PLAYER

**DIAHANN CARROLL (1935–2019)** starred in *No Strings* and became the first black to star in the romantic lead of a white Broadway play. Her work earned her a Tony Award.

## BARRIER-BREAKING TELEVISION ACTRESS                                            1963

Actress **CICELY TYSON (1924–2021)** won a regular feature role in the television drama *East Side, West Side* and became the first black to appear in a key part on a television series. She made her Broadway debut with a hit role in *The Dark of the Moon*. Tyson was universally hailed by critics for her portrayal of a sharecropper's wife in *Sounder*. She received an honorary Oscar in 2018 and became the first black actress to receive such recognition.

Cicely Tyson

# 1963 HISTORY-MAKING CHOREOGRAPHER AND DANCER

**KATHERINE DUNHAM (1909–2006)** was the first black choreographer to work at the Metropolitan Opera House. As early as the 1930s, Dunham incorporated her training in anthropology and her study of African and West Indian dances into her own techniques and dance instruction. In the early 1940s, her professional troupe, the Dunham Dancers, was a first for black Americans, setting the stage for the Alvin Ailey American Dance Theater and Arthur Mitchell's Dance Theater of Harlem. In 1989 she was awarded the National Medal of Arts. Other recognitions include the Kennedy Center Honor for Lifetime Achievement and the NASACM Image Award.

# SHAKESPEARE FESTIVAL ACTRESS     1965

**RUBY DEE (1922–2014)** was the first black actress to play major parts at the American Shakespeare Festival in Stratford, Connecticut, where she played Kate in *The Taming of the Shrew* and Cordelia in *King Lear*. Dee was known for her appearances in Broadway performances, including *A Raisin in the Sun* (1959) and *Purlie Victorious* (1961). She and her husband, Ossie Davis, shared careers in television, stage, screen, and other public appearances, and were active in civil rights.

Ruby Dee

## 1966  SEASON-OPENING OPERA SINGER

On September 16, 1966, *(MARY VIOLET) LEONTYNE PRICE (1927–)* was the first black to open a Metropolitan Opera season and to sing the title role at the opening of a new Metropolitan Opera house. She played Flora Tosca in Puccini's *Tosca*, which was televised on NBC's Opera Workshop in 1955, and became the first black to appear in opera on television. Price was the first black lyric soprano to achieve international diva status.

## PIONEERING RADIO EXECUTIVE  1967

Chicago radio executive *BERNADINE WASHINGTON (1920S–1993)* became the first black woman vice president of a radio station—WVON radio, in Chicago. She joined WVON in 1963 and became vice president and later general manager. She hosted the popular show *On Scene with Bernadine*, which presented the latest trends in the black community, including fashion and politics.

## 1968  PASSIONATE ADVOCATE REMOVING STEREOTYPES

*DIAHANN CARROLL (1935–2019)*, actress and singer, was the first black woman to star in a non-stereotypical role on television, in the weekly NBC series *Julia*. (She won the 1968 Golden Globe Award for Best Female TV Star for her role.) In the 1980s she appeared in other nighttime soaps, such as *Dynasty* and *The Colbys,* and in 2006–07 in the popular *Grey's Anatomy*. In 2011 she was inducted into the Television Academy Hall of Fame.

Diahann Carroll

## PRIME-TIME RADIO SHOW HOST  1968

*The Xernona Clayton Show* was first broadcast this year. Host *XERNONA BREWSTER CLAYTON (1930–)* became the first black person in the South to have her own show and the first black woman in the South to host a regularly scheduled prime-time television talk show.

# 1969     EMMY AWARD–WINNING FIRST

The first black actress to receive an Emmy Award was **GAIL FISHER (1935–2000)**. She won the award in 1969 for her portrayal of secretary Peggy Fair on the CBS television show *Mannix*. In 1961 Fisher was also the first black to have a speaking part in a nationally televised commercial and is the only black woman to receive the Duse Award from the Lee Strasberg Actors Studio. She was one of America's most recognized television personalities in the 1960s and 1970s. Fisher studied at the American Academy of Dramatic Arts, Lincoln Arts Center (where she was the first black accepted to the repertory theater), and the Actors Studio.

## PIONEERING VARIETY SHOW HOST     1969

*DELLA REESE (1931–2017)* was the first black woman to host a television variety show, *The Della Reese Show*. She later became the first woman of any race to host *The Tonight Show*. Reese also appeared in the television shows *Chico and the Man* (1976–78) and *The Royal Family* (1991–92). Her career was revitalized beginning in 1994 when she began playing Tess on *Touched by an Angel*. She was recognized in 1994 with a star on the Hollywood Walk of Fame.

Della Reese

# 1970     MUSIC DIRECTOR ON BROADWAY

*MARGARET ROSEZARIAN HARRIS (1943–2000)*, musician, prominent conductor, and educator, worked on Broadway, notably as music director of *Hair*. She took over that position this year on a regular basis, a pioneering engagement for a black woman. Harris was also the first black woman to conduct the symphony orchestras of Chicago, Detroit, Los Angeles, St. Louis, and other cities in America. She gained the most prominence as a conductor; however, she also composed two ballets, an opera (*King David*), and two piano concertos. Harris was recognized as a gifted musician early in life. At age ten she performed with the Chicago Symphony Orchestra.

## AWARD-WINNING CHILDREN'S LIBRARIAN AND AUTHOR                1970

**CHARLEMAE HILL ROLLINS (1897–1979)** was the first black winner of the Constance Lindsay Skinner Award (now the WNBA Award) of the Women's National Book Association. She became the first children's librarian at the George Cleveland Hall Branch in Chicago in 1932. Rollins had a regular storytelling hour, wrote book reviews, selected books for children, and held workshops for parents and teachers. She worked to dispel negative images of blacks in books for children and young adults. Rollins was the first black president of the American Library Association's Children's Services Division.

## 1970    ORIGINAL SCREENPLAY PRODUCER

**MAYA ANGELOU (MARGUERITE JOHNSON) (1928–2014)**, actress, dancer, and writer, was the first black woman to have an original screenplay produced, *Georgia, Georgia*, which she directed. Angelou was also the first black woman to have a work on the nonfiction bestseller list. Her autobiographical *I Know Why the Caged Bird Sings* (1969) evoked images of a black girl's childhood in the South, was nominated for a 1974 National Book Award, and aired as a television movie in 1979. An artist of wide-ranging talents, she was nominated for a Tony Award for acting and a Pulitzer Prize for poetry.

## BLACK HAIR MAKES WAVES                                1971

WABC-TV news reporter **MELBA TOLLIVER (1939–)** caused a stir when she changed her hair from straightened to natural, becoming the first black woman news reporter to do so. She was assigned to cover the White House wedding of Tricia Nixon that summer. Studio executives described her appearance as less attractive and warned her that she could not appear on air until she changed her hairstyle. She refused and, after public pressure because of the mandate, the station relented.

## 1971    FASHION MODEL HOSTS TALK SHOW

*The Audrey Thomas Show* became the first black half-hour news and talk show on WSNS-TV in Chicago. Host **AUDREY THOMAS (1933–**

# ALMA WOODSEY THOMAS (1891–1978)
## Visionary Artist

In 1972 Alma Woodsey Thomas became the first black woman to have a solo exhibit at New York's Whitney Museum of American Art. Her works show a variety of themes, including science, economics, religion, and society. Thomas was deeply inspired by the space program and did a number of "Space Paintings." Her most popular painting, *The Eclipse*, features a dark circle surrounded by mosaic squares in many colors.

*1996)* had been a fashion model during the 1960s, appearing in such magazines as *Ebony* and *Vogue*.

## ACADEMY AWARD NOMINEE                          1972

The first black woman nominated for an Academy Award for costume design was **ELIZABETH COURTNEY**, for *Lady Sings the Blues*.

## 1973              ARTIST MAKES SOLO EXHIBIT

The first black artist to have a solo exhibit at the Boston Museum of Fine Arts was **LOIS MAILOU JONES (1905–1998)**. Jones was responsible for organizing the art department at Palmer Memorial Institute in Sedalia, North Carolina. She also taught at Howard University. She was highly successful as a teacher and artist and influenced the lives of many fledgling black artists.

## RECORD-BREAKING RADIO              1973
## STATION OWNER

**DOROTHY EDWARDS BRUNSON (1939–2001)** became the first black woman to own a radio station when she purchased WEBB in

Baltimore. She acquired three other stations later on and in 1990 also bought WGTV, a television station in Philadelphia.

## 1973    CREATIVE LIGHTING DESIGNER

**SHIRLEY PRENDERGAST (1929–2019)** became the first black woman lighting designer on Broadway. She worked with the Negro Ensemble Company's *The River Niger*. After passing the lighting examination in 1969, she became one of the first black women to gain admission into the lighting division of United Scenic Artists Association. She designed for a number of theaters, including the Alvin Ailey American Dance Theatre, New York Shakespeare Festival, and the New Federal Theatre.

## "MS. RADIO" BECOMES STATION    1975
## MANAGER

**CATHERINE "CATHY" LIGGINS HUGHES (1947–)** became the first female radio station general manager in Washington, D.C. She began in radio as an administrative assistant to Tony Brown at Howard University in 1971 and transferred to Howard's radio station in 1973, later becoming vice president and general manager of the station. In 1980 she founded Radio One, which in 2018 was renamed Urban One, Inc., and is the largest black-owned U.S. broadcasting company.

## 1975    NEWBERY MEDAL WINNER

**VIRGINIA ESTHER HAMILTON (ADOFF) (1936–2002)** became the first black to receive the Newbery Medal, the American Library Association's most prestigious award in American children's books. Her novel *M. C. Higgins, the Great*, which won her the award, also garnered for her the National Book Award in 1975 and several other recognitions. In 1995 Hamilton became the first writer of children's books to receive a MacArthur Foundation "genius" grant. She published her first book, *Zeely*, in 1967, followed by such works as *The House of Dies Drear*, *The Time-Ago Tales of Jadhu*, *The Planet of Junior Brown*, and *M. C. Higgins, the Great*—the book that secured her literary reputation. Hamilton always considered herself a storyteller. She became known as one of the most influential figures in twentieth-century American literature.

# GLASS-SHATTERING OPRY SINGERS 1975

The Pointer Sisters, left to right, are Anita, Bonnie, and Ruth Pointer.

The first black women to perform on the Grand Ole Opry, in Nashville, Tennessee, were the Pointer Sisters. The sisters, called the "musical darlings" of the 1970s and 1980s, returned on June 8, 2002, to perform at Nashville's most prestigious social event, the Swan Ball. The sisters, **RUTH (1946–), ANITA (1948–), BONNIE (1950–2020)**, and **JUNE (1953–2006) POINTER**, were born in Oakland, California. Two of the sisters, Bonnie and June, formed a group known as Pointers and performed in the Bay Area. Anita later joined the group and, in 1972, Ruth was the last to join.

# 1975 LONG-RUNNING TELEVISION SERIES

*The Jeffersons*, which ran 11 seasons, made its debut. Starring **ISABEL SANFORD (1917–2004), MARLA GIBBS (1931–)**, and Sherman Hemsley (1938–2012), the show became the longest-running black series. The show was also the first to feature a married interracial couple, the Willises.

# PIONEERING SCIENCE-FICTION WRITER     1976

**OCTAVIA BUTLER (1947–2006)** became the first black woman science-fiction writer to be published. She suffered from unrecognized dyslexia, the consequence of which at first led to poor performance in school. However, her problem never interfered with the fantasy stories and romance that she wrote when she was 10 and 11 years old. Butler enrolled in writing courses, attended writing workshops, and participated in the Clarion Writers Workshop. She published a number of short stories, several of which were award-winning. She also wrote a number of science-fiction novels, most falling within a series. Her most successful stand-alone novel is *Kindred* (1988), which she called "grim fantasy" and not science fiction, for there is no science in it.

# 1976          BROADWAY MUSICAL DIRECTOR

**VINNETTE JUSTINE CARROLL (1922–2002)** became the first black woman to direct a Broadway musical, *Your Arms Too Short to Box with God*. In the summer of 1975, the play was commissioned for the Spoleto Festival in Italy, and the next year it opened to rave reviews in New York. She won an Obie Award in 1961 for *Moon on a Rainbow Shawl* and an Emmy Award in 1964 for *Beyond the Blues*. She received three Tony Award nominations, including one for *Don't Bother Me, I Can't Cope*. Carroll became the first black woman to play the role of Ftatateeta in George Bernard Shaw's *Caesar and Cleopatra*.

# BEST-SELLING OCTOGENARIAN     1977

**ALBERTA HUNTER (1895–1984)** was the first black to record a best-selling album at age 83. She performed in Chicago at various clubs and cabarets for blacks. In 1915 she moved to one of the top spots for whites, the Panama Cafe. In 1921 Hunter cut her first record for the Black Swan label. She switched to Paramount, where she recorded her own "Down Hearted Blues." She moved to New York, where she performed in *How Come?* at the Apollo Theater, then went on the road with the show. Hunter also worked in vaudeville on the Keith Circuit. She worked in Paris and on the French Riviera in 1927, and a year later she opened in the London production of *Show Boat*. Hunter left show business to work as a practical nurse for 20 years; forced to retire from nursing, she returned to music.

## 1977        RINGLING BROTHERS CLOWN

***BERNICE COLLINS (1957–)*** was the first black woman clown with Ringling Brothers. She attended "The Greatest Show on Earth" in Chicago and soon studied at Ringling Bros. and Barnum & Bailey Clown College. She became the first black woman clown in the show's history. Her love for animals brought her in contact with Charly Baumann, who tutored her. Collins made her debut with big cats in 1983. She returned to Ringling Bros. as a showgirl and then went back to the animals, presenting horses. Collins has presided as company manager at Big Apple Circus and later joined Cirque du Soleil's *Zumanity* in Las Vegas.

## ANTHOLOGY OF BLACK WOMEN'S     1978 HISTORY

***SHARON HARLEY (1948–)*** and ***ROSALYN M. TERBORG-PENN (1941–2018)*** published *The Afro-American Woman: Struggle and Images*, the first anthology of black women's history. They also worked with Darlene Clark Hine on her book *Black Women in America,* published in 1993. Harley was on the editorial advisory board for the book, and Terborg-Penn was an associate editor.

## 1978      NATIONALLY TELEVISED WHITE HOUSE SINGER

President Jimmy Carter on October 8 inaugurated a series of nationally televised concerts from the White House. Opera singer ***LEONTYNE PRICE (1927–)*** was the first black American to present works at the concerts.

Leontyne Price

## PIONEERING FILM DIRECTOR      1982

The first black American woman to direct a feature-length film, *Losing Ground*, was ***KATHLEEN COLLINS (1942–1988).*** She also wrote the screenplay.

# 1983     SHINING STAR OF SHOW BOAT

**LONETTE McKEE (1954–)** became the first black woman to star as Julie on Broadway, in the Houston Grand Opera's version of *Show Boat*. The character of Julie, the product of a mixed-race relationship, required her to pass for white as she headlined a show sailing down the Mississippi River in the late 1880s. McKee made a number of theater appearances on Broadway (*Showboat*, 1983), and off-Broadway (*Lady Day at Emerson's Bar and Grill*, 1986–87). Her film appearances include *The Cotton Club, Jungle Fever*, and *Malcolm X*. Among her television appearances are *The Women of Brewster Place* and *Queen*.

# PULITZER PRIZE WINNER     1983

**ALICE WALKER (1944–)** was the first black woman writer to win a Pulitzer Prize for a work of fiction. Her novel *The Color Purple* was popular but controversial. It also won the American Book Award and established her as a major American writer. Her third novel, *The Color Purple* was made into an Oscar-nominated movie and Tony-winning musical. Walker is also a poet, essayist, and short fiction writer. She graduated from the liberal Sarah Lawrence College and worked in the Civil Rights Movement in Mississippi. An ardent feminist, Walker uses the term "womanist" to describe her work. Her

Alice Walker

works include *The Third Life of Grange Copeland; In Search of Our Mother's Garden: Womanist Prose; The Temple of My Familiar; Meridian;* and *The Way Forward Is with a Broken Heart.*

# 1985     *SATURDAY NIGHT LIVE* CAST MEMBER

**DANITRA VANCE (1954–1994)** was the first black woman to join the regular *Saturday Night Live* cast, joining in the 1985–86 season. She also performed with Chicago's Second City comedy troupe.

# QUEEN OF SOUL     1986

In 1986 **ARETHA FRANKLIN (1942–2018)** was the first black woman selected for induction into the Rock and Roll Hall of Fame and

Museum. She joined a quartet directed by James Cleveland. She turned to blues in the 1960s, and in 1967 two of her albums sold more than a million copies each. Franklin won 18 Grammy Awards and in 1994 received the Grammy Legend Award.

Aretha Franklin

## 1986                                                  MEDIA TYCOON

Oprah Winfrey

*OPRAH WINFREY (1954–)* became the first black woman to host a nationally syndicated weekday talk show, *The Oprah Winfrey Show*. She started her career in Nashville, Tennessee, and later moved to Chicago. Winfrey took over *A.M. Chicago*. She formed Harpo Productions and became the first black woman in television and film to own her own production company. She ended the show and then launched the series premier of her network, OWN (Oprah Winfrey's Network). Oprah's Book Club, an on-air reading club, ran from 1996 to 2002. Winfrey launched Oprah's Angel Network. She has appeared in a number of films and in television movies. With Hearst Magazines, Winfrey introduced *The Oprah Magazine*. Her charitable programs include the Oprah Winfrey Charitable Foundation and the Oprah Winfrey Leadership Academy Foundation. Winfrey is cited as the richest woman in television history. She has appeared on the *Forbes* Celebrity 100 list of the world's most powerful celebrities in the world. Winfrey's numerous awards include honoree at the 33rd annual Kennedy Center Honors and the Presidential Medal of Freedom.

## GLASS-SHATTERING ROCKETTE                    1988

The first black Rockette at Radio City Music Hall was *JENNIFER JONES (1967–)*. A fill-in, she was scheduled to be called whenever there was a vacancy.

## 1988    BARRIER-BREAKING QUEEN OF RAP

Queen Latifah

***QUEEN LATIFAH (DANA OWENS) (1970–)*** was one of the first women to make a breakthrough in the male-dominated field of rap music. In 1989 Queen Latifah had several successes—she made her first European tour, first appeared at the Apollo in Harlem, and made her first video ("Dance for Me") and album (*All Hail the Queen*). She later appeared in such films as *Juice, Jungle Fever, House Party 2, Chicago, Ice Age 2* and *3*, and *Joyful Noise*. Her television appearances include *Fresh Prince of Bel-Air, Living Single*, and *Joyful Noise*.

## CHANGE-MAKING TELEVISION EXECUTIVE                                              1989

***JENNIFER KAREN LAWSON (1946–)*** became executive vice president of programming for the Public Broadcasting Service in Washington, D.C. As the highest-ranking black woman to serve in public television, she managed national programming for 330 stations. *The Civil War*, which was aired under her administration, drew more than 50 million viewers and became the most-watched show in PBS history.

## 1989    POWERFUL THEATRICAL PRODUCER

The first recipient of the Actors' Equity award for broadening participation in the theater was ***ROSETTA LENOIRE (1911–2002)***. The award was later named in honor of LeNoire and presented annually. LeNoire, a theatrical producer, created nontraditional casting before the phrase itself was created. She studied at the Works Progress Administration program at a theater on the Lower East Side and earned an entry into the all-black version of *Macbeth*. In 1939 LeNoire made her Broadway debut in the all-black *The Hot Mikado*. She played and acted in several television shows, such as *Search for Tomorrow, The Guiding Light*, and *Gimme a Break*.

## FILM DIRECTOR                                                               1989

***EUZHAN PALCY (1958–)*** was the first black woman director of a full-length film for a major American studio. *A Dry White Season*, starring Donald Sutherland and Susan Sarandon, deals with apartheid in South Africa.

# 1989    TRAIL-BREAKING RECORD COMPANY EXECUTIVE

The first black woman vice president of a major record company, Atlantic Records, was **SYLVIA RHONE (1952–)**. She directed promotional work for various record labels and gained a reputation as one who discovered and shaped black talent. In 1991 she was named copresident and chief executive officer of Atlantic's East-West Records and became chair and chief executive officer of Atlantic's newly formed Atco-East/West label.

Sylvia Rhone

# TRAILBLAZING ESPN ANCHORWOMAN  1990

Television sportscaster **ROBIN ROBERTS (1960–)** became the first on-air black anchorwoman for ESPN. In 1996 she was named the new host of *ABC's Wide World of Sports*, the first black woman to hold that position. She was also the first black woman to host a network-televised NFL pre-game show. In 1994 she had a series of her own on ESPN, *In the Sports Light*, and she anchored ABC's coverage of the U.S. Figure Skating Championships in 1996. Roberts won two Emmy Awards and the DAR Television Award for Merit. In 2005 Roberts became coanchor of *Good Morning America*. She took a hiatus from the show in 2012 to undergo a bone marrow transplant to treat myelodysplastic syndrome (MDS). As of 2021, Roberts is the coanchor of ABC's *Good Morning America*.

Robin Roberts

# 1991                     SYNDICATED CARTOONIST

**BARBARA BRANDON-CROFT (1958–)** became the first black woman cartoonist nationally syndicated in the white press. Her comic strip "Where I'm Coming From" appeared first in the *Detroit Free Press* and was acquired by Universal Press Syndicate in 1991.

Her cartoons were the first to center on black women. In 1982 she created "Where I'm Coming From" and took it to the editors of the black woman's magazine *Elan*. The magazine accepted her strip but ceased publication before her strip appeared. The *Detroit Free Press* first published her strip in 1989, and two years later it went national.

## BARRIER-BREAKING BLACK MODEL          1991

*KATHLEEN BRADLEY (1951–)* became the first black model on the daytime television game show *The Price Is Right*, starring Bob Barker.

## 1992          WRITER/DIRECTOR MAKES A DASH

*JULIE DASH (1952–)* became the first black woman writer and director to have a feature-length film in national distribution. The film, *Daughters of the Dust*, is the story of one day in the life of a black family living on Ibo Island, South Carolina. In 1981, Dash began work on a series of films about black women. Her drama *Illusions* was highly acclaimed and received the 1989 Jury Prize for the Black Filmmakers Foundation's Best Film of the Decade. Although she began work on *Daughters of the Dust* in 1975, Dash continued to work on the project throughout the 1980s. She relocated to Atlanta in 1986, founded Geechee Girls Productions, Inc., in 1988, and released *Daughters of the Dust*, which catapulted her to national attention.

Julie Dash

## PAINTINGS DEPICT RACE PROBLEMS          1992

*CORINNE HOWARD MITCHELL (1914–1993)* became the first black American to have a solo exhibit, *A Glimpse of Joy*, at the National Museum of Women in the Arts. She responded to the race problems in America by painting; for example, she reflected on the 1963 March on Washington by painting *The March* (1965).

# MAYA ANGELOU
## (1928–2014)

### Glass-shattering Writer and Poet

In 1993 Maya Angelou (Marguerite Johnson) became the first black inaugural poet, at the swearing-in of President Bill Clinton on January 20. She began a career as a dancer and performed in Chicago and New York; she also toured Europe and Africa in *Porgy and Bess*. Around this time, she adopted her name *Maya*. Angelou returned to the United States and continued her career as a nightclub performer. She also became a social activist and committed herself to the Southern Christian Leadership Conference. The Harlem Writer's Guild helped her along her newly chosen path of becoming a writer. In 1970 she published her first autobiography, *I Know Why the Caged Bird Sings,* and became the first black woman to have a nonfiction work on the bestseller list. She earned an Emmy nomination for her appearance in Alex Haley's television production of *Roots*, and she continued her acting career while she developed a writing career. In 1981 Angelou accepted a lifetime faculty appointment at Wake Forest University in Winston-Salem. Her numerous works include several volumes of poetry and *The Heart of a Woman*. With the publication of her sixth and final memoir, *A Song Flung up to Heaven* (2002), Angelou intended to "close the book on life," to the extent that it would be her concluding memoir. Her inaugural poem was published as "On the Pulse of Morning."

## 1993      TRAILBLAZING WRITER OF ENCYCLOPEDIA

**DARLENE CLARK HINE (1947–)** edited and published a two-volume encyclopedia, *Black Women in America*, the first major work on that subject. A second edition of the work, printed in three volumes, was published in 2005. She was director of Purdue's Africana Studies and Research Center, and later vice provost. While there she embarked on a project for the National Council of Negro Women. Her work resulted in the publication of *When the Truth Is Told: Black Women's Community and Culture in Indiana, 1875–1950*. She later established the Black Women in the Middle West project and coedited a book about these sources in 1985 under the title *Black Women in the Middle West: A Comprehensive Research Guide, Indiana and Illinois*.

## NOBEL PRIZE WINNER      1993

Toni Morrison

**TONI MORRISON (1931–2019)**, novelist, educator, and editor, was the first black American and the second American woman to win the Nobel Prize in literature. Her novel *Song of Solomon*, published in 1977, won the National Book Critics Award for fiction that year, and in 1988 she won the Pulitzer Prize for fiction for her work *Beloved*. Her other novels include *The Bluest Eye, Sula, Tar Baby, Jazz, Paradise, Love*, and *A Mercy*. Morrison became the Robert F. Goheen Professor of the Council of the Humanities at Princeton University. In 1996 the National Endowment for the Humanities named her the Jefferson Lecturer in the Humanities.

## 1994      ACADEMY AWARD SHOW HOST

When **WHOOPI GOLDBERG (CARYN JOHNSON) (1955–)** hosted the 66th annual Academy Awards telecast on March 21, she became the first black and the first solo woman ever to host the event. She served as host three additional times. She made her film debut in *The Color Purple* (1985). For her lead role as Celie, Goldberg won a Golden Globe Award, the NAACP Image Award, and an Academy Award nomination. She won an Academy Award as best supporting actress in the film *Ghost* in 1991. Her other films include *Jumpin' Jack Flash*,

*Fatal Beauty, The Long Walk Home, The Player, Sister Act, The Lion King,* and *How Stella Got Her Groove Back.* Her various television appearances include *Star Trek: The Next Generation* and *Baghdad Café,* and in 2007 she began cohosting the talk show *The View.* In 2002, Goldberg became the first black person to have won a Grammy (1985), Oscar (1991), Tony (2002), and Emmy (2002).

Whoopi Goldberg

## NETWORK TELEVISION ANCHOR     1994

**DIANN BURNS (1958–)** became the first black woman anchor at a network station in Chicago. She joined Capital Cities/ABC's WLS in Chicago as a general assignment reporter and was promoted in 1994.

## 1995     TRAILBLAZING ACTRESS BECOMES TELEVISION STAR

**HALLE (MARIA) BERRY (1966–)** became the first black to play the role of Sheba on television. The television movie *Solomon and Sheba* is based on the Old Testament of the Bible and premiered on February 26. Berry's first film, *Jungle Fever* (1991), set her on the road to stardom. In 2002 Berry was voted best female actor for the film *Monster's Ball* (2001) at the 74th Annual Academy Awards, becoming the first black woman to win the award. Among her film appearances are *Boomerang, Why Do Fools Fall in Love?, Gothica,* and *X-Men: The Last Stand.* Her

Halle Berry

television appearances have included a recurring role in *Knots Landing,* the miniseries *Queen* (1993), and *Introducing Dorothy Dandridge* (1999).

## CREATIVE DIRECTOR     1995

**HOPE CLARK (1941–)** was the first black person to direct and choreograph a major staging of the opera-musical *Porgy and Bess.* She was principal dancer with the Katherine Dunham Company and the Alvin Ailey American Dance Theater during the 1960s. She also appeared in a number of television shows, including *Hill Street Blues, The Jeffersons*, and *As the World Turns*. Clark's Broadway appearances include *Don't Bother Me I Can't Cope* and *Purlie*. Her choreography for *Jelly's Last Jam* (1992) earned her a Tony Award nomination. In 1995 she won the award for directing *Porgy and Bess*.

## 1996        CABLE NEWS NETWORK ANCHOR

*LORI STOKES (1962–)* became the first anchor on Microsoft and NBC's cable news network, MSNBC. She was promoted from anchor on *Good Morning Washington*, a weekend program.

## GROUNDBREAKING ARTIST-IN-        1997
## RESIDENCE

The Ford Foundation named *ANNA DEAVERE SMITH (1950–)* its first artist-in-residence. Her assignment was to help plan a "new initiative on the civic role of the arts" and to assist the foundation in integrating artistic and cultural perspectives across its program areas. In 1996 Smith also received a "genius grant" for theater work from the John D. and Catherine T. MacArthur Foundation. The playwright, performance artist, and actress is known for her unique performance. Her plays present a cross-section of Americans from the 1980s to the 1990s.

## 1999        *ACCESS HOLLYWOOD* WEEKEND
## ANCHOR

The first black woman weekend anchor for the nationally syndicated entertainment magazine *Access Hollywood* was *SHAUN ROBINSON (1962–)*.

## BAND DIRECTOR        1999

*NORMA SOLOMON WHITE (1934–)* became the first woman to direct the Florida A&M "Marching 100." When White was a student at the university (1951–55), she was the first female member of the band.

## 1999 FILM CORPORATION EXECUTIVE

The first black woman executive at Twentieth Century Fox Film Corporation in Los Angeles was **MARYANN JOHNSON**. She was named director of television music administration. Her responsibilities were to track music in the corporation's television shows, which included *Ally McBeal*, *The X-Files*, and *The Simpsons*.

## PULITZER PRIZE–WINNING PLAYWRIGHT 2002

**SUZAN-LORI PARKS (1963–)** became the first black woman to win a Pulitzer Prize for drama, for her play *Topdog/Underdog*. The play premiered in July 2001 at the nonprofit Public Theater off Broadway. *Topdog/Underdog* is a dark comedy with only two characters—brothers Lincoln and Booth. Parks received a $500,000 MacArthur Fellows grant in 2001.

Suzan-Lori Parks

## 2002 OSCAR-WINNING LEAD ACTRESS

**HALLE (MARIA) BERRY (1966–)** won an Oscar for her lead role in *Monster's Ball* and became the first black actress to win the award in that category in Academy Award history. Presented in Hollywood ceremonies on March 24, 2002, the Oscar was awarded for her portrayal of a death row widow who forged a relationship with a white prison guard. Oscar night was a momentous one for black actors in Hollywood. For the first time in almost four decades, a black actor won an Oscar for a lead role.

## RECORD-SETTING SURVIVOR STAR 2002

**VECEPIA "VEE" TOWERY (1966?–)** became the first black to win $1 million on the CBS show *Survivor*, in May. She was a member of the network's fourth installment of *Survivor* called *Survivor: Marquesas*.

## 2005    PIONEERING TELEVISION PRODUCER

The first African American woman to create and produce a top-ten series on network television was **SHONDA LYNN RHIMES (1970–)**. She became widely known for the popular medical drama *Grey's Anatomy*, first produced on ABC this year. The show ranked among the top ten most-watched television programs during its first four seasons. Rhimes launched a spin-off of the show in 2007 with *Private Practice*. Her success with *Grey's Anatomy* led to more television shows, including *Scandal, How to Get Away with Murder*, and *The Catch*. Rhimes left the shows in 2017 and signed a multiyear contract with Netflix.

## QUEEN TAKES A STAR                                      2007

The first rap artist to receive a star on the Hollywood Walk of Fame was **QUEEN LATIFAH (1970–)**.

## 2007                             PRIZE-WINNING WRITER

Children's author, poet, and prose writer for adults **LUCILLE CLIFTON (1936–2010)** was the first black to win the Ruth Lilly Poetry Prize. The $100,000 award is one of the largest and most prestigious literary honors in the United States. Established in 1986, the annual prize honors the lifetime achievements of a U.S. poet. Two of Clifton's 11 books of poetry were nominated for a Pulitzer Prize. She also wrote one book of prose and 19 children's books.

## AWARD-WINNING DISNEY ACTRESS         2009

The full-length movie *The Princess and the Frog* opened on December 11 with the first black female lead in a Disney animated feature. Rising black star and Tony Award–winning actress **ANIKA NONI ROSE (1972–)** provides the voice for the princess (Tiana). The film is set in New Orleans (the Big Easy) and its boggy surroundings in the 1910s and 1920s. The movie highlights the spirit of black Cajun soul that defines the culture of New Orleans.

Anika Noni Rose

## 2012 — AWARD-WINNING SCREENWRITER

Ava DuVernay

*AVA DUVERNAY (1972–)* was the first black woman to win the best director award at the 2012 Sundance Film Festival. She won for her second film, *Middle of Nowhere*. In 2017 she was the first black female director to receive an Oscar nomination for Best Documentary Feature for *13th*. The next year, she became the first woman of color to direct a feature film with a budget of $100 million or more for the film *A Wrinkle in Time*. DuVernay made her directorial debut in 2008 with the film *This Is the Life*. She won an African-American Film Critics Association award in 2010 for her first narrative feature film called *I Will Follow*. Her breakthrough film, *Selma*, was released in 2014.

## LATE NIGHT TELEVISION WRITER — 2014

Comedian and writer *AMBER RUFFIN (1979–)* joined *Late Night with Seth Meyers* and became the first black woman to write for a late-night network talk show in the United States. Ruffin also writes on Comedy Central/Broadway Video's *Detroiters*, and she regularly narrates on *Drunk History*.

Amber Ruffin

## 2014 — PASSIONATE TELEVISION COHOST

Tamron Hall

The first African American woman to cohost *The Today Show* was *TAMRON HALL (1970–)*. Hall abruptly left the show in early 2017, after being forced out to make room for popular television host Megyn Kelly. She became an Emmy-nominated daytime anchor for MSNBC and host for the program *MSNBC Life with Tamron Hall*. In September 2019, she began to host a new talk show on NBC.

# MISTY COPELAND
## (1982–)

### Ballerina Breaks Barrier

Misty Copeland took the lead in *Swan Lake* in 2015 at the Metropolitan Opera House in New York City and in June became the first African American performer to serve as a principal dancer for the American Ballet Theatre (ABT). She also joined the cast of the Broadway revival of Leonard Bernstein's *On the Town*. Copeland studied under ballet instructor Cindy Bradley and joined the studio company of ABT, becoming a soloist. She starred in such productions as *The Nutcracker* and *Firebird*. Of mixed ethnic heritage, Copeland endured a difficult family life but found solace in dancing routines, which she performed at home. At age 13, she moved in with her ballet teacher's family, continued her training, and performed in several productions, including *The Chocolate Nutcracker*. Beyond ballet, Copeland published her own calendar in 2013. She published her memoir, *Life in Motion: An Unlikely Ballerina,* and *Firebird*, an award-winning children's picture book. She inspired a Barbie doll that wore a costume similar to the one she wore in *Firebird*. The doll is a part of the Barbie Sheroes program, which spotlights female heroes who break boundaries.

## PIONEERING MAJOR NETWORK EXECUTIVE　　2016

***CHANNING (NICOLE) DUNGEY (1969–)*** became the first black American president of ABC Entertainment Group, making her the first black American president of a major broadcast network. She

became a production executive with Warner Brothers, where she helped to develop and supervise such films as *The Bridges of Madison County* and *The Devil's Advocate*. In February 2016 she became president of ABC Studios and oversaw the development of shows such as *Scandal, How to Get Away with Murder, Nashville,* and *Once upon a Time.* On May 29, 2018, she made the news for canceling the *Roseanne* reboot due to a racist tweet that actress Roseanne Barr posted about a former advisor to President Barack Obama.

Channing Dungey

## 2017   COLOR BARRIER-BREAKING BACHELORETTE

*RACHEL LINDSAY (1985–)* became the first black bachelorette on the 13th season of ABC's *The Bachelorette.* She selected Bryan Abasolo as her mate; they became engaged and later set their wedding for summer 2019.

## TRAILBLAZING ACTRESS/SINGER    2017

On November 11, *TIFFANY HADDISH (1979–)*, an actress and singer, became the first black female to host *Saturday Night Live (SNL).* In 2018 she won an Emmy for Outstanding Guest Actress in a Comedy Series for hosting *SNL.* In October 2019, Haddock became host for ABC television's revival of *Children Say the Darndest Things.* She received a Grammy Award for best comedy album for *Black Mitzvah* in 2021. In addition to acting and comedy work, she also voices cartoon characters, including that of Tiffany Haddock in *The SpongeBob Movie: Sponge on the Run.*

Tiffany Haddish

## 2017   EMMY-WINNING COMEDY WRITER

On September 17, *LENA WAITHE (1984–)* became the first black woman to win an Emmy for Outstanding Writing for a Comedy

Series. *Master of None* was cocreated with Aziz Ansari. After receiving the award, Waithe delivered an empowering message to her LGBTQIA family. She wrote and produced *Queen & Slim*, which was released by Universal Pictures in fall 2019.

Lena Waithe

## OSCAR-WINNING ACTRESS                    2017

**VIOLA DAVIS (1965–)** won an Oscar for Best Supporting Actress for her role in the film adaptation of August Wilson's play *Fences*. With this award, she became the first black to win a triple crown—an Oscar, Emmy, and Tony. Davis made her screen debut in 1996, when she appeared in *The Substance of Fire*, followed by guest spots in various television shows and films. Her starring role in the television series *How to Get Away with Murder* from its beginning in 2014 helped make the show a major success.

Viola Davis

## 2018            EMMY AWARD WINNERS

**TIFFANY HADDISH (1979–),** Ron Cephas Jones, **SAMIRA WILEY (1987–)**, and Katt Williams achieved milestones this year by winning Emmy Awards in guest star categories, marking the first time that four black actors were so honored in the same category in the same year. Haddish and Williams won for best guest actress and actor in a comedy series for their work on *Saturday Night Live* and *Atlanta*, respectively.

## HUGO AWARD–WINNING NOVELIST       2018

**N. K. JEMISIN (1972–)** became the first person ever to win the Hugo Award for Best Novel three years in a row and the only black writer to win the award. In 2016 she was the first black to win the award for

Best Novel, for *The Fifth Season*. In 2017 she won again for its sequel, *The Obelisk Gate,* and in 2018 for *The Stone Sky*. Also in 2018, she published "The Broken Earth" series, a trilogy of her Hugo Award–winning novels.

## 2018                   BILLBOARD AWARD WINNER

Janet Jackson

**JANET JACKSON (1966–)** became the first black ever nominated to receive *Billboard*'s Icon Award. She is also the only member of the legendary Jackson family, which includes Michael Jackson, to be nominated for an Academy Award. In 2018 she was inducted into the Rock and Roll Hall of Fame. In 2014 she was considered the third-most-awarded recording artist of all time, ranking behind her brother Michael and Beyoncé.

## INAUGURAL POET                                    2021

**AMANDA GORMAN (1998–)**, only 22 years old, became the youngest inaugural poet in U.S. history when she read her poem "The Hill We Climb" at the inauguration of President Joe Biden on January 20. In her five-minute reading, she called for healing and unity in the United States. Following this appearance, she performed at Super Bowl LV. In 2014 Gorman was named the first Youth Poet Laureate of Los Angeles. Three years later, she became the country's first National Youth Poet Laureate. The Los Angeles native experienced chronic ear infections as an infant, followed by an auditory processing disorder that resulted in a speech impediment. In 2016 she founded a nonprofit called One Pen One Page to help youth to use their voices and eliminate inequality by becoming educated. Her first children's book, *Change Sings: A Children's Anthem*, has become a popular work.

## 2021          "QUEEN BEE" WINS GRAMMYS

The first artist to win 28 Grammy Awards is **BEYONCÉ GISELLE KNOWLES-CARTER (1981–)**. Beyoncé (also called Queen Bee), is a singer-songwriter, actress, and entrepreneur who rose to fame in the late

Beyoncé

1900s when she formed the singing-rapping group Destiny's Child. The group dissolved several times to allow each singer to pursue individual projects. In 2004 the group officially disbanned. Beyoncé continued to rise in fame and dominated the 2010 Grammy Awards by receiving six that year, the most Grammys collected by a female artist in a single night. By 2021 she had 28 Grammys, the most won by a female artist. Her acting debut came in 2001 with the television movie *Carmen, a Hip Hopera* and continued with her role in *The Fighting Temptations, The Pink Panther*, and *Dreamgirls*. She has been nominated for a Golden Globe and an Academy Award.

# Business

A critical analysis of slavery in America will reveal countless ways in which black women brought from Africa their talents and innate ability. Women in Africa were, in fact, involved in business dealings well before they became enslaved Americans. When they crossed America's shores, they were forced to devote their talents largely to the service of white enslavers. They also served their own communities, and after emancipation they were able to apply their talents more broadly.

Early black business clientele lived primarily outside the South, where white clientele either did not know or did not care if the product came from black people. This era produced women who did exquisite embroidering and fashionable dressmaking primarily for whites. They were people like former slave and pastry chef Duchess Quaimo and tradeswoman Elleanor Eldridge, also a former slave. As time passed, however, black women contributed to the economic development of their community. The enduring businesses of black women beginning with this early period and continuing today included beauty shops, the manufacturing of beauty products, and training beauty-care workers. For example, Christiana Carteaux Bannister operated her shampooing and hair-dyeing business in Massachusetts and Rhode Island but catered to whites. Madame C. J. Walker, Sarah Spencer Washington, and Annie Turnbo Malone remain the most popular icons of the early beauty industry. That Walker and Malone became millionaires is astonishing. Their shops and others like them were incubators for politicians and civil rights workers who needed a safe haven in which to plan and promote their work.

As early as 1903, the nation saw the first black-created and black-run bank—Saint Luke's Penny Thrift Savings Bank. Founder Maggie Lena Walker, a feminist, made passionate pleas to young black women to work diligently and become a source of feminine power. Her plea characterizes the success of other black women who became important in the black and larger communities.

The power of African American women business leaders increased over the years. Many became involved in the financial industry as bank founders and/or bank presidents. They founded and led advertising agencies, opened automobile dealerships, became plant managers of major automobile and other manufacturing industries, opened successful restaurants, and owned newspapers. They also pioneered as heads of corporations like Xerox. In recent years, more African American women moved into leadership positions of prominent and well-established major retail businesses. They include women like Ann Fudge, the first black woman to head a major company—the Maxwell House Coffee division of Kraft General Foods; Ursula Burns, chief executive of Xerox Corporation and the first black female CEO of a Fortune 500 company; and Rosalind (Roz) Brewer, the first woman and the first black American to lead a division of Walmart and Sam's Club. Today's black women keep up with trends in successful entrepreneurship and engage in e-business often seen in products like jewelry, fashion, and cosmetics.

Recognitions given to black women entrepreneurs and/or business leaders are well deserved and point to the success of women long disregarded or minimized in the media.

## POOR SLAVE BECOMES RICH ENTREPRENEUR                    1866

**BIDDY MASON (1818–1891)** was the first known black woman property owner in Los Angeles, California. Born into slavery in Georgia or Mississippi and named Bridget, she and her master, Robert Smith, took the strenuous journey first to the Utah Territory and then to California, where Mason legally gained her freedom on January 21, 1856. All members of her family were freed as well. Mason worked as nurse and midwife—as she had done en route to the West—and saved her money. Her earnings and careful investment became the foundation that enabled her grandson Robert to be called the

Biddy Mason

# NANCY GREEN (1834–1923)

## America's Aunt Jemima

Nancy Green, a former slave from Montgomery County, Kentucky, was the first Aunt Jemima and the world's first living trademark. She made her debut in 1893 at age 59 at the Columbian Exposition in Chicago. The Aunt Jemima Mills Company distributed a souvenir lapel button that bore her image and the caption, "I'se in town honey." The caption later became the slogan on the company's promotional campaign. Green was the official trademark for three decades, touring the country and promoting Aunt Jemima products. The Aunt Jemima character, a variant of the mammy image, has perpetuated racial and gender stereotyping. Characteristically, the mammy icon in American culture is that of a plump black woman household servant who is soft-witted, comical, and headstrong and who nurtures the children of her white master. Aunt Jemima, on the other hand, is a polite, indulgent cook who is closely associated with pancakes and kitchen products. Her image has been used on products that bore the Aunt Jemima label while the mammy and Jemima images have been seen in housewares, dolls and other toys, household decorations, and in literature, film, radio, and elsewhere. Acknowledging that the image is a racial stereotype, Quaker Oats retired the Aunt Jemima brand in 2020.

richest black in Los Angeles around 1900. A very religious and charitable woman, Mason opened her house for the establishment of the first African Methodist Episcopal church in the city in 1872. She is also said to have opened the first day care nursery for homeless community children.

# 1903     FIRST BLACK WOMAN BANK PRESIDENT

*MAGGIE LENA WALKER (1864–1934)* became the first black woman bank president when she founded the Saint Luke Penny Savings Bank in Richmond, Virginia. The bank began as an insurance society in

Maggie Lena Walker

which Walker became active. When she retired in 1933, the bank was strong enough to survive the Great Depression, and it is still operational. Walker urged blacks to save their nickels and dimes, turn them into dollars, and finance their own homes, since white-owned banks would not do so. An ardent feminist, she urged women to improve themselves educationally and economically. She fought for women's suffrage and also worked in voter registration campaigns. She was an instrument in the formation of the Virginia Lily Black Republican Party. In March 1902 Walker founded *The St. Luke Herald,* a newspaper that illuminated black concerns and strengthened communication between the community and the Order of St. Luke, a black organization that dealt with the concerns of the race. The daughter of a formerly enslaved washerwoman, she became one of the wealthiest and most influential black women of the early twentieth century. Her spacious home in Richmond has been declared a National Historic Landmark.

## MILLIONAIRE HAIR-CARE MAGNATE        1910

*MADAME C. J. WALKER (1867–1919)* is believed to be the first black woman millionaire. However, supporters of Annie Turnbo Malone (1869–1957) dispute this. Both women produced hair-care products for black women during the period; it is asserted that Walker worked as a salesperson for Malone products. Both became very wealthy by around 1910. Sarah Breedlove McWilliams Walker, known as Madame C. J. Walker, was born in Louisiana to indigent former slaves. She became interested in the hair problems of black women, and after moving to Denver, she began to manufacture hair products and eventually produced five hair-care

Madame C. J. Walker

products. Her company began with door-to-door selling techniques; she eventually established a chain of beauty parlors across the country, the Caribbean, and South America. Walker selected Indianapolis as her headquarters. She employed 5,000 black commissioned agents, who demonstrated her techniques and sold her products. She became wealthy and built a palatial mansion, Villa Lewaro, on the Hudson River in Irvington, New York. It became a gathering place for black leaders and entertainers. In 1993 investment banker Harold Doley bought the house and in 1958 turned it into a temporary decorators' museum to attract black designers and raise money for charity. The mansion has become a private residence.

## 1930s        LEADING MILLINER BLAZES TRAIL

**MILDRED BLOUNT (1907–1974)**, a leading milliner in the 1930s and 1940s and a civil rights advocate, was the first black American to design hats for Hollywood films. She also successfully fought for inclusion in Hollywood unions, which restricted membership to whites. She took a job at Madame Clair's dress shop, created hats from small pieces of clothing, and later moved to the John-Frederics company— the first black on staff. There she created 87 miniature hats for the New York World's Fair, resulting in her rapid rise as a milliner. Then she made hats for the film *Gone with the Wind* and became known among established milliners in New York City and in Hollywood. She made hats for other films as well. Blount left John-Frederics, moved to California, and founded her own company in Hollywood. Among her clients were Hollywood stars and private clients like singer Marian Anderson.

## TRAILBLAZER SAVINGS AND                                    1946
## LOANS EXECUTIVE

The first black woman to head a savings and loan institution was **LOUISE K. QUARLES LAWSON (1927?–2004)**. She became a clerk at Illinois Service Federal Savings and Loan Association in 1946 and spent 57 years at the financial institution. In 1930, a group of black businessmen on Chicago's South Side founded the institution and encouraged African Americans to buy their own homes. Lawson successfully served in an industry dominated by white men and helped the Chicago institution become one of the largest black-owned savings and loan companies in America. In 1976, she was appointed to President Jimmy Carter's Advisory Committee on Small and Minority Businesses.

## 1950s        PIONEERING NUTRITIONIST

**ALVENIA FULTON (1907?–1999)** became the first black to establish a health food store and vegetarian restaurant in Chicago. After opening her businesses in the late 1950s, she continued to work at her Fultonia

Health and Fasting Institute until she retired. Fulton encouraged what she called therapeutic healing and recommended that her clients cleanse their bodies. Fulton was the author of *The Fasting Power* and *The Nutrition Bible*.

## PASSIONATE LABOR UNION EXECUTIVE 1954

The first woman president of a packinghouse local was **ADDIE L. WYATT (1924–2012)**. When she failed to get a clerical job at a meat packinghouse in Chicago, she took a union position, joined the United Packinghouse Workers, and later became the union local's president. In 1968 the union merged with the Amalgamated Meat Cutters Union. Wyatt became an international vice president of the union in 1976 and was the first black woman to hold this leadership role in an international union. As a member of the national executive board of the Amalgamated Meat Cutters and Butcher Workmen, Wyatt became the first black woman labor executive in 1976.

## 1971 ADVERTISING AGENCY EXECUTIVE

**BARBARA GARDNER PROCTOR (1933–2018)** opened her own business this year and became the first black woman in Chicago to found an advertising agency. She wrote descriptive comments for jazz album covers and also worked in several advertising companies before deciding to form her own company.

## PIONEERING RAILROAD ENGINEER 1976

**EDWINA J. "CURLIE" JUSTUS (1943–)** was the first black woman engineer for the Union Pacific Railroad. The path to her position was partially paved by William "Bill" Riley, the railroad's first African American engineer at its Bailey Yard in North Platte, Wyoming. In 1973, Justus began as a traction motor clerk in North Platte, Wyoming, and then she was hired as a yard hostler, moving locomotives and cars in the train yard. When she became an engineer, she started with short trips to Cheyenne, Gering, and Scottsbluff. She felt fear during a railroad stop in Sidney, Nebraska, where she was the only black person in town. Justus was friendly with hobos, or "unauthorized passengers," whom she met along the routes. After 22 years, she retired in 1998 and

# RUTH JEAN BASKERVILLE BOWEN

## (1924–2009)

### Historical Booking and Talent Agent

Ruth Jean Baskerville Bowen was the first black woman to establish a successful booking and talent agency in New York City. She had done personal relations work for Dinah Washington, and her firm, Queen Booking Corporation, represented a number of black singers. Bowen began in 1959 and within ten years owned the largest black-owned agency in the world. At one time she was publicist for singer Dinah Washington, who encouraged Bowen to pursue a career as publicist. Bowen retained David Dinkins, later mayor of New York City, as her attorney and then obtained a booking license from the State of New York. As she devoted more time to Washington and became her personal manager, she hired other personnel to help with her publicity business, then known as Queen Artists.

has since then lived in Omaha. At age 73, she enjoyed the celebrations given in her honor, including the Union Pacific Railroad exhibit in the Union Railroad Museum in Council Bluffs, Iowa. The exhibit was called "Move Over, Sir: Women Working on the Railroad."

# 1977    HISTORY-MAKING BANK EXECUTIVE

The first woman to become vice president of Continental Bank of Philadelphia was **EMMA CAROLYN (BAYTON) CHAPPELL (1941–2021)**. In 1990 Chappell became the first chair and chief executive officer of the newly founded United Bank of Philadelphia, which opened for service on March 23, 1992. By 1995 the bank was named *Black Enterprise* magazine's Financial Company of the Year. Through her efforts, Chappell contributed significantly to economic development of Philadelphia's black community. She was a founder of the Rainbow Coalition and served as treasurer of Jesse Jackson's campaign for president of the United States in 1984.

# CAROLINE ROBINSON JONES
## (1942–2001)
### Advertising Agent "Does Chicken Right"

Caroline Robinson Jones was the first black female vice president of a major advertising agency, Batten, Barton, Durstine and Osborn (BBDO). In 1968 she cofounded Zebra Associates, a full-service agency. During the 1970s and 1980s, she worked for several agencies before helping to found Mingo Jones in 1977. In 1986, she established Creative Resources Management, which was later operated as Caroline Jones Advertising and Caroline Jones, Inc. One of the firm's most recognized slogans was "We do chicken right," developed for Kentucky Fried Chicken. Jones became an advertising pioneer who broke race and sex barriers in the industry.

## INSURANCE BROKERAGE FIRM ON WALL STREET                    1977

The E. G. Bowman Company was the first major American black-owned commercial insurance brokerage firm on Wall Street. **ERNESTA G. PROCOPE (1931–)** founded the company in 1953.

## 1981    PIONEERING STOCK EXCHANGE MEMBER

**GAIL PANKEY-ALBERT (1954–)** owned her own trading company and bought a seat on the New York Stock Exchange, reportedly the first minority woman to do so.

## LABOR UNION LEADER                                        1981

**BARBARA B. HUTCHINSON (1924–2013)** was the first black woman member of the American Federation of Labor and Congress of Indus-

# DOLORES DUNCAN WHARTON
## (1927–)
### Corporate Executive

In 1979 Dolores Duncan Wharton became the first black and the first woman on the board of Gannett Company. She is also the first black and first woman director for the Kellogg Foundation and Phillips Petroleum. She founded the Fund for Corporate Initiatives Inc. and became its chair and corporate director.

trial Organizations (AFL-CIO) executive council. Hutchinson was director of women's affairs for the American Federation of Government Employees.

## 1982    BUSINESS EDUCATOR BREAKS BARRIER

**SYBIL COLLINS MOBLEY (1925–2015)** was the first black woman member of the board of Sears, Roebuck and Company. Mobley taught in the business school of Florida Agricultural and Mechanical College (later Florida A&M University), where she became a dean in 1974. At first only a few companies recruited from the school's business department, but she convinced a number of Fortune 500 companies to recruit her students. Mobley became highly respected in the business community and was sought out for her expertise.

## PIONEERING BANK EXECUTIVE    1982

**MILDRED GLENN** became president of the New World National Bank in Pennsylvania and was the first black woman bank president in the state. New World National Bank is the only minority bank in the state.

## 1984     FINANCIAL FUTURES SPECIALIST

**CHRISTINE BELL** was the first black woman financial futures specialist for Prudential-Bache Securities in Chicago.

## EMPLOYEES UNION LEADER     1984

**ALTHEA WILLIAMS** was the first black woman president of the Michigan State Employees Association.

## 1984     TEACHER'S UNION EXECUTIVE

**JACQUELINE BARBARA VAUGHN (1935–1994)** was the first black woman president of the Chicago Teachers Union. In 1968 she became a secretary for the Illinois Federation of Teachers, and in 1972 she was elected union vice president. She led the nation's strongest local union, and as result of the strikes that she led in 1985 and 1987, teachers saw a number of salary increases and perks. Union concessions in fall 1993 were made to avert a strike that might have shut down the school system.

## TREND-SETTING STILL     1984
## PHOTOGRAPHER

**MICHELLE V. AGINS (1956–)** was the first black woman still photographer admitted to the International Photographers of the Motion Picture and Television Industries union. She was personal photographer to then-Chicago mayor Harold Washington.

## 1987     CHANGE-MAKING AUTOMOBILE
## DEALER

**BARBARA JEAN WILSON (1940–)** was the first black woman automobile dealer. Wilson was president of Porterfield Wilson Pontiac, GMC Truck, Mazda, and Honda in Detroit, Michigan; Ferndale Honda in Ferndale, Michigan; and Porterfield's Marina Village in Detroit.

## AUTOMOBILE COMPANY EXECUTIVE          1990

**SHELEME S. SENDABA (1949–)** was the first black vice president of Nissan Motor Corporation in the United States. Sendaba worked at General Motors before going to Nissan.

## 1992          UTILITY COMPANY EXECUTIVE

**ROBERTA PALM BRADLEY (1947–)** was the first woman to head a major public utility, Seattle City Light. She has served on a number of boards, including United Way, the Vallejo Chamber of Commerce, and the Vallejo Salvation Army.

## SWEET GEORGIA BROWN IN TOWN          1993

**GEORGIA BROWN'S** restaurant opened its doors in Union Station this year and became the first African American restaurant in downtown Washington, D.C. It became a popular hangout for African American VIPs. Its bronze ceiling scroll is deliberately reminiscent of the grand oak trees that are seen in Southern states. The honey bee is included in the restaurant's logo and reflects the contribution of more than 50 crops in the state of Georgia.

## 1993          BUSINESS WOMAN OF THE YEAR

**PEARLINE MOTLEY (1933–2016)** was the first black honored as American Business Woman of the Year. She received the award from the American Business Women's Association in 1993. Motley was the manager of the Federal Women's Program of the Agricultural Stabilization and Conservation Service in Kansas City, Missouri.

## BLACK WOMAN DIRECTS          1994
## AFRICAN BANK

Sworn in by treasury secretary Lloyd Bentsen, **ALICE M. DEAR** was the first black woman and the second black American to serve as U.S. executive director of the African Development Bank headquartered

# ANN M. FUDGE

## (1951–)

## Corporate Executive

Ann M. Fudge became the first black woman to head a major company in 1994, when she was appointed president of the Maxwell House Coffee division of Kraft General Foods in 1994. Her success in corporate America began in 1977, when Fudge joined Minneapolis-based General Mills Company and in 1978 was named assistant product manager. Four years later, she was made product manager with responsibility for four brands. Honey Nut Cheerios was developed under her leadership and became one of the division's top performers. In 1986 Fudge joined Kraft General Foods, where she revived old brands such as Shake 'N Bake and Stove Top Stuffing, both high profit-makers for Kraft. She held several management positions before being named executive vice president in 1993 and president a year later.

in Abidjan, Ivory Coast. A pioneering entrepreneur, Dear opened her own consulting firm and directed a wide range of global businesses.

## 1994     HISTORY-MAKING BANK LEADER

**CATHERINE DAVIS-CARTEY** became the first black vice president of Michigan National Bank's private banking division in Farmington Hills, Michigan. Prior to her appointment, she was a relationship manager for high-network clients at the bank.

## PIONEERING ASSEMBLY PLANT MANAGER                           1994

Ford Motor Company named **DEBORAH STEWART KENT (1953–)** manager of the Ohio Assembly Plant in Avon Lake, making her the first black woman to manage an assembly plant in the firm's worldwide manufacturing system. In 1992 she became the first black woman in the history of the company to serve as assistant plant manager in an assembly plant. By 1993 Stewart worked through her Chicago office to oversee the work of 2,700 employees. After her appointment in Chicago, the Taurus/Sable became the bestselling car in the nation. Kent first worked with General Motors and was promoted in plants in St. Louis; Bowling Green, Kentucky; and Detroit. She joined Ford in 1987 as chassis area manager at its Wixom, Michigan, assembly plant. During her employment, the 1988 Town Car and the 1989 Lincoln Continental were rated best in their class for chassis.

## 1995    BANK PRESIDENT BLAZES TRAIL

Nashville's Citizens Savings Bank & Trust Company, the oldest continuously operating minority-owned bank in the country, named *DEBORAH SCOTT-ENSLEY (1954–)* its chief executive officer and seventh president. With the appointment, she became the first woman to hold the post at the bank. She headed the bank when it closed its downtown office and relocated to the black community near Fisk and Tennessee State Universities and Meharry Medical College. There the bank aimed to strengthen its focus as a community-oriented institution.

## TREND-SETTING BREWERY MANAGER    1995

Miller Brewing Company, headquartered in Milwaukee, named *I. PATRICIA HENRY (1947–)* manager at its North Carolina brewery in Eden. Henry became the first woman to hold a top management post at an American brewery. She oversaw all of the plant's operations, including the production of eight million barrels of beer annually. Prior to her promotion, she served as brew master.

## 1996    HAIR-CARE CHIEF OFFICER

The president and chief executive officer of Soft Sheen Products, Inc., in Chicago, *TERRI GARDNER* was the first woman to hold the office. Gardner positioned the firm to continue its record-breaking success as the top black hair-care products company.

## MAJOR LAW FIRM PARTNER                    1996

**JUDITH ALANE COLBERT (1960–)** became the first black woman in Oklahoma to be named a shareholder and partner in a major law firm. She became a partner with Hall, Estill, Hardwick, Gable, Golden & Nelson, P.C., located in Tulsa.

## 1996                    MANUFACTURING COMPANY FOR OLYMPICS

The first African American licensee for the 1996 Olympic Games in Atlanta was Terry Manufacturing Company of Roanoke, Alabama. It contracted to sell woven pants, shirts, and shorts for all of the games. The company was founded in 1963 by **VELMA TERRY** and her husband, J. A. Terry, during Alabama's tumultuous civil rights era. The building became one of the largest black-owned businesses in America. The company made camouflage and other apparel for the U.S. Department of Defense and uniforms for the National Hockey League, McDonalds Corporation, and the U.S. Forest Service. Once successful, the company closed in 2003 after a scandal concerning fraud. Approximately 300 workers, mostly black women, lost their jobs.

## PIONEERING CASINO MANAGER EMERGES                    1996

Named general manager of the original Harrah's Tunica Casino in Tunica, Mississippi, **KAREN SOCK** became the first black woman to hold such a position. She gave oversight to Harrah's daily operations and was placed in charge of 500 employees and a $50 million operation. She left in 1997 and became senior vice president of administration and assistant general manager of Grand Casino Tunica.

## 1996                    CONSULTING FIRM PARTNER

**PAMELA THOMAS-GRAHAM (1963–)** was named partner in the largest management consulting firm in the world, McKinsey & Company—the first black woman to hold this post at the firm. Prior to her promotion, she was the company's senior engagement manager.

## PUBLIC RELATIONS LEADER                    1997

*INEZ Y. KAISER (1918–2016)* was named the 1997 National Minority Advocate of the year. She was the only black included in the National Hall of Fame of Women in Public Relations.

## 1997          PIONEERING BOARD MEMBER

*MARY K. BUSH (1948–)*, president of the international consulting firm Bush and Company, Washington, D.C., was the first black woman elected to the board of directors of Texaco, Inc.

## BUILDING INDUSTRY SPECIALIST          1997

*EDITH STUBBLEFIELD WASHINGTON (1948–)*, a certified construction specialist and president of the Stubblefield Group in Toledo, Ohio, was elevated to fellow at the Constructions Specifications Institute. She became the first black so honored for service to the institute and for contributing to continuing education for those in the building industry.

## 1998          SPOKESMODEL "HEAD AND SHOULDERS" ABOVE OTHERS

When actress *LARK VOORHIES (1974–)* was named national advertising campaign spokesmodel for Head & Shoulders, she became the first black woman celebrity in the country to fill that role. Voorhies has appeared on television in such shows as *Saved by the Bell*, *In the House*, *Days of Our Lives*, and *The Bold and the Beautiful*. She also starred in the Def Jam movie *How to Be a Player*.

Lark Voorhies

## LAW FIRM PARTNER                    1998

*DENISE GRANT* became the first black partner with the international corporate law firm Shearman & Sterling located in New York City.

## 1998　PIONEERING MOTORCYCLE DEALER

When **KATHERINE JOHNSON** opened her own Harley-Davidson motorcycle dealership in Horn Lake, Mississippi, on December 12, she became the first black woman licensed for the dealership in the company's history. A black recruiter at Harley's Milwaukee headquarters encouraged her to consider the motorcycle business. Her store includes a full-service repair shop, and it sells clothing and accessories that bear the Harley logo.

## REGULATORY EXECUTIVE　　1999

**JOSET B. WRIGHT (1956–)** became the first black president of Ameritech Illinois. She was in charge of government, regulatory, and external relations in the state. Wright joined the company in 1987 and moved up to become vice president of procurement and property services that same year.

## 1999　STOCK EXCHANGE COMPANY LEADER

Cathy Hughes

Radio One, founded by **CATHERINE "CATHY" LIGGINS HUGHES (1947–)**, became the first company headed by a black woman to be traded on the stock exchange. The company, which went public in 1999, was the largest black-owned and operated broadcast company in America with 26 stations. The network, now known as Urban One, has 62 stations and is worth more than $2 billion. All of this growth has taken place since founder Hughes bought her first station in Washington, D.C., in 1980. Urban One concentrates on an urban-oriented format, offering a blend of music and talk. Hughes is now chairperson of the board.

## CHANGING-MAKING MARKETING　　1999
## EXECUTIVE

When **PAULA A. SNEED (1947–)** was named chief marketing officer for Kraft Foods in Northfield, Illinois, she became the first black to hold this position at the company. She was made responsible for media services, advertising services, ethnic marketing, and other operations. Sneed joined General Foods Corporation in 1977 and later was promoted to executive vice president and general manager of the Desserts Division (1991–1995). Since joining Kraft Foods North America, she was senior vice president of marketing services (1995–1999) and then chief marketing officer in 1999. Sneed was also president of Kraft's E-Commerce Division. In 2005, she became executive vice president for the firm Global Market Resources and Initiatives. She became chairperson and chief executive officer of Phelps Prescott Group LLC (PPG), a company that she cofounded.

# 1999 PIONEERING TELEVISION MUSIC EXECUTIVE

**MARYANN JOHNSON (1948–)** was promoted to director of TV Music Administration for Twentieth Century Fox Film Corporation in Los Angeles, becoming the first black woman executive in the department.

# BOUNDARY-BREAKING AUTOMOBILE DEALER 1999

**ELLENAE L. HENRY-FAIRHURST (1943–)** became the first black to own a Nissan-Infinity car dealership in North America. The dealership, which is a part of Nissan North America's initiative to assist minority entrepreneurs, opened this year in Huntsville, Alabama. Until then only 13 of the approximately 1,070 Nissan dealerships in North America were black-owned, and none of the black-owned dealerships carried the luxury Infinity line.

# 1999 CASINO HUMAN RESOURCES EXECUTIVE

When named vice president of human resources at MGM Grand Detroit Casino, **LISA J. LINDSAY WICKER** became the first black woman to hold the position at the casino.

## PHARMACEUTICAL BUSINESS LEADER   2000

*MYRTLE STEPHENS POTTER (1958–)* became the first black woman to head a department in a major pharmaceutical business when she was named president of the BristolMyers Squibb U.S. Cardiovascular/Metabolics business.

## 2001       PIONEERING ENGINEERING FIRM EXECUTIVE

The first woman and the first black senior vice president of Aerospace's Engineering and Technology Group was *WANDA M. AUSTIN (1954–)*. In 1979 she joined Aerospace Corporation. Before her promotion to senior vice president, she was general manager of the firm.

## AUTOMOBILE FIRM EXECUTIVE              2007

A former vice president for Volvo Parts North America, *STEPHANIE R. DAWKINS* was promoted to senior vice president at AB Volvo, making her the company's first black senior vice president. She became president and CEO of Stephanie R. Dawkins International, Inc.

## 2007       TRAILBLAZING MANUFACTURING ENGINEER

Alicia Boler-Davis

*ALICIA BOLER-DAVIS* joined General Motors in 1994 as a manufacturing engineer and steadily climbed the ranks. In 2007 she became the first black woman plant manager at a General Motors Corporation vehicle-assembly plant. She began her new post in October, at the GM plant in Arlington, Texas. Previously, Boler-Davis was assistant plant manager at the Pontiac Assembly. Her goal was to become an officer at GM. Boler-Davis was named U.S. vice president, Customer Experience in February 2012 and later in the year vice president, Global Quality and U.S. Customer Experience. General Motors promoted her to senior vice president of Global Connected Customer Experience in December 2014, and she led the company's Global Manufacturing Operations. In June 2016 she was promoted to executive vice president for Global Manufacturing. In 2018 she continued to be recognized as the highest-ranking black woman in the entire automotive industry. She left GM in April 2019 to join Amazon.

## GENERAL MOTORS SETS TREND                2008

**CRYSTAL WINDHAM (1973?–)**, who was appointed director of General Motors' North American Passenger Car Design, became the first black woman director in the carmaker's history. The appointment meant that she oversees interior design for GM's global midsize, compact, and small cars. Windham was a lead designer on the 2008 Chevy Malibu. Windham was also a major player in designing the 2007 award-winning Saturn Aura.

## 2008?            PIONEERING BANK EXECUTIVE

**KIMBERLY YOUNG LEE** is the first black woman president and chief executive officer of New Orleans–based Dryades Savings Bank. Federally chartered in 1994, the bank is a leading black-owned financial institution that serves Orleans and Jefferson Parishes.

## POWERFUL CHIEF EXECUTIVE                2009

**URSULA BURNS (1958–)**, president of Xerox Corporation, became the company's chief executive officer on July 1 and the first black woman to head the company. Xerox, maker of printers and copiers, is the largest company in the United States to be headed by a black woman. She is also the first black female CEO of a Fortune 500 company and the first of her race and gender to run an S&P 100 company, with sales of $17.6 billion in 2008. In 2010 she became chair of the board. At Xerox she quickly distinguished herself by multitasking successfully and flagging problems that she observed. She focused on improving customer service and the

Ursula Burns

company's financial health. Her rise to the top reflected Xerox's commitment to gender and racial diversity. Unable to revive Xerox, Burns stepped down as CEO in 2016 and resigned as chair of the board the following year.

# 2012 GLASS CEILING–BREAKING EXECUTIVE

**ROSALIND (ROZ) BREWER (1962–)** made history this year by becoming the first woman and the first black American to lead a division of a Walmart brand—Sam's Club. She joined the company in 2006 as regional vice president and was later named president of Walmart East. For 22 previous years, she was a scientist and then president of the Global Nonwovens Sector of Kimberly Clark. Brewer was appointed to the Starbucks board of directors in March 2017 and in 2018 became the chief operating officer and group president of Starbucks. In 2014, 2015, and 2016, she was named one of the "Most Powerful Women in the World." In March 2021 she left Walmart and became the first black chief executive officer for Walgreens Boots Alliance, Inc., and the only black woman leading a Fortune 500 company.

# Civil Rights and Protests

Civil rights and protests are an integral part of American history. Most black people came to America against their will and were denied their human rights. They responded in many ways to demonstrate their disapproval of such treatment. In 1867, the U.S. Congress gave black men the right to vote, but not black women.

Black and white abolitionists founded antislavery societies to work in the interests of enslaved blacks. Black women warriors for racial justice also founded black antislavery groups. For example, in 1832 a group of African American women who called themselves "females of color" founded the Female Anti-Slavery Society of Salem, Massachusetts. Thus, African American women saw a need to work in their own interests as well as that of the entire race. In 1832, Maria W. Stewart, a women's rights activist, journalist, and educator, was the first to speak out publicly in defense of women's rights and antislavery issues. Other members of the race followed.

Black women were actively involved in the Underground Railroad. Tenacious leader Harriet Tubman led about 300 enslaved people to freedom. Women continued their agitation and were involved in movements predating the modern Civil Rights Movement that is generally dated in the mid-1950s. In 1944, civil rights pioneer Irene Morgan (Kirkaldy) refused to surrender her seat to whites in Virginia, an act that led the courts to strike down segregation in interstate transportation. America's high school and college students launched the

Sit-in Movement, and many young white students joined their efforts. Women also trained students and led and participated in marches, especially in the South.

The Montgomery Bus Boycott of 1955 catapulted Rosa M. Parks to the forefront of the Civil Rights Movement. She refused to surrender her seat to a white man on a bus in Montgomery and was arrested and jailed. The boycott ended 13 months later, when the U.S. Supreme Court declared Montgomery's racial bus seating unconstitutional. The massive boycott in Montgomery marked the beginning of the modern Civil Rights Movement. From then forward, the nation celebrated her efforts and rewarded her by naming schools, streets, and other places in her honor and, later, by creating a postage stamp in her memory. In 2013, the legendary civil rights pioneer became the first African American woman honored with a full-length statue in the U.S. Capitol's National Statuary Hall.

Two years after the historic Million Man March and Day of Absence was held in 1995, 21 blocks from the Capitol Building in Washington, D.C., black women held the first Million Women March in Philadelphia. Organizers aimed to strengthen the cohesiveness of black women in all arenas, beginning with education, employment, politics, and business.

Civil rights leadership from then on saw the widespread activities of black women in practically every area known. They founded, led, and participated in women's organizations; entered political arenas; accepted memberships on corporate boards; established businesses; became mayors of cities; and some became millionaires. Now black women in America have spread their trailblazing and groundbreaking achievements throughout the nation and in other countries. They continue to demonstrate their tenacity, enthusiasm, strength, and nerve in the struggle to dismantle racial barriers. Their work rests on the shoulders of Harriet Tubman, Sojourner Truth, Rosa Parks, and other pioneers in the cause for social justice. Their work is documented throughout the chapters in this work.

# AMERICA'S FIRST FREE BLACKS 1622

**MARY** and Anthony **JOHNSON** and family were the first known free blacks. They lived in Old Accomack, later Northampton County, in the Virginia colony. In 1651, Anthony Johnson, John Johnson, and John Johnson Sr. were the first black landowners in Virginia. Anthony Johnson and his wife were among the 23 black servants in the 1624–25 census of the colony. In 1653 Anthony Johnson became the first black

# MARIA W. STEWART

## (1803–1879)

### Women's Rights Activist

Maria W. Stewart, journalist and educator, was the first American-born woman to speak publicly on political themes to a mixed audience of men and women. On September 21, 1833, she was perhaps the first black woman to lecture in defense of women's rights. Her public speeches, delivered in Boston, also made Stewart the first black woman to lecture on antislavery issues. The importance of education and the need for blacks to be unified in the struggle for liberation were also themes in her speeches and writings. Stewart was an acknowledged militant who was willing to accept armed conflict if necessary. Her militancy was intricately entwined with her religious commitment. In her final speech delivered in 1833, titled a farewell address, Stewart noted the disfavor with which the black community viewed her. She settled finally in Washington, D.C., where she taught school. She also worked at Freedmen's Hospital, opened a Sunday school for neighborhood children, and obtained a government pension as the wife of a U.S. Navy veteran. She used this money to print an expanded version of a book she had written earlier. Stewart was both an example of and an advocate for the right of women to be heard on the important issues of the day.

on record as a slave owner. However, by 1662, slavery had been made hereditary in the colony by a decree assigning freedom or slavery according to the condition of the mother. Still, free blacks in Virginia retained the right to vote until 1723.

# 1832 · PASSIONATE ADVOCATORS FOR WOMEN'S RIGHTS

The **FEMALE ANTI-SLAVERY SOCIETY** of Salem, Massachusetts, was formed in February by a group of African American women who called themselves "females of color." The society's constitution made no reference to slavery but "called for mutual improvement and the promotion of the welfare of color." In 1834 the organization changed its name to the Salem Female Anti-Slavery Society and had a racially mixed membership. By then its constitution stated that slavery was a sin and called for its prompt abolishment. It noted that people of color had a right to a home in the United States. Sarah Parker Remond, a leading public speaker, was one of its early members.

## BARRIER-BREAKING RIDERS                              1854

The first successful suit to end segregation in street cars was won this year. Activist and teacher **ELIZABETH JENNINGS GRAHAM (1826?–1901)** is said to be the first black woman to win a lawsuit against a New York streetcar company. Even though slavery was illegal in New York in the years before the Civil War, racial segregation was legal. Blacks were allowed to ride street cars only if white passengers accepted them aboard. If they complained, black riders were required to leave the cars. On July 16, Jennings (then unmarried) and her friend Sarah Adams boarded a streetcar. Apparently, whites protested, and the conductor asked the two women to disembark. When Jennings refused to leave, a conductor, later joined by a police office, forcibly removed her, leaving her injured. She filed a lawsuit against the Third Avenue Railway Company, was successful in the suit a month later, and was awarded $225 in damages. While she won the suit, 20 years passed before segregation ended on the city's streetcars.

## 1936            GROUNDBREAKER FOR JUSTICE

**SUE BAILEY THURMAN (1903–1996)** was the first black woman to have an audience with human rights leader Mahatma Gandhi. She met with Gandhi to discuss nonviolent resistance in the struggle for political freedom and social change. She is also credited with helping to establish the first integrated church in the United States and with being the first black student to be awarded the bachelor's degree in music by Oberlin Conservatory (1926).

## RACIAL JUSTICE ADVOCATE                              1944

**IRENE MORGAN (KIRKALDY) (1917–2007)** refused to give up her seat on an interstate bus to a white person in Gloucester, Virginia. She was jailed and fined $100 for resisting arrest. This occurred nearly a decade before Rosa Parks gained recognition for a similar action on a local bus in Alabama. In July 1944 Morgan, who lived in Baltimore, boarded a bus at Hayes Store, took a seat in the rear, and refused to give her seat to a white couple. Morgan resisted and was fined for kicking the Middlesex County sheriff who tried to remove her and for scratching the deputy who took her to jail. NAACP lawyer Thurgood Marshall was successful in his appeal to the U.S. Supreme Court on Morgan's behalf. The court then struck down segregation in interstate transportation. Gloucester County honored her on its 350th anniversary in 2000, and in 2001 President Bill Clinton awarded her the Presidential Citizens Medal for "taking the first step on a journey that would change America forever."

# 1951 PROTESTORS FOR CIVIL RIGHTS

The nation's first civil rights assassination occurred in the Christmas bombing at the Mims, Florida, home of **HARRIETTE** and Harry **MOORE**. They have been called the only husband and wife team to die in a civil rights struggle in the nation. The case remains officially unsolved. The Moores were teachers and administrators in Brevard County public schools but were fired from their jobs in 1946 due to their activism.

# PIONEERING CIVIL RIGHTS ACTIVIST 1955

*CLAUDETTE COLVIN (1939–)* was a pioneer in the Civil Rights Movement in Alabama. She refused to give up her seat to a white passenger on a city bus in Montgomery months before Rosa Parks defined local law and became famous for her action. After her protest, Colvin was arrested on several charges; she was released from jail after her minister paid her bail. The NAACP considered using her case to challenge the segregation laws but decided against it due to her age and the fact that she became an unwed mother. Instead, Colvin became one of the four plaintiffs in the *Browder v. Gayle* case, which led to the court's ruling in 1956 that Montgomery's

Claudette Colvin

segregated bus system was unconstitutional. Although Colvin's protest was significant, it was largely ignored by the public and only marginally alluded to in many public sources.

# 1955      MONTGOMERY BUS BOYCOTT

A statue of Rosa Parks sitting in the bus can be viewed at the National Civil Rights Museum in Memphis, Tennessee.

The boycott of public buses in Montgomery, Alabama, marked the beginning of the modern black Civil Rights Movement. On December 1, **ROSA PARKS (1913–2005)** was jailed for refusing to give up her seat on a city bus to a white passenger, thus prompting the historic 381-day Montgomery Bus Boycott. The local black community then formed the Montgomery Improvement Association (MIA) to join the fight to desegregate the buses and elected Martin Luther King Jr. as president. The MIA filed a suit in the U.S. District Court on February 1, 1956, designed to declare Alabama's segregation laws unconstitutional. On June 2, a lower court declared such segregation unconstitutional, and the Supreme Court upheld the ruling, ordering integration on December 20, 1956.

## CHANGE AGENT FOR JUSTICE      1958

**CLARA SHEPARD LUPER (1923–2011)** led the first sit-ins to win concessions in a Southern state in modern times. The movement occurred in restaurants in Oklahoma City beginning August 19. The NAACP Youth Council members, for which Luper was advisor, decided to stage a sit-in at a Katz Drug store lunch counter in downtown Oklahoma City. The group of 6- to 13-year-olds endured violent protests for days until they were served. Then Katz Drug store integrated their lunch counters in four other states. Protests continued at other restaurants, hotels, and parks in Oklahoma City. Throughout the early 1960s, the group helped to end segregation in the state's public accommodations. Luper followed the technique of nonviolence, participated in other marches and demonstrations, and was jailed.

## 1989 WOMEN'S RIGHTS ORGANIZER

**BARBARA ARNWINE (1951?–)** became the first black woman to head the male-dominated Lawyers Committee for Civil Rights Under Law. She worked in North Carolina for the Durham Legal Assistance Program, then moved to Raleigh to work at the head office. Her concern for women's rights and the need to clarify the real roles that black women played in the United States led her to organize the National Conference on African American Women and the Law.

## PIONEERING GLOBAL RIGHTS ACTIVIST 1994

The first black to become executive director of the International Human Rights Law Group was **GAY JOHNSON McDOUGALL (1947–)**. She became director of the Southern Africa Project of the Lawyers' Committee for Civil Rights under Law. In 1994 McDougall was named to the Independent Electoral Commission in South Africa, whose charge was to run South Africa's first all-race elections. In her position as executive director of the Global Rights organization from 1994 to 2006, she was an advocate for human rights around the world.

## 1997 MILLION WOMAN MARCH

The first **MILLION WOMAN MARCH** was held in Philadelphia on October 26. More than 300,000 American women attended. Speakers included Representative Maxine Waters, Winnie Mandela, and Sister Souljah. Organizers of this march aimed to strengthen the cohesiveness of black women from all walks of life. The women addressed such issues as women in prison, the beginning of independent black schools, employment, and women in politics and business.

# AWARDED FOR DISOBEDIENCE          2013

Rosa Parks is immortalized among other American heroes at the U.S. Statuary Hall on Capitol Hill.

**ROSA PARKS**, legendary civil rights pioneer, became the first African American woman to be honored with a full-length statue in the U.S. Capitol's National Statuary Hall. President Barack Obama unveiled the statue on February 27 after praising her for "confronting segregation by refusing to give up her seat on a city bus" and adding that her efforts "should inspire all Americans to face up to today's challenges." Her singular act of disobedience occurred in Montgomery, Alabama, on December 1, 1955, and sparked a boycott that led to the integration of public buses in Montgomery and inspired countless others to protest, paving the way for nation-altering legislation.

# 2013          MARTYRS FOR CIVIL RIGHTS

President Barack Obama signed legislation to award the Congressional Gold Medal to four black girls who were killed in an Alabama church bombing on September 15, 1963. Cited were **ADDIE MAE COLLINS (1949–1963), CAROLE ROSAMOND ROBERTSON (1949–1963), CYNTHIA DIONNE WESLEY (1949–1963)**, and **CAROL DENISE McNAIR (1951–1963)**, who lost their lives in a bomb blast that white supremacists planted at the 16th Street Baptist Church in Birmingham.

# Education

Black women are pioneers of progress in education. They have long shared with public officials their concern for educating black youth and worked to sustain a system of educating young people and adults. Depending on state regulations, black people were relegated to segregated education by law, could attend mixed-race schools, were denied admission to schools, or could establish privately funded schools for their own education. They protested in many states and overturned de jure segregation in others.

As these efforts continued, black women seized opportunities to educate women and children, and they became teachers, school principals, and school founders. In 1852 the Society of Friends established the Institute for Colored Youth in Pennsylvania as a coeducational classical high school. Fannie Jackson Coppin became principal of the school in 1869. In 1886 Lucy Laney founded the coeducational Haines Normal and Industrial Institute in Augusta, Georgia. Mary McLeod Bethune, later a well-known educational leader, founded Daytona Educational and Industrial Training School for Negro Girls in 1904. The school admitted boys two years later. As the need for education in the black community continued, in 1923 the school merged with Cookman Institute for Boys and became Bethune-Cookman College (now University). Charlotte Hawkins Brown founded Palmer Memorial Institute in Sedalia, North Carolina, first known as the Alice Freeman Palmer Institute. Palmer attracted increasing numbers of black youth from upper-middle-class black families and became known as a "finishing school."

Black teachers were needed especially in the small, rural schools throughout the South. The Jeanes Fund, founded by Anna T. Jeanes, provided funds to address this problem, and in 1908 Virginia Estelle Randolph became one of the first Jeanes teachers. Her work covered Virginia, North Carolina, and Georgia, while other teachers in the Jeanes movement covered additional southern states.

As higher educational opportunities for white women grew rapidly between 1865 and 1900, the black community experienced a similar need for their women. Thus, schools for black women were established, including Hartshorn Memorial College, Montgomery Industrial School for Girls, and Mary Holmes Seminary. Later, these schools merged with others and became coeducational. The pattern of development of two institutions founded during this period differs somewhat. In 1883 the Methodist Episcopal Church opened Bennett College in Greensboro, North Carolina. At first coeducational, in 1926 the school became Bennett College for Women. Spelman College opened in Atlanta in 1881. Both institutions continue as the nation's only black colleges for women.

Institutions now known as historically black colleges and universities (HBCUs) were established as early as 1832, when Cheyney State College was founded under another name. HBCUs are privately or publicly supported. In addition to those founded by a black woman, many maintained male leaders for a long time. Others later hired their first black woman leader. They include Johnnetta Betsch Cole, Anna Cherrie Epps, Elmira Mangum, Lila D. McNair, Carolyn Reed Wallace, and Dorothy Cowser Yancy. Similarly, black women who are current or past presidents of mainstream institutions include Carmen Twillie Ambar, Mary Dana Hinton, Shirley Ann Jackson, Ruth J. Simmons, Valerie Smith, and Lori White.

Black women were also school integrationists, school principals, heads of academic departments, school superintendents, and heads of school boards or boards of trusts, and received terminal degrees from mainstream and professional schools. These women serve as role models for young, emerging, and current leaders in education.

## HISTORIC BOARDING SCHOOL                       1829

**SAINT FRANCIS ACADEMY OF ROME** in Baltimore, Maryland, was the first boarding school for black girls. The school was established by the Oblate Sisters of Providence, a group of black nuns who were French educated. The only secondary school for black women, Saint Francis became well known and attracted young women from all across the country as well as from Canada. The school became coeducational by 1865 and was known then as the Saint Francis Academy.

# 1850 TREND-SETTING COLLEGE GRADUATE

Lucy Ann Stanton

The first black woman to graduate from college was *LUCY ANN STANTON (MRS. LEVI N. SESSIONS) (1931–1910)*. She completed the two-year "ladies'" course and received a bachelor's degree from Oberlin College on December 8, 1850, then taught school in the South during Reconstruction. Two other women also have been called the first black woman college graduate. *GRACE A. MAPPS (1835?–1897)* was the first black woman to obtain a degree from a four-year college—Central College, McGrawville in New York. She apparently finished in 1852 and joined Charles Lewis Reason (1818–1893), then recently named head, at the Institute for Colored Youth in Pennsylvania. *MARY JANE PATTERSON (1840–1894)* was the first black woman to earn a bachelor's degree from the four-year "gentleman's" course at Oberlin College in 1862.

## HBCU TEACHER/ADMINISTRATOR 1859

*SARAH JANE WOODSON EARLY (1825–1907)* became the first regular black teacher at Wilberforce, where she served as principal. She was an active worker on behalf of antislavery and temperance causes. Her efforts resulted in recognition from the state committee of Tennessee's Prohibition Party, which hired her to lecture throughout the state in 1887. She was also the only woman delegate from the Southern states at the Congress of Representative Women in 1893 at the Columbian Exposition in Chicago. It has been suggested that Early's father, Thomas Woodson (1790?–1879?), was the child of Sally Hemings and Thomas Jefferson.

Sarah Jane Woodson Early

## 1863   TREND-SETTING SCHOOL PRINCIPAL

***SARAH J. (SMITH THOMPSON) GARNET (1831–1911)*** was the first black woman to be appointed principal in the New York public school system. Garnet was a founder of Brooklyn's Equal Suffrage League and superintendent of the Suffrage Department of the National Association of Colored Women. She worked to achieve suffrage for women for most of her life.

## HISTORY-MAKING SCHOOL LEADER     1869

***FANNY JACKSON COPPIN (1837–1913)*** became the first black woman to head a major educational institution for blacks, the Institute for Colored Youth of Philadelphia. When Coppin graduated from Oberlin College in 1865, she became principal of the Institute's female department. She began her teaching career while still an Oberlin student, teaching voluntarily in an evening school that she established for newly freed blacks. When she moved to Philadelphia, her activities resulted in the establishment of a home and nurse training courses for poor black women in 1888, opening of the institute's industrial department in 1889, and another school, the Women's Exchange and Girls' Home, in 1894.

Fanny Jackson Coppin

## 1870   RACIAL BARRIER-BREAKING STUDENT

The first black to teach white college students in Kentucky was ***JULIA BRITTON HOOKS (1852–1942)***. She was one of the first black women in the United States to attend Berea College. W. C. Handy, one of the early trailblazing black musicians, was one of her students. After moving to Memphis, she was an active advocate for the Memphis black community and used proceeds from her concerts to found the Negro Old Folks and Orphans Home in 1891. She was also involved in establishing the Negro Juvenile Court Detention Home. She later opened her own music school, which welcomed both black and white students.

## COLLEGE GRADUATE A "FIRST" FOR THE SOUTH

**1875**

*VIRGINIA E. WALKER (BROUGHTON) (1856?–1934)* studied at Fisk University for ten years before receiving her bachelor's degree in May of this year and is said to be the first black woman in the South to graduate from college. She is recognized as a religious feminist who was one of several Baptist women who used the Bible to defend women's rights during the latter decades of the nineteenth century and early in the twentieth century.

**1879**

## HISTORY-MAKING EDUCATOR

Josephine Silone Yates

*JOSEPHINE SILONE YATES (1859–1912)*, teacher, journalist, and clubwoman, was the first black American certified to teach in the public schools of Rhode Island. She later became an outstanding teacher at Lincoln Institute in Jefferson, Missouri, and president of the National Association of Colored Women.

## COLLEGE FOUNDED FOR BLACK WOMEN

**1881**

*SPELMAN COLLEGE* in Atlanta was the first institution of higher education established in Georgia to educate black women. Founded by two teachers in a church basement, the school opened on April 11, 1881, as the Atlanta Baptist Female Seminary. In 1884, upon the receipt of a large gift from John D. Rockefeller, the name Spelman was adopted in honor of Rockefeller's wife Laura's parents.

**1883**

## COLLEGES OPENED FOR BLACK WOMEN

*HARTSHORN MEMORIAL COLLEGE*, the first black women's college in the country, opened on November 7 in Richmond, Virginia, with

58 students. It was chartered on March 13 as "an institution of learning of collegiate grades for the education of young women." The college awarded its first degrees in 1892, when three young women graduated. In 1918 Hartshorn students began enrolling in courses at Virginia Union University; by 1922 Hartshorn had entered into an agreement for educating its students at Virginia Union. Rather than merge with Virginia Union, in June 1928 Hartshorn officials closed the college department and focused on its high school. In 1932 the college trustees conveyed the school's property to Virginia Union, merged with the school, and became Hartshorn Memorial College in the Virginia Union University.

## OBERLIN'S FIRST BLACK GRADUATE        1889

**HARRIET "HATTIE" ALETHA GIBBS MARSHALL (1869–1941)**, concert artist, pianist, and educator, was the first black to complete the entire course at Oberlin Conservatory of Music in Ohio. Her degree was awarded in 1906 because the school did not actually give degrees in music when she completed her course. In 1890 Marshall founded a music conservatory at Eckstein-Norton University in Cane Springs, Kentucky, the first and for a time the only such school for blacks.

## 1895        FREEDOM FIGHTERS IN EDUCATION

Mary Church Terrell

**MARY CHURCH TERRELL (1863–1954)** was the first black woman to serve on the Washington, D.C., Board of Education. In 1896 she was cofounder and first president of the National Council of Colored Women. She went to Ohio for her early schooling, attending first the Antioch College Model School, then a public school in Yellow Springs, and finally the public high school in Oberlin. In 1885 she began her professional career at Wilberforce College but left after a year to teach in the Latin department of the Colored High School in Washington, D.C. She became the leader of the Colored Women's League. This group later merged with Boston's Federation of American Women and two other groups to become the National Council of Negro Women. Terrell became known for her work as a political activist and civil rights pioneer. She once led successful desegregation protests against discrimination in restaurants in Washington.

# MARY McLEOD BETHUNE

## (1875–1955)

### Visionary College Founder

Mary McLeod Bethune was founding president of the Daytona Educational and Industrial Training School for Negro Girls in Daytona Beach, Florida, in 1904. The school merged with Methodist-supported Cookman Institute in Jacksonville. The institution became known as Bethune-Cookman College (now University) and retained Bethune as its president. Bethune taught at Haines Institute in Augusta. On October 3, 1904, she founded the Daytona school. She accepted a full-time federal position in Washington, D.C., and resigned the presidency, which she returned to in 1946 and 1947. Bethune was well known for her work in the black women's club movement. One of her best-known writings is her "Last Will and Testament," which serves as an inspiration for black people; it was subsequently published in a number of collections.

## PIONEER LAW SCHOOL GRADUATE          1897

The first black woman to graduate from a law school in the South was **LUTIE A. LYTLE (1875–1955)**, who received her law degree from Central Tennessee College. Lytle also used the names Lytle-McNeil and Cowan. Central Tennessee College, located in Nashville, was founded in 1865, and by 1897 it claimed to be "the first and leading school established for the education of colored attorneys in the whole South." She was the first black woman licensed to practice law in

Tennessee and perhaps in the South. She returned to her hometown of Topeka and became the first black woman admitted to the Kansas bar. In 1898, she returned to Central Tennessee College and joined the law faculty, becoming the first woman law professor at a chartered law school in the country and perhaps in the world.

## 1897        RACIAL IDENTITY STIMULATES SENSATION

**ANITA HEMMINGS (1872–1960)** was the first black to graduate from Vassar College. Since she was very light-skinned, few realized that she was black. Her declaration of racial identity upon graduation created a sensation in the press and caused "dismay" for the college administration.

## HISTORY-MAKING COLLEGE GRADUATE                    1900

The first black woman to graduate from Smith College in Northampton, Massachusetts, was **OTELIA CROMWELL (1873–1972)**, educator and author.

## 1907        PIONEERING SCHOOL FOUNDER

Charlotte Hawkins Brown

**CHARLOTTE (EUGENIA) HAWKINS BROWN (1883–1961)** became the founding president of Palmer Memorial Institute in Sedalia, North Carolina. She began her career as an educator in 1901 in a rural school near McLeansville. When the American Missionary Association closed its small schools in 1902, she remained in the area and opened her own school. The school began to attract increasing numbers of black youth from upper-middle-class black families and families from outside the South. It became known as a "finishing school," as well as a first-rate academic institution. After the school closed, its facilities became a part of historically black Bennett College in Greensboro, North Carolina, but its site was not used. The Charlotte Hawkins Brown Historical Foundation, incorporated in 1983, maintained exhibits and a state visitors' center housed in the former Carrie M. Stone Teachers Cottage. The entire campus was designated a state historic site.

## FIRST JEANES TEACHER                                    1908

Virginia E. Randolph

***VIRGINIA E(STELLE) RANDOLPH (1870–1958)*** was the first black Jeanes teacher. Anna T. Jeanes, a Philadelphia teacher, provided one million dollars to initiate a fund for teachers who worked with other teachers to encourage improvements in small black rural schools. The Jeanes teacher program was fashioned after Randolph's notable practices in Henrico, Virginia. Through the Jeanes movement that covered the period from 1908 to 1968, Randolph brought about improvements in the lives of thousands of teachers, children, and community residents. Randolph left the Henrico school when she became a Jeanes teacher, working overtime in Virginia, North Carolina, and Georgia. Her success led to expansion of the Jeanes movement, with Jeanes teachers supervising industrial education and building community support for black schools all over the South. The Virginia Randolph Fund, established as a tribute to her in 1936, was merged with the Anna T. Jeanes Foundation, which had been renamed the Negro Rural School Fund. These funds were later merged with others that became the Southern Education Fund.

## 1909            SCHOOL HONORS FORMER SLAVE

***CHARLOTTE ANDREWS STEPHENS (1854–1951)*** became the first black to have a school named in her honor, in Little Rock, Arkansas. A larger school was later erected on the same site and named in her honor as well. For 70 years, Stephens taught at every level in Little Rock's schools as well as in schools in other areas. She was Little Rock's first black teacher.

## PIONEERING TEACHER AND SOCIAL WORKER                    1911

The first black permanent teacher in Albany, New York, was **HARRIET LEWIS VAN VRANKEN (1891–1996)**. She also became the first black social worker in that city in 1939. Two years later, she became the first black senior social worker in upstate New York, a post that she retained until she retired.

## 1921      HISTORY-MAKING TRIO OF DOCTORAL DEGREES

Eva Dykes

**EVA (BEATRICE) DYKES (1893–1986)**, **SADIE TANNER MOSSELL ALEXANDER (1898–1989)**, and **GEORGIANA R. SIMPSON (1866–1944)** were the first three black American women to earn doctorates. They received their degrees in 1921. Dykes was the first to complete requirements for a Ph.D. However, the commencement exercises of Alexander and Simpson were both held before hers. Alexander received her degree in economics (the first black American to earn a degree in the field) from the University of Pennsylvania, and Simpson earned her degree in German at the University of Chicago. Simpson attended commencement exercises on June 14, making her the first black American woman to receive a doctorate.

## PIONEERING TEACHER AND SOCIAL WORKER                    1922

**BESSYE JOHNSON BANKS BEARDEN (1888–1943)**, political and civic worker, was the first black woman member of the New York City Board of Education. She founded and was the first president of the Colored Women's Democratic League. She also worked closely with the National Council of Negro Women. She was the first black woman in the country to sign public school diplomas, after having become chair of the board. Bearden achieved another first when she became deputy collector in internal revenue for New York's 3rd Collection District in 1935.

# VIRGINIA PROCTOR POWELL FLORENCE
## (1903–1991)
### First Professional Librarian

In 1923 Virginia Proctor Powell Florence became the first African American woman to receive professional training in librarianship in the United States. She was trained at Carnegie Library School, graduated from Oberlin College in 1919, and was admitted to the library school in 1922. Although she completed her course in one year, the school withheld her diploma for seven years due to uncertainty about placing its first black graduate in a position. Florence served in the New York Public Library from 1923 until 1927. In 1927 she was the first African American to sit for and pass the New York high school librarian's examination.

## 1924     RECORD-SETTING LIBRARIAN

J. P. Morgan Jr. incorporated his library of rare books and manuscripts into an educational institution dedicated to the memory of his father. He named **BELLE da COSTA GREENE (1883–1950)** as the first library director. She guided the collecting and organizing of the treasures in the Morgan library since 1905, when J. Pierpont Morgan owned it; she made it into one of the world's greatest libraries. She was known and respected in libraries, museums, galleries, and aristocratic houses throughout Europe, and she stood as one of the great figures in the art and bibliophile world. When she represented the Morgans abroad, Greene wore couturier clothes and patronized luxury hotels. (She was born Greener, but she dropped the second *r* from the spelling of her last name.)

## PIONEERING BRANCH LIBRARIAN     1924

The first black appointed as a branch librarian for the Chicago Public Library was **VIVIAN GORDON HARSH (1890–1960)**, who was appointed on February 26. In 1941 the branch library was named in her honor. When the George Cleveland Hall Branch Library opened on January 16, 1932, Harsh was at its helm. She received a grant in 1934 from the Julius Rosenwald Fund to travel to leading bookselling centers in the country to buy books about blacks for the library. She placed the new acquisitions in one wing of the library and named the collection the Special Negro Collection. Harsh also began a series of public forums and invited as speakers such noted blacks as Zora Neale Hurston, Carter G. Woodson, and Charles S. Johnson. After she died, the Chicago Public Library renamed the collection the Vivian G. Harsh Collection of African American History and Literature. That name was retained when the collection was moved to new quarters in the Carter G. Woodson Regional Library Center.

## 1924                 LIBRARY BOARD MEMBER

*FANNIE BARRIER WILLIAMS (1855–1944)*, lecturer, civic leader, clubwoman, and journalist, was the first black and the first woman to serve on the Library Board of Chicago. In 1895 she had been the first black member of the Chicago Women's Club. In 1891 she also assisted Daniel Hale Williams in the founding of Provident Hospital and Training School for Nurses, one of the first black-controlled medical centers in the country. She was a founder and a primary leader of the National League of Colored Women in 1893, and she also became active in the women's suffrage movement.

## TREND-SHATTERING LIBRARIAN       1926

The New York Public Library appointed *CATHERINE ALLEN LATIMER (1895?–1948)* as reference librarian in charge of the Division of Negro Literature and History located in the 135th Street Branch, making her the first black professional librarian in the system. Later, she headed the collection, which was eventually renamed the Schomburg Center for Research in Black Culture.

## 1927              LAW DEGREE RECIPIENT

*SADIE (TANNER MOSSELL) ALEXANDER (1898–1989)* was the first black woman to receive a law degree from the University of Pennsylvania School of Law. Later she became the first black woman to enter the bar and practice law in Pennsylvania. She obtained bach-

Sadie Alexander

elor's, master's, and doctoral degrees in economics from the University of Pennsylvania and was one of the first three black women who earned a doctoral degree in the United States. Alexander was the first black woman to serve as assistant city solicitor in Philadelphia and as secretary of the National Bar Association.

## PIONEERING LAWYER                                    1927

*EDITH (SPURLOCK) SAMPSON (1901–1979)* was the first woman of any ethnic background to receive a Master of Law degree from Loyola University in Chicago. She was admitted to the Illinois bar the same year she graduated, and she was among the first black women to practice before the Supreme Court (1934). Sampson was also the first black person to be appointed a delegate to the United Nations (1950) and the first black woman elected judge in the United States (1962).

## 1929                    RECORD-SETTING EDUCATOR

*JANE ELLEN McALLISTER (1899–1996)* became the first black woman in the United States to receive a doctorate in education, which was awarded from Teachers College of Columbia University. In 1925 she was involved in opening the first extension classes for black teachers in Louisiana.

## TEACHERS HAVE THEIR SAY                              1930

*SADIE DELANY (1889–1999)* became the first black domestic science teacher at the high school level in New York City's public schools. After teaching first at a mostly all-black elementary school, she obtained her position as New York's first black high school domestic science teacher with a measure of subterfuge—to keep from being identified as a black person, she did not report for the job until the first day of class. She continued to teach in New York high schools until retiring. In 1993, Sadie and her sister Bessie's autobiography, *Having Our Say: The Delany Sisters' First 100 Years,* was published, and they became celebrities.

## 1931    PIONEERING LAWYER AND JUDGE

The first black woman to graduate from the Yale University Law School was **JANE MATILDA BOLIN (1908–2007)**. At age 31, she became the first black woman appointed judge in the United States, in the Domestic Relations Court (later known as Family Court) of New York City.

## TRAILBLAZING LIBRARY ADMINISTRATOR/EDUCATOR                                      1932

**VIRGINIA LACY JONES (1912–1984)** became the first black woman to earn an advanced degree in library science, when she graduated from Columbia University with a master's in library science. She joined the faculty at Atlanta University, teaching in Atlanta's new library school. Jones entered the University of Chicago in 1943 and received a Ph.D. degree. She returned to Atlanta and became the second dean of Atlanta University's School of Library Service. When the Atlanta University Center consortium of four historically black Atlanta institutions was formed in 1981, Jones was named director of the Center's Robert R. Woodruff Library.

Virginia Lacy Jones

## 1933    PROTESTS FOR JUSTICE

**ETHEL THOMPSON OVERBY (1892–1997)** became the first black woman principal in the Richmond, Virginia, school system. She headed Elba School and later the Albert V. Norrell School. Overcrowded conditions at Elma spurred Overby to push for a 12-month school program. She was successful and included parent education in the curriculum.

## RECORD-SETTING DOCTORAL RECIPIENT                                      1933

The first black woman to earn a doctorate in bacteriology was **RUTH ELLA MOORE (1903–1994)**.

# ALICE JACKSON STUART

## (1913–2001)

### Determined Student Seeks Admission

Alice Jackson Stuart attempted to integrate the University of Virginia in 1935 and became the first black person known to seek admission to a white graduate or professional school in the state. After her admission was denied, the state set up a tuition supplement for black students to study in graduate schools outside Virginia. She accepted the supplement and enrolled at Columbia University. She taught at a number of high schools and universities. In 1950 the supplement program was declared unconstitutional, and the state's public university graduate programs were gradually integrated. She joined the NAACP's lawsuit challenging segregation in public colleges and universities.

## 1935                    HISTORY-MAKING LIBRARIAN

The first public library for blacks in Raleigh, North Carolina, opened in a storefront on East Hargett Street. **MOLLIE HUSTON LEE (1907–1982)** was its founder. Later the Richard B. Harrison Library, as it was named, received national recognition for its service to the aged, disadvantaged, blind, and illiterate. The collection, basically one of black books and materials, grew in quality, and the library received annual appropriations from the North Carolina State Library. In 1972 the collection was officially named the Mollie Huston Lee Collection of Black Literature. She became supervisor of Negro School Libraries in North Carolina and was instrumental in the founding of the North Carolina Negro Library Association.

## EDUCATOR AND ACTIVIST                    1936

**GERTRUDE ELISE McDOUGALD AYER (1885–1971)**, activist and educator, was the first black woman to have a full-time principalship in a New York City public school after desegregation of the school system. (Sarah Garnet was the first black woman principal in 1863, in a black school.) Ayer was strongly committed to the education and training of African Americans.

## 1937                    A FIRST FOR HARVARD

The first black woman to earn a doctorate from Harvard University's Graduate School of Education was **ROSE BUTLER BROWNE (1897–1986).** In 1969 her alma mater, now known as Rhode Island College, dedicated a women's residence hall and medical facility in her honor.

## PIONEER DEGREE HOLDER                    1937

**CLARA B. WILLIAMS (1885–1994)** became the first black to receive a bachelor's degree from New Mexico College of Agriculture and Mechanic Arts (now New Mexico State University). When she graduated, some students boycotted ceremonies. However, when the school awarded her an honorary degree in 1980, she received a standing ovation.

## 1937                    PIONEERING SOCIOLOGIST

The first black to receive a doctorate in sociology was **ANNA R. JOHNSON JULIAN (1904–1994)**, who graduated from the University of Pennsylvania. She also earned her bachelor's and master's degrees there and was the first black person there to be awarded Phi Beta Kappa honors. Julian was a visible victim of racism when the home she shared with husband Dr. Percy Julian in a previously all-white Chicago suburb was firebombed. Bodyguards were hired to protect the home.

## PIONEERING CPA                    1939

The first black woman certified public accountant was **MARY T. WASHINGTON**. She graduated from Northwestern University.

# 1940       RECORD-SETTING SCULPTOR

*ELIZABETH CATLETT (1915–2012)* was the first person to receive a master of fine arts degree in sculpture from the University of Iowa. She was denied living quarters in the school's residence halls because of her race. American Realist painter Grant Wood, who was on Iowa's faculty, influenced her to depict her race in her work; as a result, she did a limestone sculpture of a black American mother and child for her thesis. For this work, she won first prize in sculpture from the American Negro exposition in Chicago in summer 1940. That same summer, she won first prize in sculpture in the Golden Jubilee National Exposition held in Chicago.

# PIONEERING GEOLOGIST       1942

Geologist and geographer *MARGUERITE THOMAS WILLIAMS (1895–1991)* became the first black person to earn a doctorate in geology in the United States.

# 1944       SCHOOL BOARD LEADER

*RUTH WRIGHT HAYRE (1910–1998)* was the first black to become a regular high school teacher in Philadelphia. She was elected to the Philadelphia Board of Education, and in 1990 she was the first black (and the first woman) elected president of the board. She became a district superintendent in Philadelphia in 1963.

# HONORARY DEGREE HOLDER       1946

On February 21, 1946, *MARY McLEOD BETHUNE (1875–1955)*, educator and civic leader, became the first black to receive an honorary degree from a white college in the South; she received the degree from Rollins College.

## 1946    PIONEER NURSING EDUCATOR/ ADMINISTRATOR

After she received her master's degree in 1946, **ESTELLE MASSEY (RID-DLE) OSBORNE (1901–1981)** became the first black woman instructor in New York University's department of nursing education. She became the first educational director of nursing at Freedmen's Hospital School of Nursing, later to become the College of Nursing at Howard University. She became the first black director of nursing at City Hospital No. 2, known later as the Homer G. Phillips Hospital Training School. In 1943 she became consultant to the National Nursing Council for War Service and was the first black consultant on the staff of any national nursing organization. She remained an advocate for black nurses.

## FIRST REFERENCE LIBRARIAN    1946

**DORIS EVANS SAUNDERS (1921–2014)** was the first black reference librarian in the Chicago library system. She became librarian for the Johnson Publishing Company in 1949 and head of the company's book division in 1961. She influenced Johnson Publishing to fill the gap in information about black people and publish more books on black themes. Saunders grew up under the influence of librarian and children's writer Charlemae Hill Rollins (1897–1979).

## 1949    BOUNDARY-BREAKING LAW SCHOOL STUDENT

**ADA LOIS SIPUEL FISHER (1924–1995)** became the first black admitted to the University of Oklahoma Law School. In 1945 she was denied admission to Oklahoma's law school. The letter denying her admission stated quite clearly that her race was the reason she was denied. She filed several suits in state courts, followed by appeals in the U.S. Supreme Court. Meanwhile, the State Board of Regents voted to establish a segregated law school at all-black Langston University, intending for Fisher to enroll there. In 1949 the state legislature passed a law allowing admission of blacks to Oklahoma graduate courses on a segregated basis. In 1950 the U.S. Supreme Court overturned all laws requiring segregation at the graduate level. Fisher received her law degree in 1951, practiced law immediately after graduation, and returned to Langston to teach in 1957. The university recognized her in 1978 by having a day in her honor and in 1991 by awarding her an honorary doctorate.

## OKLAHOMA STATE'S FIRST BLACK STUDENT

### 1949

*NANCY RANDOLPH DAVIS (1926–2015)* became the first black student to enroll at Oklahoma State University. Much later, the university dedicated a new residence hall in her honor and named a series of scholarships after her.

## 1949    MATHEMATICIANS OF DISTINCTION

The first two black women to receive doctorates in mathematics were *MARJORIE LEE BROWNE (1914–1979)*, from the University of Michigan, and *EVELYN BOYD GRANVILLE (1924–)*, from Yale University.

## LAW SCHOOL GRADUATE

### 1950

*JUANITA E. JACKSON MITCHELL (1913–1992)* was the first black woman to graduate from the University of Maryland's law school and the first black woman to practice law in Maryland. She received her law degree from the University of Maryland 23 years after it had denied her admission.

## 1952    MECHANICAL ENGINEERING GRADUATE

*YVONNE CLARK (1929–2019)* became the first woman to receive a bachelor's degree in mechanical engineering from Howard University. She became head of the Department of Mechanical Engineering at Tennessee State University. Clark was also the first woman ever hired by the Nashville Ford Motor Company at its glass plant. Despite applying during the 1950s, she was not hired until 1971.

Yvonne Clark

# TRENDSETTER IN POLITICAL SCIENCE    1954

The first black woman to receive a doctorate in political science was *JEWEL LIMAR PRESTAGE (1931–2014)*. She became dean and professor of political science in the Benjamin Banneker Honor College at Prairie View Agricultural and Mechanical College.

# 1956        BARRIER-BREAKING ALABAMA STUDENT

*AUTHERINE JUANITA LUCY (FOSTER) (1929–)* became the first black student admitted to the University of Alabama on February 3, 1956. A riot followed, and she was suspended that evening. She was expelled February 29 for making "false" and "outrageous" statements about the school. Lucy had completed her undergraduate degree at Miles College in Alabama. In 1989 she entered the Alabama's graduate program in elementary education.

# CHANGE-MAKING LAW SCHOOL GRADUATE                                    1956

*LILA FENWICK (1932–2020)* became the first black woman to graduate from the Harvard Law School. The school was one of the first university law schools to admit blacks but one of the last to admit women.

# 1957        PASSIONATE ADVOCATE FOR SCHOOL INTEGRATION

*DAISY GATSON BATES (1914–1999)*, then president of the Arkansas state branch of the NAACP, led nine black students to integrate Central High School in Little Rock, Arkansas, on September 25 of this year. In 1998 the U.S. Senate voted to award Congressional Gold Medals to the nine at a White House ceremony. Arkansas declared the third Monday in February as Daisy Gatson Bates Day. When Arkansas moved slowly to follow the U.S. Supreme Court's 1954 desegregation order, the NAACP, under Bates's leadership, protested. Bates and other NAACP officials were arrested and charged with violating a new law requiring organizational information. Bates was convicted and fined, but the decision was later reversed. Fifty years after Central High School's integration, the nation reflected on the legacy of the town and the Little Rock Nine in a celebration in Little Rock that included the opening of the school as a National Historic Site.

## VERSATILE EDUCATOR                                          1958

**HELEN WALKER WILLIAMS** became the first black woman hired as a permanent teacher in the Rhode Island school system. She taught English and social studies at Esek Hopkins Junior High School in Providence.

## 1960  RISK-TAKING NEW ORLEANS STUDENT

Ruby Bridges

**RUBY BRIDGES (HALL) (1954–)** became the first black student enrolled at William Frantz Elementary School in New Orleans. She was escorted to school by federal marshals, who joined her at the school for celebration of Black History Month in 2001. The significance of Hall's enrollment was recognized in Norman Rockwell's painting *The Problem We All Live With,* which shows Hall entering school. In 1995, *The Story of Ruby Bridges,* her picture book for children on which Harvard psychologist Robert Cole collaborated, was published. The book led to the establishment of the Ruby Bridges Foundation, which focuses on helping schools establish diversity programs.

## STUDENTS INTEGRATE UNIVERSITY        1961

**CHARLAYNE HUNTER-GAULT (1942–)** and Hamilton Earl Holmes (1941–1995) were the first black students to enroll at the University of Georgia, on January 10. Students rioted in protest of their admission, and they were temporarily suspended in the interest of their safety. Nevertheless, both students graduated from the institution in 1963. Hunter-Gault worked at the *New Yorker* magazine until a 1967 Russell Sage Fellowship led her to study at Washington University in St. Louis. Holmes, whom the university initially rejected as academically unqualified, graduated Phi Beta Kappa. He became the first black medical student at Emory University in 1967 and became an orthopedic surgeon.

## 1964                    CHANGE-MAKING LIBRARIAN

*JESSIE CARNEY SMITH (1930–)* became the first black to receive a Ph.D. in library science from the University of Illinois. In 1976–77, she became the first black national president of Beta Phi Mu, the honor society for persons with graduate degrees in library science. Smith was honored again in 1985, this time as the first black to be named Association of College and Research Librarian of the Year.

## TREND-SHATTERING UNIVERSITY          1965
## STUDENTS

The first black student to graduate from the University of Alabama, on May 30, 1965, was *VIVIAN MALONE (JONES) (1942–2005)*. In 1956, *AUTHERINE JUANITA LUCY (FOSTER) (1929–)* was the first black student enrolled in the university. Malone and another black student, James Hood, had to be escorted by the National Guard to registration. After graduation, Malone worked for the Justice Department and the Veteran's Administration and retired in 1996 from her position as director of the Federal Office of Environmental Justice in the Environmental Protection Agency. She was also executive director of the Voter Education Project.

## 1966                    FIRST BLACK PROFESSOR

*VIVIENNE MALONE-MAYES (1942–1995)* became the first black professor at Baylor University in Waco, Texas. She had been denied admission to the university just five years earlier.

## SELF-ELEVATING FORMER MAID          1969

*LILLIAN LINCOLN LAMBERT (1940–)*, a one-time maid, was the first black woman to earn an M.B.A. from Harvard Business School. While there, she and other black students began a recruitment program to attract more black students and also established an African American student union.

# JACQUELYNE JOHNSON JACKSON

## (1932–2004)

### Medical School Educator

Jacquelyne Johnson Jackson, sociologist and civil rights activist, became the first full-time black faculty member at Duke University Medical School in 1968. She became the medical school's first black tenured faculty member. She was also the first woman chair of the Association of Black Sociologists. Jackson received her doctorate in 1960, becoming the first black woman to earn a doctorate in sociology from Ohio State University. Later she was the first black postdoctoral fellow at Duke's Center for the Study of Aging and Human Development. She was actively involved in the Civil Rights Movement and participated in the 1963 March on Washington; she was in Jackson, Mississippi, during the riot when three young black men were shot.

## 1970　　　　　LAW SCHOOL GRADUATE

**ELAINE R. JONES (1944–)** graduated from the School of Law at the University of Virginia and became the first black woman to be admitted and to graduate from the school. A tireless and effective civil rights worker, under Jones's leadership equal education and voting rights legislation have received continuing attention.

## AGITATOR FOR CHILDREN'S RIGHTS　　1972

The first black woman elected to the Yale University Corporation was **MARIAN WRIGHT EDELMAN (1939–)**, a lawyer, children's rights activist, and head of the agency that she founded in 1973, the Children's Defense Fund. In 1980 she became the first black (and the second woman) to head the Spelman College Board of Trustees. She became a very active participant in the student protests in the South and was arrested after a large sit-in at Atlanta's City Hall. She took her first job as one of the first two interns with the NAACP's Legal Defense and Education Fund in Jackson, Mississippi, and later opened her own law office. Edelman moved to Washington with a grant to study how to obtain legal justice for the poor. She directed Harvard's Center for Law and Education while establishing the Children's Defense Fund.

Marian Wright Edelman

## 1972        PIONEERING WOMAN PHYSICIST

**WILLIE HOBBS MOORE (1934–1994)** became the first black woman to receive a doctorate in physics. She received three degrees from the University of Michigan. Much of her research has been published in scientific journals.

## MIT'S RECORD-HOLDING PHYSICIST        1973

**SHIRLEY ANN JACKSON (1946–)** received a doctorate in theoretical elementary particle physics. She was the first black woman in the United States to receive a doctorate in physics from Massachusetts Institute of Technology. She joined AT&T Bell Laboratories, where she conducted research on topics relating to theoretical material sciences.

## 1973 PIONEERING SCHOOL BOARD MEMBER

**MARIANNA WHITE DAVIS (1929–)** was the first black woman member of the South Carolina Board of Education. She later served as acting president of Denmark Technical College in South Carolina.

## PIONEERING UNIVERSITY        1976
## CHANCELLOR

The first black woman to head a major research university in the United States was **MARY FRANCES BERRY (1938–)**. She was named

Mary Frances Berry

chancellor of the University of Colorado at Boulder this year. Berry has had an enviable career in a variety of spheres. A Nashville, Tennessee, native, she was born into a family of extremely poor circumstances, which resulted in her being placed in an orphanage for a period of time. She credits mentorship from one of her black high school teachers with motivating her and helping her to overcome the trauma of her early years. In 1970 she took a faculty position at the University of Colorado. She was Colorado's first director of the Afro-American Studies and was named provost for the Division of Behavioral and Social Sciences. After a year as chancellor, Berry remained on the faculty at Colorado until 1980. She was assistant secretary of education in the U.S. Department of Health, Education, and Welfare from 1977 to 1980. She was the first black woman to be named chief educational officer of the United States. In 1980 she joined the faculty at Howard University and was appointed to the U.S. Commission on Civil Rights that same year. In 1987 Berry became the Geraldine R. Segal Professor of American Social Thought at the University of Pennsylvania.

# 1976     HARVARD'S FIRST BLACK TENURED PROFESSOR

**EILEEN JACKSON SOUTHERN (1920–2002)** was the first African American woman to receive a tenured professorship in any discipline at Harvard. A specialist in Renaissance European and African American music, she was professor of music and Afro-American studies at the university. Previously, Southern chaired the university's Afro-American Studies Department (1975–79).

# CHANGE-MAKER FOR GOVERNING BOARD     1977

**WENDA WEEKES MOORE (1941–)**, a Minneapolis civic leader, was the first black chairperson of the University of Minnesota Board of Regents. She was appointed to the board in 1973, elected to the board in 1975, elected vice chair of the board in 1975, and then moved up to become chair.

# 1978                  DISTINGUISHED TEACHER AT BERKELEY

**BARBARA T. CHRISTIAN (1944?–2000)** was the first black tenured professor at the University of California, Berkeley. In 1986 she was the first black promoted to full professor and in 1991 the first black to receive the Distinguished Teaching Award from the university. Christian, an acclaimed professor in African American Studies, was considered one of the first scholars to focus national attention on such black women writers as Toni Morrison and Alice Walker. She joined the faculty at Berkeley in 1972 and played a central role in founding the African American studies department.

# SUBMARINE NAVIGATION ANALYST          1979

The first black woman to graduate from Yale University with a degree in mechanical engineering was **GWENDOLYN BOYD (1955–)**. After graduating from Yale, Boyd was an analyst in submarine navigation systems at the Applied Physics Laboratory at Johns Hopkins University. She is an ordained elder in the A.M.E. Church. In 2013, she became the first woman president of Alabama State University.

# 1979          YALE'S FIRST BLACK TENURED PROFESSOR

The first black woman to become tenured at Yale University was **SYLVIA ARDYN BOONE (1939–1993)**. She was visiting lecturer in Afro-American studies at Yale and taught a course on black women. She also began a black film festival.

# FIRST SCHOOL          1981
# SUPERINTENDENT

**RUTH B(URNETT) LOVE (HOLLOWAY) (1935–)** was the first black and the first woman superintendent of the Chicago school system. The system faced budget problems, issues with its desegregation plan, and additional political issues. Love instituted new programs, including discipline codes and "Adopt-a-School," which had positive results. She relocated

Ruth B. Love

to San Francisco and formed Ruth Love Enterprises, an educational consulting firm.

# 1981        PIONEERING COLLEGE PRESIDENT

**YVONNE KENNEDY (1945–2012)** became the first black woman junior college president in Alabama, when she took the position at Bishop State Community College in Mobile. She also became the first black woman to head a state college in Alabama.

# GROUNDBREAKING CHEMICAL        1981
# ENGINEER

The first black woman to earn a doctor of science degree in chemical engineering was **JENNIE R. PATRICK (YEBOAH) (1949–)**. She received her degree from the Massachusetts Institute of Technology, having received a bachelor's degree in chemical engineering from the University of California, Berkeley.

# 1981        CALIFORNIA'S GLASS CEILING
# BREAKER

**JEWEL PLUMMER COBB (1924–2017)** became president of California State University at Fullerton. She was the first black woman appointed in the system and is believed to be the first to head a major public university on the West Coast. She wrote extensively, often about the role of women in science. Her work as a biologist is praised in scientific circles; buildings bear her name at Douglass College and at California State, Fullerton; and her portrait, as a distinguished black scientist, hangs in the National Academy of Sciences.

# SCHOOL BOARD MEMBER        1982

**BETTYE J. DAVIS (1938–2018)**, state representative and senator, was the first black woman elected to the Anchorage, Alaska, Board of Education.

## 1984    TREND-SETTING COLLEGE LEADER

The first woman of any race to become president of Wilberforce University was *YVONNE WALKER-TAYLOR (1916–2006)*. She held the administrative positions of dean and vice president—both "firsts" for a woman at Wilberforce. Walker-Taylor was highly visible nationally, appearing on television, testifying before congressional committees, and participating in a variety of professional and community associations.

## LAW SCHOOL DEAN                1987

*MARILYN VIRGINIA YARBROUGH (1945–2004)* became the first black law school dean in the South and the only black woman law school dean in the country, when she was hired at the University of Tennessee at Knoxville.

## 1987      SPELMAN'S SISTER PRESIDENT

Johnnetta Cole

Educator and anthropologist *JOHNNETTA (BETSCH) COLE (ROBINSON) (1936–)* was the first black woman president of Spelman College. She was affectionately called "Sister President," a title that she assumed in 1987. She resigned from Spelman in June 1997 and later became a member of the faculty at Emory University. Then she became president of Bennett College for Women. Cole served as director of the Smithsonian Institution's National Museum of African Art. In 2017 she became senior consulting fellow for the Andrew Mellon Foundation.

## AGENT OF CHANGE FOR EDUCATION    1988

*BLENDA JACQUELINE WILSON (1941–)* became the first black woman to head a public university in Michigan when she was appointed chancellor of the University of Michigan–Dearborn. From 1992 to 1999, she was president of California State University at

# NIARA SUDARKASA

## (1938–2019)

### HBCU President

In 1986 Niara Sudarkasa, educator and anthropologist, became the first woman president of Lincoln University in Pennsylvania. She taught at the University of Michigan, where she was the first black woman promoted to full professor in the arts and sciences division and the first tenured black woman professor. Her research on African women and the application of this research to the African American family structure contributed to her international reputation as a researcher. In 1996 she became the first black chair of the Pennsylvania Association of Colleges and Universities. She was also well known for her political activism, which came to the fore during the 1970s. Her activism extended to stress the need for equal access to higher education. To emphasize her ties to Africa, Gloria Marshall changed her name to Niara Sudarkasa.

Northridge, the only woman in the United States to head a branch of the nation's largest public university system at the time.

# 1990   PROMINENT SCHOOL BOARD LEADER

*GWENDOLYN CALVERT BAKER (1931–2019)* was the first black woman president of the New York City Board of Education. She moved to the nation's capital to become chief of Minorities and Women's Programs for the National Institute of Education. She later served as vice president and dean of Graduate and Children's Programs at the prestigious Bank Street College of Education. Baker was noted for her abiding interest in multicultural education. She was named to the board of the Greater New York Saving Bank in 1992, the first black and the first woman ever chosen.

## UNIVERSITY PRESIDENT                                           1990

**MARGUERITE ROSS BARNETT (1942–1992)** took office as the first woman and first black president of the University of Houston. When appointed, she became one of only three women to lead institutions with more than 30,000 students and the only black to head a major research institution at the time. In 1986 she had been named the first black woman chancellor of the University of Missouri, Saint Louis.

Marguerite Ross Barnett

## 1990            HISTORY-MAKING UNIVERSITY PRESIDENT

**DOLORES E. CROSS (1938–)** was the first black woman president of Chicago State University. She was also the first woman to head a four-year college in the Illinois system of public higher education. In 1999 she became the first woman president of Morris Brown College in Atlanta. She also held an academic administrative post at City University of New York, and she was the first black senior administrator at the University of Minnesota. Cross became an accomplished marathon runner.

## PIONEER LEADER OF UNIVERSITY            1991
## SYSTEM

**DOLORES MARGARET RICHARD SPIKES (1936–2015)** became president of the Southern University and A&M College system, the first woman in the United States to head a university system. She was also the first woman to head a public college or university in Louisiana. In 1971 Spikes became both the first black graduate and the first Southern University graduate to earn a doctorate in mathematics from Louisiana State University.

## 1992            SUPERINTENDENT OF THE YEAR

The first black and the first woman superintendent of the South Bend Community School Corporation in Indiana was **VIRGINIA BROWN**

*CALVIN (1945–)*. In 1996 she was named Superintendent of the Year, the first black to hold that honor.

## RECORD-SHATTERING COLLEGE FUNDRAISING     1992

*SPELMAN COLLEGE* in Atlanta became the first black college to receive a single gift of $37 million, until then the largest gift ever made to a historically black college. The gift from the DeWitt Wallace/Spelman College fund was established in the New York Community Trust by the Reader's Digest Association. The funds were earmarked for scholarships and to build a curriculum development program within the honors program.

## 1992     COMMUNITY COLLEGE ADMINISTRATOR

*BELLE SMITH WHEELAN (1951–)* became president of Central Virginia Community College. She was the first black woman to serve as president of a two- or four-year public institution of higher education in the Commonwealth of Virginia.

## ACADEMIC LEADER     1993

*CONDOLEEZZA "CONDI" RICE (1954–)* became the youngest and first black chief academic officer at Stanford University, serving as provost from 1993 to 1999. Rice had served as senior director of Soviet and East European Affairs on the National Security Council from 1991 to 1993.

## 1993     HBCU PRESIDENT

*JOANN HORTON* became the first woman president of Texas Southern University, one of the nation's largest historically black colleges. Among the positions held before moving to Texas Southern, she headed the 15 institutions and 28 campuses of the Iowa community college system. She left the post in 1995 and in 1998 became president of Kennedy-King College in Chicago.

## PIONEERING UNIVERSITY DEAN            1993

**BARBARA WILLIAMS WHITE (1943–2019)** became the first black dean at the University of Texas at Austin, where she headed the School of Social Work.

## 1994     GEORGIA SCHOOL BOARD MEMBER

**FRANCES EDWARDS** became the first black woman elected chair of the school board for DeKalb County, Georgia. Previously she was vice chairperson of the board.

## HISTORY-MAKER IN GENETICS            1994

**GAIL MARIE HAWKINS** received a doctorate in genetics from Stanford Medical School, becoming the first black ever to receive the degree. She was also the first black woman to graduate from the University of California at Davis with a bachelor's degree in genetics.

## 1994            UNIVERSITY BOARD MEMBER

**C(ECELIA) ELLEN CONNALLY (1945–)** became the first black to head the Board of Trustees of Bowling Green State University.

## CHANGE AGENT IN COLLEGE            1994
## ADMINISTRATION

**CAROL SURLES (1947?–)** was named president of Texas Woman's University, the first black to hold the post. Earlier in her career, she held administrative posts in Florida, Mississippi, and Michigan. Since her Texas appointment, in 1999 she was named president of Eastern Illinois University in Charleston, the first black woman to hold this position.

# SHIRLEY A. R. LEWIS

## (1937–)

## HBCU President

In 1994 Shirley A. R. Lewis was named president of Paine College in Augusta, Georgia, the school's first woman president. She had worked at both Vanderbilt University and Meharry Medical College; she was the first associate dean of academic affairs at Meharry. She was executive director of the Black College Fund for the United Methodist Church for five years, after which she was promoted to assistant general secretary for the General Board of Higher Education and Ministry of the United Methodist Church in Nashville, Tennessee.

## 1994 HUMAN ENVIRONMENT ADMINISTRATOR

*RETIA SCOTT WALKER* was appointed dean of the University of Kentucky's College of Human Environmental Sciences, making her the first black woman to hold the post. Walker was previously faculty administrator at the University of Maryland, Eastern Shore.

## BARRIER-BREAKING COLLEGE PRESIDENT 1994

Johnson C. Smith University in Charlotte, North Carolina, named *DOROTHY COWSER YANCY (1944–)* its twelfth president and the first woman to head the school in its 127-year history. She became president of Shaw University in Raleigh in 2009 and again in 2001.

## 1995    PHILANTHROPIC SALARIED WORKER

**OSEOLA McCARTY (1908–1999)** contributed her life savings, $150,000, to the University of Southern Mississippi, establishing a scholarship fund for black students. This was the first time that a black person had funded such a program at the school. For 78 years, McCarty worked as a laundress, saved her money, and invested it wisely. She accumulated an estate, the bulk of which she gave to the University of Southern Mississippi, and received wide recognition, including an honorary degree from Harvard University in 1996.

## HISTORY-MAKING COLLEGE LEADER    1995

**RUTH SIMMONS (1945–)** became the first black president to lead one of the "Seven Sisters" schools, Smith College in Northampton, Massachusetts. She was also the first black to head an upper-tier college. In 2001 she became the first black and first woman president of an Ivy League school when she became president of Brown University in Providence, Rhode Island. A former president of Smith College, she is also the first woman to head two of the nation's premier institutions. She retired in 2012 and in 2017 was named eighth president of Prairie View A&M University.

Ruth Simmons

## 1995         EXPERT FOR HEARING-IMPAIRED

**LILLIE RANSOM** became the first black president of Maryland School for the Deaf, located in Frederick, Maryland. She is an expert in deaf education and was vice president of the Board of Trustees for the school.

## HBCU PRESIDENT                          1995

**LOIS STOVALL WILLIAMS** became the first woman president of Knoxville College and the 22nd president in the college's 120-year history.

**1995**

# RECORD-SETTING COLLEGE PRESIDENT

**JACQUELYN M. BELCHER** was named president of Georgia Perimeter College, the first black woman to head the third largest institution in the University System of Georgia. She was also the first black woman head of any institution in the system and the first black person to head a Georgia institution that is not historically black.

# ELECTRICAL ENGINEER                                  1995

**CASSANDRA SWAIN** became the first black woman to earn a doctorate in electrical engineering from Vanderbilt University. She worked as an engineering researcher for AT&T Bell Laboratories in Holmdel, New Jersey.

**1996**

# SUPERINTENDENT OF THE YEAR

**VIRGINIA BROWN CALVIN (1945–)** became the first black to be named Indiana State Superintendent of the Year. She was also the first black and first woman superintendent in the history of the district represented by the South Bend Community School Corporation.

# DEGREE-HOLDING JUDGE                               1996

Illinois Circuit Court Judge **MARY MAXWELL THOMAS (1943–)** became the first black woman judge to receive a master of judicial studies degree from the University of Nevada, Reno. The program was available to sitting judges who graduated from law schools accredited by the American Bar Association.

**1997**

# WISCONSIN'S SUPERINTENDENT OF THE YEAR

**ROSA A. SMITH** was named superintendent of the Columbus, Ohio, public schools, becoming the first woman to head the 63,000-student district. In 1997 the former superintendent of the Beloit, Wisconsin, school district was named Superintendent of the Year in Wisconsin.

# CYLENTHIA LaTOYE MILLER

## (1962–)

## Law School Class President

Cylenthia LaToye Miller was the first black woman to serve as president of her law school class at the Detroit College of Law in 1996. This was the oldest independent, continuously operating law school in the country until 2018, when it began integration into Michigan State University as its College of Law.

## RECORD-BREAKING EDUCATOR          1997

The first black faculty member of the National Defense University in Washington, D.C., was **NEDRA HUGGINS-WILLIAMS**. A graduate of Fisk University, she received her doctorate from the University of Utah.

## 1997          HBCU PRESIDENT

**MARIE V. McDEMMOND (1946–)**, the first woman and the third president of Norfolk State University, took office in July. She came to the university from Florida Atlantic University, where she was vice president for finance and chief fiscal officer (the first woman to hold that post in the Florida State University System). While at Florida Atlantic, she was elected president of the Southern Association of College and University Business Officers, the first black woman to hold this office.

## PIONEERING COLLEGE LEADER          1998

The appointment of **JOYCE F. BROWN (1947–)** as president of the Fashion Institute of Technology in New York made her the first black and first woman head of the school. She was both president and chief executive officer of the school's advisory group, the Educational Foundation for the Fashion Industries.

# 1998                                    COLLEGE PRESIDENT

The first black female layperson to be named president of Marygrove College in Detroit was **GLENDA DELORES PRICE (1939–)**.

# AMA-FOUNDED COLLEGE LEADER          1998

**MARGUERITE ARCHIE-HUDSON (1937–)** became the first woman president of Talladega College in Alabama. Former slaves and the American Missionary Association founded the liberal arts college in 1867.

# 1998                          HEALTH SCIENCES EDUCATOR

**MARILYN K. EASTER (1957–)** became the first black associate professor and chair at the College of Notre Dame in Belmont, California. She was named chair of the new health services program.

# LEADS CENTER OF HEALTH                1998
# DISPARITIES

**FANNIE G. GASTON-JOHANSSON (1938–)** became the first black woman tenured professor at Johns Hopkins University. In 2007 she became the first chair of the School of Nursing in the Department of Acute and Chronic Care at the university. An internationally renowned nursing educator, researcher, and clinical practitioner, Gaston-Johansson also became director of the Center on Health Disparities Research and leader of the international and interdisciplinary Minority Global Health Disparities Research Training Program.

# 1998                                      HBCU PRESIDENT

Philander Smith College in Little Rock named **TRUDIE KIBBE REED (1947–)** as president. She was the school's 11th president and first woman president. Reid left her post in 2004 to become president of Bethune-Cookman University until retiring in 2012.

# HISTORY-MAKING LAW SCHOOL PROFESSOR

## 1998

The first tenured minority woman on the Harvard Law School faculty was *(CAROL) LANI GUINIER (1950–)*. She made headlines in 1993 when President Bill Clinton nominated her to head the Civil Rights Division of the U.S. Department of Justice. She later withdrew her name, citing concern over allegedly controversial ideas relating to race and voting rights in some of her writings. She worked in the Civil Rights Division of the Justice Department during the Jimmy Carter Administration, and she was the chief litigator on voting rights for the NAACP Legal Defense and Education Fund from 1981 until she moved to Pennsylvania. Many of her writings appeared after her work with the NAACP, where her experiences in the courts may have helped to shape her views.

Lani Guinier

## 1998                    LIBRARY BOARD CHAIR

*GLORIA TWINE CHISUM (1930–)*, psychologist and library administrator, was the first black and first woman chair of the board of trustees of the Free Library of Philadelphia.

## SEMINARY'S ALL-WOMEN CLASS          1998

The first all-woman class of doctoral graduates from the United Theological Seminary of Dayton, Ohio, graduated this year. They were also the first class of all black women in the school's 150-year history. The women were *MICHELE DELEAVER BALAMANI, SHIRLIMARIE McAROY-GRAY (1948–2011), BARBARA A. REYNOLDS (1942–),* and *CYNTHIA WIMBERT-JAMES*. Six more black women were expected to graduate later in the year.

## 1998                    BARRIER-BREAKING MINING ENGINEER

The first black woman to graduate from the University of Arizona in Tucson with a degree in mining engineering was *ERICA BAIRD*.

## UNIVERSITY VICE PRESIDENT 1999

**GAIL F. BAKER** became the first black to hold the title of vice president at the University of Florida. She was promoted from her position as director of university communications to vice president for public relations. She was also the chair of the Department of Public Relations in the College of Journalism and Communications. She later became vice president and provost of the University of San Diego.

## 1999      PIONEERING COLLEGE LEADER

Shirley Ann Jackson

**SHIRLEY ANN JACKSON (1946–)** became the first black president of Rensselaer Polytechnic Institute in Troy, New York. Shortly after she took office, the school received the largest financial donation in its history. She received a bachelor's degree in physics in 1968 from Massachusetts Institute of Technology and became the first black woman to earn a doctorate from the school. In July 1995 she took office as chair of the United States Nuclear Regulatory Commission, making her the first woman and the first black to hold that office. Jackson has served on a number of state and federal government committees and as a trustee of MIT.

## HBCU PRESIDENT 1999

St. Augustine's College (now University) in Raleigh, North Carolina, named **DIANNE BOARDLEY SUBER (1949?–)** president, making her the first woman president of the school.

## 2000      DUAL DEGREE HOLDER

**COLLEEN SAMUELS (1960?–)** received a law degree as well as a master's degree in social work from Yeshiva University in New York, becoming the first person to simultaneously earn the two degrees there.

## DISTINGUISHED SCHOLAR AND PROFESSOR                    2001

The University of Iowa College of Law named **ADRIEN KATHERINE WING (1956–)** as the Bessie Dutton Murray Distinguished Professor of Law. The author of more than 60 publications, Wing is the first black woman to be awarded an endowed chair at the institution.

## 2001    PIONEERING ALUMNA LEADS HBCU

**CAROLYNN REID-WALLACE (1947–)** became the first woman president of Fisk University. Her career prior to her Fisk appointment includes a variety of administrative posts in higher education, the Corporation for Public Broadcasting, and the National Endowment for the Humanities. President George H. W. Bush appointed her assistant secretary for postsecondary education at the Department of Education in 1991.

## HBC PRESIDENT                                          2001

Livingstone College in Salisbury, North Carolina, named **ALGEANIA W. FREEMAN (1949–)** its 11th president, making her the first woman to head the institution.

## 2001    SPACE FLIGHT CENTER GRADUATE

The first black woman to receive a doctorate from NASA's Goddard Space Flight Center was **APRILLE J. ERICSSON-JACKSON (1963–)**. She was also the first black woman to receive a doctorate in mechanical engineering from Howard University as well as the first American to receive a doctorate with the aerospace option.

Aprille Ericsson-Jackson

# BUILDING HONORS SCHOOL INTEGRATIONISTS                    2001

University of Georgia in Athens renamed and dedicated a building in honor of its first black students—**CHARLAYNE HUNTER-GAULT (1942–)** and Hamilton Earl Holmes (1941–1995)—on the fortieth anniversary of the school's integration. The structure that became the Holmes-Hunter Academic Building is the same structure at which the two tried to register 40 years earlier.

# 2002                                            ACADEMIC LEADER

**DARLYNE BAILEY** became dean and vice president for academic affairs at Teachers College, Columbia University. She also became a full professor in the university's School of Social Work.

# HISTORY-MAKING TEEN GRADUATE            2007

Girl genius **BRITTNEY EXLINE (1992–)EN**, then 15 years old, became the youngest black female ever accepted to an Ivy League school, the University of Pennsylvania. She received a full scholarship that covered the $50,000 tuition at the university. In high school, Exline studied Spanish, French, Japanese, Russian, Arabic, and German. A gifted dancer as well, she has studied jazz, tap, and ballet.

# 2007           IVY LEAGUE-TRAINED TRIPLETS

**ASHLEY, BRITTANY**, and **COURTNEY HENRY (1985–)** received bachelor's degrees from Dartmouth College, becoming the first set of triplets to graduate from the Ivy League school. The triplets, then 21 years old, have remained together through life. They were born on the same day, attended the same schools, and always lived together. They attended a Christian Seventh Day Adventist school and graduated in 2003 with the shared distinction as "valedictorian" of their 60-student class.

## HBCU PRESIDENT                    2008

**CLAUDETTE WILLIAMS** was installed as president of Edward Waters College in St. Augustine, Florida, becoming the first women to head the 143-year-old institution.

## 2008    HARVARD'S NEW UNDERGRADUATE LEADER

Harvard College, the undergraduate division of Harvard University, named **EVELYNN M. HAMMONDS (1953–)** dean of that division, making her the first black and the first woman to hold that post. In 2005, she became the first black senior vice provost for diversity at Harvard.

## COLLEGE DEAN                    2009

The first black and the first woman to be named dean of Columbia College was **MICHELE MOODY-ADAMS**. She moved up from her position as Hutchinson Professor and director of the program on ethics and public life.

## 2009    DOCTORAL GRADUATE IN MATHEMATICS

The first black woman to earn a Ph.D. in mathematics from Florida Atlantic University was **MARY HOPKINS**. Her dissertation revolves around communicative ring theory, a part of abstract algebra.

## LAW SCHOOL DEAN                    2009

The first African American to serve as dean of the University of Maryland's School of Law is **PHOEBE HADDON**. She joined the 185-year-old law school's administration after serving as a distinguished member of Temple University's Beasley School of Law. In 1976, the fourth-generation lawyer became the first black American to edit the *Duquesne Law Review*.

## 2009        BOARDING SCHOOL'S LEADER

***AUTUMN ADKINS*** became the sixteenth president and the first black woman to head Girard College. The boarding school, located in Philadelphia, was founded by a nineteenth-century merchant banker who wrote that he wanted to educate many "poor, White, male, orphans."

## NOTRE DAME'S PIONEER      2010 VALEDICTORIAN

Notre Dame University had its first black valedictorian in its 161-year-history this year. ***KATIE WASHINGTON (1989–)***, who earned the honor, presented the valedictory address during commencement exercises on Sunday, May 16, in the school's stadium.

## 2014      YALE'S ASTROPHYSICS GRADUATE

***JEDIDAH C. ISLER***, a Virginia Beach, Virginia, native, became the first black woman to receive a Ph.D. in astrophysics from Yale University. Isler graduated from Norfolk State University and received a master's degree in physics from the Fisk-Vanderbilt Master's-to-Ph.D. Bridge Program.

## RACIAL BARRIER-BREAKING      2014 LIBRARIAN

***SANDRA PARHAM*** became the first black director of library services at David Lipscomb University in Nashville, Tennessee. She left that position in 2020 and became library executive director of Meharry Medical College.

## 2015      GLASS CEILING BREAKER AT SWARTHMORE

The appointment of ***VALERIE SMITH (1956–)*** as Swarthmore College's 15th president and the first black woman to lead the school was praised by scholars as a major breakthrough for black women at the academy. A distinguished scholar of African American literature and culture, she left her post as dean of the college at Princeton University.

# EMILIE M. TOWNES

## (1955–)

### Pioneering Divinity School Dean

In 2013 Emilie M. Townes was named dean of the Vanderbilt University Divinity School, becoming the first black woman to hold that position. She left her post at Yale Divinity School, where she was the Andrew W. Mellon Professor of African American Religion and Theology and associate dean of academic affairs. She is the author or coeditor of several books. Her writings have focused on womanist topics in the field of religion and ethics, and she is known for her spirituality practice.

## PIONEERING LEADER AT OBERLIN          2016

The first black president of Oberlin College was **CARMEN TWILLIE AMBAR (1968–)**. The 15th president of the school, she served as president of Cedar Crest College since 2008, after a successful tenure as vice president and dean of Douglass College at Rutgers University.

## 2018                              HBCU PRESIDENT

In January, **WILMA MISHOE** was named interim president and in June elevated to president of Delaware State University, becoming the first woman to hold the latter post.

## HBCU PRESIDENT                              2018

**LILY D. McNAIR** became the first female president of Tuskegee University on July 1. Previously, she was provost and senior vice president for academic affairs at Wagner College. She was the first black woman in the Department of Psychology at the University of Georgia.

## 2018               UNIVERSITY PRESIDENT

***GLORIA J. GIBSON*** was named president of Northeastern Illinois University, making her the first black woman in his position in the school's 150-year history.

## LAW SCHOOL DEAN             2019

***VERNA L. WILLIAMS*** became the first African American dean of the University of Cincinnati College of Law. She graduated from Georgetown University and Harvard Law School.

## 2019         LAND-GRANT INSTITUTION PRESIDENT

***FELECIA M. NAVE*** made history by becoming the first woman president of Alcorn State University, the oldest public, historically black, land-grant institution in the United States.

# Journalism

America's black press had its beginning in 1827. Black journalism demonstrated from the beginning a near total commitment to the cause of racial justice. Although there are claims that the early black presses were not exclusively aimed at black readers, the fact is that there were protest-oriented and focused on the then-current critical issues: slavery, lynching, and the nation's brutality against black men, women, and children. Journalists of the early black press supported the work of black women activists and the important work of Ida B. Wells (Barnett). Clearly, black women were important in developing the black press. Sometimes they were society editors for black newspapers founded or edited by black men, or staff writers or correspondents for news services.

In 1753 abolitionist Mary Ann Shadd (Cary) became the first black woman editor of a newspaper in North America. She was editor and financier of the *Provincial Freeman*, published in Canada. The first newspaper written for and by women was the *Woman's Era*. It began in 1894 and published news and atrocities of black women's clubs throughout the country. This was the official organ of the National Association of Colored Women. Josephine St. Pierre Ruffin and her daughter Florida Ruffin Ridley were the early editors. In 1885, editor, journalist, and feminist Gertrude (Emily Hicks) Bustill Mossell began the first black woman's weekly column in the *New York Freeman*. She wrote on woman's suffrage and devoted her paper to the interest of women.

Other black women played important roles in the history of the black press. Charlotta Bass bought the *California Eagle* in 1912, becoming the first woman to publish a newspaper in the United States. Elizabeth B. Murphy Moss (Phillips), better known for her work with her family's newspaper, the *Baltimore Afro-American*, was the first black woman certified as a war correspondent in 1944. Three years later, Alice Dunnigan became the first black woman accredited to the White House. In another direction, Hazel Garland became the first female head of a nationally circulated black newspaper, the *Pittsburgh Courier*, while Ethel Payne was the only black newswoman assigned to cover the Vietnam War for Sengstacke Newspapers.

Women also made a difference in the broadcast media, among them Charlayne Hunter-Gault, the first black woman to anchor a national newscast, *The MacNeil/Lehrer Report*; Vicki L. Mabrey, a member of CBS's *60 Minutes II*; Carole Simpson, the first black woman to anchor a major network nightly newscast during weekdays; and Norma R. Quarles, the first woman in New York City to coanchor a 6:00 P.M. news program. History preserves the legacy of prominent broadcast journalist Gwen Ifill, the first black woman to host a prominent talk show on national television. She received widepread attention in 2008 when she moderated the vice-presidential debate between Sarah Palin and Joe Biden, and again in 2016, when she moderated a debate between Democratic candidates Hillary Clinton and Bernie Sanders.

Black media journalists are easily seen on television, sometimes with local stations or as White House correspondents for major anchor chains. Black women sports broadcasters include Robin Roberts, the first on-air black anchorwoman for ESPN, and Maria Taylor, the first black female reporter for ESPN's *College Game Day* and ABC's *Saturday Night Football*. Other areas in which black women journalists have contributed include periodicals, photojournalism, and press secretary.

# PIONEER JOURNALIST                                    1885

Editor, journalist, and feminist ***GERTRUDE (EMILY HICKS) BUSTILL MOSSELL (1855–1948)*** began the first black woman's weekly column in the *New York Freemen*. Her column, "Our Women's Department," appeared in the first issue of the *Freeman*, in December. Mossell introduced her column with the subject of women's suffrage. An educator and feminist, Mossell campaigned for equal rights and women's rights.

She taught in New Jersey and in Delaware but left teaching after she married because married women were not allowed to teach. Then she developed her career in journalism and became active in women's rights and in social reform movements.

Gertrude Bustill Mossell

## 1894  PROMINENT NEWSPAPER EDITORS

The first newspaper written for and by women was the **Woman's Era**; it published news and activities of women's clubs throughout the country. The official organ of the National Association of Colored Women, **JOSEPHINE ST. PIERRE RUFFIN (1842–1924)** and her daughter, **FLORIDA RUFFIN RIDLEY (1861–1943)**, were editors until 1900. Josephine, a clubwoman, civic leader, and reformer, was a founding member of the Women's Era Club, the National Federation of Afro-American Women, the National Association of Colored Women, and the Northeastern Federation of Women's Clubs. Florida was also a clubwoman as well as a writer, educator, and social worker.

## GROUNDBREAKING JOURNAL  1940 FOR WOMEN

**SUE BAILEY THURMAN (1903–1996)** was the founder-editor of *Aframerican Women's Journal,* the first published organ of the National Council of Negro Women. (In 1949 the title of the journal was changed to *Women United.*)

## 1944  LEADER OF THE BLACK PRESS

**ELIZABETH B. MURPHY MOSS (PHILLIPS) (1917–1998)** was the first black woman certified as a war correspondent during World War II. However, due to illness, she returned without filing a report. Moss later became vice president and treasurer of the Afro-American

# CHARLOTTA BASS
## (1874–1969)

### First in the Press

Publisher Charlotta (A. Spears) Bass is thought to be the first woman to own and publish a newspaper in the United States. She bought the *California Owl* in 1912 and ran it for some 40 years. Bass was the Progressive Party's vice presidential candidate in 1952, another first for a black woman. Through her journalistic and political interests, she worked tirelessly on behalf of the elimination of racism and sexism. She moved to Los Angeles and took a part-time job with the *Eagle*. When Bass assumed control of the paper in 1912, she renamed it the *California Eagle*. The film *Birth of a Nation,* injustice in the military during World War I, the 1919 Pan-African Conference, the 1931 alleged rape case in Scottsboro, Alabama, and discrimination in employment were among the concerns that came under the paper's scrutiny. Bass ran unsuccessfully for three political offices. She was the first black grand jury member for the Los Angeles County Court.

Company and publisher of the largest black chain of weekly newspapers in the United States, the *Baltimore Afro-American* (aka *The Afro* or *The Afro-American*) group.

## PIONEER ACCREDITED JOURNALIST        1947

***ALICE DUNNIGAN (1906–1983)*** of the Associated Negro Press was the first black woman accredited to the White House and the State Department and the first to gain access to the House of Representatives and Senate press galleries. Dunnigan was also the first black elected to the Women's National Press Club. In 1948 she became the first black news correspondent to cover a presidential campaign, when she covered Harry S. Truman's whistlestop trip. She became chief of the Associated Negro Press in Washington. She continued to write after leaving government service, publishing her autobiography in 1974 and a second book in 1979.

Alice Dunnigan

## 1950 · MAINSTREAM NEWSPAPER'S PIONEER JOURNALIST

**MARVEL (JACKSON) COOKE (1903–2000)** was the first full-time black woman reporter on a mainstream newspaper, the *Daily Compass*. In 1926, during the middle of the Harlem Renaissance, she moved to New York City and began her career as an editorial assistant to W. E. B. Du Bois in 1926 at the *Crisis*, which positioned Cooke to meet many of the artistic and literary figures of the era. She left the *Crisis* in 1928 and joined the *Amsterdam News*. She became assistant managing editor of Adam Clayton Powell's *People's Voice* in 1935. In 1949 she moved to the *Daily Compass*, and because she was black, she had access to news events about blacks that she wrote about in the paper. This included a series of articles about the exploitation of black domestic workers in the Bronx. She went undercover in the Bronx and gained firsthand knowledge of what she called the "Bronx Slave Market."

## MANAGING EDITOR · 1963

**ARIEL PERRY STRONG** became the first woman to head *Tan* (later *Black Stars*) magazine as managing editor. She was a proofreader for *Tan*, *Ebony*, and *Jet* magazines.

## 1965 · RADIO ANNOUNCER

The first black radio announcer at the United Nations was **BEATRICE "BEA" MOTEN-FOSTER (1937–2011)**. She broadcast her show

# JOAN MURRAY (1937–)

## Television Correspondent

The first major black woman general-assignment, on-camera newscaster for CBS-TV's New York affiliate, WCBS-TV, was Joan Murray (1937–). The *New York Times* called her the first accredited black woman television news correspondent in the country. From 1963 to 1964 she was an on-air interviewer for NBC-TV. She was also a hostess, writer, and production assistant with Kitty Carlisle's *Women on the Move*, and in April 1965 she joined WCBS-TV News. A pilot as well, Murray learned to fly when she filmed the New York documentary, *The Small Plane Boom*. In 1966 she was copilot and official WCBS news reporter for the Powder Puff Derby, officially the cross-country Trans-Continental Women's Air Race. In 1969 she founded and became executive vice president of Zebra Associates, the first integrated advertising agency with black principals and then the largest black-owned and managed advertising agency.

*African Profiles* until 1969, interviewing over 100 ambassadors, presidents, and foreign ministers. She obtained recipes from the officials' wives or their cooks. While living in Indianapolis in 1976, she formed a cookbook committee and later published a book of her own—*200 Years of Black Cookery*—that incorporated African recipes and her own as well. In October 1989 she became host of her own television show, *The Bea Moten-Foster Show*, that aired in Indianapolis on weekdays. This also made her the first black woman television announcer in Indianapolis; already she was the city's first woman radio announcer. She had a daily radio cooking program on WGRT Gospel Radio. A resident of Muncie, Foster had a career in business as marketing director and owned the Bea Moten Charm and Modeling School.

## JOURNALIST AND FREELANCE WRITER                      1968

**ELEANORA ELAINE TATE (1948–)** became the first black woman journalist to work at the *Des Moines Register* and *Tribune* newspapers.

In 1966 she became news editor for the *Iowa Bystander*, an African American weekly. Her work with the *Bystander* and *R&T* brought her in touch with a number of high-profile figures. Tate relocated to Tennessee in 1976, where she joined the *Jackson Sun* for one year. In 1977 she became a freelance writer for the Memphis *Tri-State Defender* and later, with the late photographer Zack E. Hamlett III, established a small public relations company with a news service. She has written fiction stories, poems, articles, book reviews, and books.

## 1969          TELEVISION REPORTER

**MAL JOHNSON (1924–2007)** was the first black woman television reporter to cover the White House. In 1970 she became the first woman national correspondent for Cox Broadcasting Corporation, on WKBS-TV. She hosted *Coffee Break* and *Let's Talk About It*. She was senior correspondent from 1969 to 1972 and director of community relations for Cox Enterprises from 1973 to 1992.

## ATLANTA'S PIONEERING JOURNALIST      1971

The *Atlanta Constitution* hired **TINA McELROY ANSA (1949–)** for its copy desk for the morning edition, making her the first black woman to hold that position. Ansa became an acclaimed novelist, whose work broke new ground in black American literature. She held several positions with the paper and later moved to the *Charlotte Observer*, first as copy editor then as editor, from the late 1970s to 1981, after spending a year as a freelance journalist. Ansa found inspiring the firsthand accounts of older black women who had worked as midwives or who had other beliefs, rituals, and real-life experiences to relate. Her writings reflect these experiences as well as those of her own family.

## 1972       LEADER OF THE BLACK PRESS

**HAZEL B. GARLAND (1913–1988)**, editor-in-chief of the *Pittsburgh Courier*, was the first woman head of a nationally circulated black newspaper in the United States. Her columns were published in various editions of the *Courier*. Her contact with the *Courier* in 1943, when she was a reporter for the local YWCA in Pittsburgh, led to her appointment in 1946 as a full-time staff member. She wrote the column "Things to Talk About." In 1966 John Sengstacke purchased the paper and renamed it the *New Pittsburgh Courier*, and Garland became women's and entertainment editor. She was named editor-in-chief in 1972.

## GOAL-SETTING NURSING JOURNAL EDITOR                                    1973

The first black editor-in-chief of the national journal *Nursing Research* was **MARY ELIZABETH CARNEGIE (1916–2008)**. Carnegie studied at Lincoln School for Nurses in Washington, D.C., one of the few schools in the city that accepted black students. Her concern for equality of black women and women of all races in nursing remained a theme for Carnegie. Carnegie joined Veterans Administration Hospital in Tuskegee, Alabama, one of only two U.S. federal hospitals that employed black nurses. She was assistant director of Hampton Institute's proposed new collegiate nursing program in 1943. As Carnegie was recognized as being the person primarily responsible for developing the program, her career flourished. She became dean of the nursing program at Florida Agricultural and Mechanical College (now University). In 1953 she began a career in nursing journalism when she became assistant editor of the *American Journal of Nursing*. She became associate editor and later senior editor of *Nursing Outlook*. She was also editor of *Nursing Research*.

## 1974                          POPULAR MANAGING EDITOR

**AUDREY T. WEAVER (1908–1996)** was named managing editor of the *Chicago Defender,* making her the first woman to hold this position with a major newspaper. She was previously city editor and had been associate editor for *Jet* magazine. In 1973 and 1974 Weaver was a juror on the Pulitzer Prize Committee.

## ROLE-SETTING NEWSCASTER                                    1978

**CHARLAYNE HUNTER-GAULT (1942–)** was the first black woman to anchor a national newscast, *The MacNeil/Lehrer Report*. She left that post in 1997 when she moved to South Africa. In 1999 she joined CNN in Johannesburg as bureau chief. In January 1961 she and Hamilton Holmes were the first two black students to attend the University of

Georgia, where they were confronted with a student riot protesting their admission. Hunter-Gault's first job after graduating from the university was as a secretary for *The New Yorker* magazine. While there, she contributed articles to a feature section and wrote short stories. She edited articles for *Trans-Action* and covered the Poor People's Campaign in Washington, D.C. This coverage led to her first television job: investigative reporter and anchorwoman of the evening local news at WRC-TV in Washington. A ten-year position at the *New York Times* followed, after which she went on to *The MacNeil/Lehrer Report*.

Charlayne Hunter-Gault

## 1982      PIONEERING PUBLISHER

**PAMELA McALLISTER JOHNSON (1945–)** became the first black woman publisher of a mainstream paper, the *Ithaca Journal*, in December 1982.

## EMMY-WINNING TELEVISION REPORTER      1986

**VALERIE COLEMAN-MORRIS (1946–),** a veteran television reporter in Los Angeles, was named weekday anchor for KCBS-TV in Los Angeles, becoming the first black in that time slot. She received three Emmy Awards for her work.

## 1987      FOREIGN EXCHANGE JOURNALIST

**YELENA KHANGA (1962–)** received an award from the Soviet Union that allowed her to work several years as an exchange journalist with the *Christian Science Monitor*. She was the first woman to receive the honor.

## HISTORY-MAKING TELEVISION ANCHOR      1989

**CAROLE SIMPSON (1941–)** substituted for Peter Jennings on Wednesday, August 9, this year and again on Thursday night, becoming

# DANA TYLER (1958–)

## Television News Anchor

In 1990 Dana Tyler and Reggie Harris formed the first black anchor team in a major metropolitan city for WCBS-TV in New York City. Tyler, who graduated from Boston University, is the great-granddaughter of Ralph Waldo Tyler, the first black war correspondent during World War I.

the first black woman to anchor a major network newscast during weekdays. She was also the first black woman television newsperson in Chicago. Her career in broadcast journalism began in 1965, when she was news reporter for Chicago's WCFL Radio. She became the first black reporter on WMAQ-TV in Chicago in 1970 and was promoted to a weekend anchor post. Simpson moved to Washington, D.C., and became reporter for NBC News. Then she was a general assignment correspondent for ABC News, still based in Washington. She was promoted to weekend anchor of *World News Saturday* in 1988. Simpson covered George H. W. Bush when he was vice president and president. She also covered many breaking news stories, including Nelson Mandela's release from prison in South Africa in 1990.

## 1990     BARRIER-BREAKING PRESS SECRETARY

**LYNETTE MOTEN (1954–)** became the first black woman press secretary for a U.S. senator. She worked with Thad Cochran, a Republican from Mississippi, in his Washington, D.C., office.

## EDITORIAL PAGE EDITOR     1990

**CYNTHIA ANNE TUCKER (1955–)** was the first black woman to edit the editorial page at a major daily newspaper, the *Atlanta Constitution*. She joined the newspaper in 1976 and left in 1982 to become a reporter for the *Philadelphia Inquirer*. Tucker was editorial writer and later columnist for the *Atlanta Journal*.

## 1990 NEWSPAPER BUREAU CHIEF

The first black chief of the *Detroit Free Press* city-county bureau was **CONSTANCE C. PRATER (1963–)**. She became a reporter for the newspaper in 1989. In 1990 Prater was local president of the National Association of Black Journalists.

## HEARING-IMPAIRED NEWSPAPER EDITOR 1990

**CONNIE BRISCOE (1952–)** became the managing editor of the *American Annals of the Deaf*, the first black and the first hearing-impaired person to hold the position at Gallaudet University. She was hired as editorial assistant for the Joint Center for Political and Economic Studies in Washington, D.C. She knew lip-reading and used a hearing aid in school. She learned sign language, became involved in deaf culture, and chose a career that would accommodate her impairment. Briscoe moved to Gallaudet University in Washington, an institution for the hearing impaired; there she was editorial assistant and by 1990 was managing editor for the school's journal.

## 1992 MAJOR NEWSPAPER EDITOR

On December 1, **PEARL STEWART (1950–)** became the first black woman editor of a major U.S. daily, the *Oakland Tribune*, with a circulation of over 100,000. Under a Freedom Forum grant, Stewart became journalist-in-residence at Howard University for 1994–95. She worked for United Press International and the *San Francisco Chronicle,* then joined the *Oakland Tribune*.

## PULITZER PRIZE–WINNING FEATURE WRITER 1994

**ISABEL WILKERSON (1960–)**, Chicago bureau chief of the *New York Times*, won the 1994 Pulitzer Prize for feature writing and became the first black to win for individual reporting. Wilkerson also won the George Polk Award and a John Simon Guggenheim Fellowship.

Isabel Wilkerson

## 1994          HISTORY-MAKING EDITOR
## OF *THE CRISIS*

The first woman editor of *Crisis*, the national magazine of the NAACP, was **DENISE CRITTENDON (1954?–)**. For 14 years, she was a reporter for the *Detroit News*.

## TRAILBLAZING EXECUTIVE EDITOR          1996

**LORRAINE BRANHAM (1952–)** became executive editor of the *Tallahassee Democrat*, the first black and the first woman to hold the position. Branham was previously associate managing editor of the *Philadelphia Inquirer*.

## 1997          NEWSPAPER DIRECTOR

**JACQUELINE MARIE THOMAS (1952–)** became the first woman and the first black director of the 160-year-old *Baltimore Sun*. Thomas began her career as reporter for the *Chicago Sun Times* and later became associate editor of the *Louisville Courier Journal and Times*. She left to become associate editor of the *Detroit Free Press*. From 1992 to 1997 she was Washington bureau chief for the *Detroit News*.

## NEWSPAPER'S VICE PRESIDENT          1998

The first woman of color to become a vice president at the *Daily News* of New York was **C. ADRIENNE RHODES (1961–)**. She was promoted from her position as director of communications and media relations for the nation's fourth largest newspaper.

## 1999          NATIONALLY RECOGNIZED
##                BROADCAST JOURNALIST

Gwen Ifill

**GWEN IFILL (1955–2016)** was hired as moderator of Public Broadcasting Service's *Washington Week in Review*, becoming the first black woman to host a prominent political talk show on national television. The veteran news reporter began her work in journalism in 1977, when she was a reporter for the *Boston Herald-American*. She left that post and became a reporter for the *Baltimore Evening Sun*. She joined the *Washington Post* in 1984 as political reporter. From 1991 to 1994 Ifill was first congressional correspondent for the *New York Times*' Washington, D.C., bureau, then became White House correspondent. Her first assignment as congressional correspondent was to join other reporters on a bus that trailed presidential candidate Bill Clinton. She served as panelist and occasional moderator from 1992 to 1999, before becoming moderator and managing editor of *Washington Week in Review*. When she made her debut on the show in fall 1999, producers began an advertising campaign for it called "TV's Voice of Reason Has a New Face." Ifill was also senior political correspondent for *The News Hour with Jim Lehrer*. She received widespread public attention when she moderated the vice-presidential debate between Alaska governor Sarah Palin and Senator Joe Biden on October 2, 2008. In 2009 her book *The Breakthrough: Politics and Race in the Age of Obama* was published.

## TELEVISION JOURNALIST          1999
## EXPANDS REACH

The first black woman to introduce herself to the sound of a television show's trademark stopwatch was **VICKI L. MABREY (1956–)**. She appeared with a team of well-respected journalists on CBS's *60 Minutes II*, a spin-off of the network's show *60 Minutes*. She became a production assistant with WBAL-TV in Baltimore and was promoted to general assignment reporter for that station. From 1992 to 1995, Mabry was a Dallas-based correspondent for CBS News, and was later reassigned to CBS News in London, England, where she remained

# KEIJA MINOR

## Magazine Editor

Keija Minor was named editor of *Brides* magazine in 2012, becoming the first black to rise to the top spot at Conde Nast, the parent company of the *New Yorker, Vanity Fair, Q,* and *Vogue.* She also became the first black to head a magazine in Conde Nast. She worked in corporate law before leaving to work with the now-defunct *Travel Savvy* and became its editor-in-chief. Later she worked with *Los Angeles Confidential, Gotham* magazine, and *Upton,* an upscale magazine for African Americans, which she edited. She joined *Brides* in 2011.

from 1995 to 1998. During the London assignment, she covered the fatal car crash in Paris involving Princess Diana and received two Emmy Awards for her work.

# 2001    FINANCIAL INDUSTRY NEWSWOMAN

**ELEANOR DIXSON-HOBBS** became the first woman and the first black publisher of the 165-year-old daily newspaper *American Banker*, the banking and financial industry's premiere source of daily information, news, and analysis.

# MAJOR NEWSPAPER STAFFER                2018

**MONICA DRAKE** was the first black woman to have her name printed on the masthead of the *New York Times*. She became known as the brains behind "52 Places to Go," a popular travel section that she started; then she hired a travel writer to bring the list alive. With this, Drake was given a new role as assistant managing editor and would oversee special digital projects. In addition to her travel section, she began a new project called "Surfacing" and helped coordinate the paper's Olympics coverage.

# 2019        FIRST FOR THE *HARVARD CRIMSON*

***KRISTINE E. GUILLAUME (1998?–)*** became leader of the *Crimson's* "146th Guard" after becoming the first black woman and the third black president of the volunteer organization at Harvard University. Elected in 2018 while a junior majoring in literature, history, and African American studies, she aimed for a more diverse and digital future for the *Harvard Crimson*.

# Military

African American women's military history is scant, especially before 1948. On July 26 of that year, President Harry S. Truman issued Executive Order 9981, signaling an end to legal segregation in the U.S. military. Previously, blacks served in the military, but they did so in racially segregated units. The Korean War (1950–1972) was a test of racial integration in the making, and America saw an overall gain of blacks especially in the army.

The history of black women and the military is another story. Harriet Tubman, known as a conductor on the Underground Railroad, was a nurse, cook, and laundress for Union troops in South Carolina. She led Union troops in a raid, becoming the only woman during the Civil War to plan and carry out an armed expedition against enemy forces. Congress approved the first all-black units in the regular army in 1867; they became known as Buffalo Soldiers, or the U.S. Colored Troops. Cathay Williams was the first and only known female Buffalo Soldier. She disguised her gender, altered her name, and enlisted in the 38th Infantry in 1866 and served on the frontier. In 1875 her true identify was discovered, yet she was undisputedly the first black woman to serve as a soldier in the U.S. Army before women were officially allowed to enlist.

Black women served the military in a number of capacities. During World War II, Lieutenant Harriet Ida Pickens and Ensign Frances

Eliza Wills were the first commissioned in the Women Accepted for Volunteer Emergency Services (WAVES). Over 4,000 joined the Women's Auxiliary Army Corps (WAAC), a year later known as the Women's Army Corps (WAC). After Congress introduced the Draft Nurse Bill, the Army Nurse Corps and the U.S. Navy ceased racial exclusionary practices. By the end of the war, 76,000 black nurses served in hospitals in the United States and several foreign countries. In 1942 the Women's Auxiliary Army Corps (WAAC) was created and made it possible for more black women to serve in the military than before. Among the racially integrated women were Charity Adams Earley, who became the first black woman commissioned in the WAAC, and Harriet M. West Waddy, who became the first black woman major in the WAAC.

The first black member of the Regular Army Nurse Corps was Nancy Leftenant-Colon, who joined in 1945. The Coast Guard Women's Reserve, known as the SPARs (which stood for the Coast Guard's motto, *Semper Paratus*—Always Ready), admitted black women in 1944; Yeoman Second Class Olivia Hooker became the first black SPAR. In 1994 Irene Trowell-Harris became the first black woman brigadier general and the highest-ranking black in the National Guard. Women also joined the U.S. Marine Corps and in time became officers. Gilda Jackson was the first colonel in the marines, in 1997. Black women continued to climb the ranks in the military. In 2000 Lillian Fishburne was the first black woman admiral in the U.S. Navy. Michelle J. Howard achieved a number of firsts: the first woman of any race to be promoted to four-star admiral (2018); the first woman executive officer on an American warship, the USS *Tortuga*; and the first woman to command a U.S. Navy combat vessel.

The first black woman to guard the Tomb of the Unknowns at Arlington National Cemetery was Danyell Wilson, a sergeant in the U.S. Army. She made her first walk as a tomb sentinel in 1997.

The Military Academy (West Point) saw its first black woman leading the Long Gray Line in 2017, when Simone M. Askew became the first captain of the 4,400-member Corps of Cadets—the highest position in the cadet chain of command.

As members of the U.S. armed forces, black women have served their country well. Some were prisoners of war, while thousands paid the ultimate price during the Gulf War, in the Middle East war on terror, and other combats.

## HARRIET TUBMAN'S DIFFERENT ROLE 1863

*HARRIET ROSS "MOSES" TUBMAN (1821?–1913)*, known for her work as a conductor on the Underground Railroad, was a nurse, cook, and laundress for Union troops in South Carolina. She led Union troops in a raid along the Combahee River in June 1863, becoming the only woman during the Civil War to plan and carry out an armed expedition against enemy forces.

Harriet Tubman

## 1866 HISTORY-MAKING BUFFALO SOLDIER

*CATHAY WILLIAMS (1844?–1893?)* was the first and only known female Buffalo Soldier. She was born into slavery and worked for the Union Army during the Civil War. She disguised her gender and, under the altered name William Cathey, enlisted in the 38th Infantry in 1866. As a Buffalo Soldier, she and her company marched from Fort Riley, Kansas, to Fort Union, New Mexico, on July 2, 1867. In October they were dispatched to Fort Cummings in New Mexico for eight months, where they served as protection from Native Americans. She suffered from illnesses at various times until she was medically discharged on October 14, 1868. It was not until 1875 that her true gender was discovered. She was the only documented black woman to serve as a soldier in the U.S. Army before women were officially allowed to enlist. Born in Independence, Missouri, she was reportedly the daughter of a free black man and a slave mother. Later she was taken to Little Rock and worked for the army as a laundress and cook. Then she was placed in the service of General Philip Sheridan and experienced life on the front lines as his troops marched on the Shenandoah Valley.

## AMERICA'S FIRST WAAC 1942

President Franklin D. Roosevelt signed the act that created the Women's Auxiliary Army Corps (WAAC) on May 15. *CHARITY ADAMS EARLEY (1918–2002)* became the first black woman commissioned in that voluntary and integrated unit. By World War II's end, she was the highest-ranking black officer in the service. Commissioned as a

# OLIVIA HOOKER (1915–2018)

## History-making SPAR

The Coast Guard Women's Reserve was created on November 23, 1942, when President Franklin D. Roosevelt signed Public Law 772. The Women's Reserve became known as SPAR, an acronym based on the Coast Guard's motto "*Semper Paratus*—Always Ready." Black women were initially denied admission into the organization. In October this year, the first black SPAR was Yeoman Second Class *Olivia Hooker (1915–2018)*. Altogether, only five black women were recruited for SPARs, representing tokenism; they were trained at Manhattan Beach Training Station in New York and were assigned to district offices of the Coast Guard without regard to race. Hooker and her family lived in Tulsa during the Tulsa Massacre of 1921 in which from three dozen to 300 or more blacks lost their lives. She became an activist, joined the Tulsa Race Riot Commission (now known as the Tulsa Race Massacre Centennial Commission), and just before she died at age 103, was one of the last known survivors of the race massacre.

lieutenant, Earley was named company commander of the women's Basic Training Company on her post. A year later, the organization became known as the Women's Army Corps (WAC).

# 1943 FIRST WAAC MAJOR

On August 21 *HARRIET M. (WEST) WADDY (1904–1999)* became the first black woman major in the Women's Army Auxiliary Corps (WAAC), which later became the Women's Army Corps (WAC). During the Great Depression, she worked as an aide to noted educator and civic leader Mary McLeod Bethune, who no doubt influenced Waddy's decision to join the WAAC. During World War II, Waddy was one of the two highest-ranking black officers in the WAAC and served as its wartime advisor on racial issues. She was promoted to lieutenant colonel in 1948. Waddy was an active recruiter of black women for the WAAC and served for a time as an aide to its director,

Oveta Culp Hobby. She also campaigned against the existing racial discrimination in the military.

## PIONEER WOMEN IN WAVES 1944

The first black women were sworn into the WAVES this year. The U.S. Navy accepted only 72 enlisted women and two officers. Bessie Garrett became the first black woman admitted. Lieutenant **HARRIET IDA PICKENS** and Ensign **FRANCES WILLIS** were the first black women that the WAVEs commissioned; they completed their training on December 13 this year. The WAVEs were incorporated into the regular navy in 1948, 30 years before the WACs were incorporated into the regular army.

## 1945 FIRST NURSE IN THE NAVY

**PHYLLIS MAE DAILEY** was the first black woman to serve as a nurse in the U.S. Navy.

## WORLD WAR II BATTALION 1945

More than 700 enlisted members of the **WOMEN'S ARMY CORPS' 6888**[th] **BATTALION** were sent to England, becoming the only battalion of black women to serve overseas during World War II. The battalion was formed after civil rights organizations and black newspapers accused the military of denying black women meaningful jobs. The women arrived in Britain, where they sorted mail, some of which had been stored for months. The commander, Charity Adams (Earley), noted that white women who served in Europe at that time were assigned to tasks equivalent to their male counterparts.

## 1948 PIONEERING ARMY NURSE

**NANCY LEFTENANT-COLON (1920–)** became the first black member of the Regular Army Nurse Corps. She joined the army reserve nurse corps in February 1945. At the time of her enlistment, black nurses were poorly regarded and denied the status of regular nurse, but in 11 months she was promoted from second to first lieutenant. Her performance as a nurse was no doubt a factor in the acceptance of her 1948 application for admission into the Regular Army Nurse Corps. During her service career, she was a U.S. Air Force flight nurse. Leftenant-Colon retired from the army with the rank of major. She achieved another "first" as the only woman to be president of the Tuskegee Airmen. She was president of the group from 1989 to 1991.

## HISTORY-MAKING ARMY MEDICAL OFFICER                               1955

*CLOTILDE DENT BOWEN (1923–2011)*, who was commissioned in the U.S. Army this year with the rank of captain, became the first black woman medical officer in the army. When she was promoted to colonel, she was the first black woman to receive this rank. Bowen began accumulating "firsts" before she entered the army. When she graduated from Ohio State University Medical School in 1947, she was the first black woman to receive a medical degree from the institution. Bowen's medical specialty was neuropsychiatry. During the Vietnam War, she served in that country and was awarded the Bronze Star and the Legion of Merit in 1971 in recognition of her service; the Meritorious Service Medal was given to her in 1974. Before she entered the army, she practiced in New York City and was associated for a time with Harlem Hospital.

## 1964                                         ARMY NURSE COLONEL

*MARGARET E. BAILEY (1915–2014)* became the first black colonel in the Army Nurse Corps. After 20 years in the army, she was made a lieutenant colonel. In 1970 she was promoted to full colonel.

## AIR FORCE OFFICER                                            1968

The first black woman colonel in the U.S. Air Force was *RUTH LUCAS (1920–2013)*, who was promoted to that rank on November 25. After Lucas graduated from Tuskegee Institute (now University) in 1942, she enlisted in the Women's Army Corps. She completed officer training, received her commission, and was assigned to several posts during the course of World War II. Lucas remained in the army and became a temporary lieutenant colonel in 1962 and a regular lieutenant colonel in 1963. Five years later, she was made a full colonel.

# 1971 HIDDEN NAVY FIGURE

Raye Montague

***RAYE (JEAN JORDAN) MONTAGUE (1935–2018)*** is said to have broken barriers as a hidden figure at the U.S. Navy. A registered professional engineer with the navy, she was the first person to design a ship using a computer. As the Vietnam War raged, President Richard Nixon ordered the navy to produce ships at a faster rate than previously done. She was directed to design a ship, defied expectations, used a computer program that she had designed, and within 18 hours and 26 minutes, her specifications for the FFG-7 frigate (the Perry-class) were complete. On January 22, 1984, Montague became the navy's first female program manager of ships (PMS-309, Information Systems Improvement Program). Her civilian equivalent rank was that of captain. Her career with the navy began in 1956, when she was a digital computer systems operator. Widely honored for her achievements, she was awarded the U.S. Navy's Meritorious Civilian Service Award (the navy's third-highest honorary award) in 1972.

## NAVY CHAPLAIN 1974

***VIVIAN McFADDEN*** was the first black woman U.S. Navy chaplain.

# 1974 COMMISSIONED OFFICER FROM ALABAMA

***JUANITA BELL (1952–)*** became the first black woman from Alabama to be commissioned by any armed service. She received her commission as a second lieutenant after being enrolled in the Air Force Reserve Officers Training Corps (AFROTC) program. She had a leadership role in her AFROTC program, coordinating corps activities and giving oversight to cadet training in the General Military course.

## BARRIER-BREAKING NAVY PHYSICIAN 1975

***DONNA P. DAVIS*** became the first black woman physician in the Naval Medical Corps.

# CLARA L(EACH) ADAMS-ENDER

## (1939–)

Distinguished Nursing Chief

Clara L(each) Adams-Ender was the first black, first woman, and first nurse to graduate with a master's degree from the U.S. Army Command and General Staff College in 1976. In July 1967 she was the first woman in the army to receive the Expert Field Medical Badge, and in 1982 she was the first black Army Nurse Corps officer to graduate from the Army War College. Adams-Ender became the first black nurse appointed chief of the nursing department at Walter Reed Army Medical Center in Washington, D.C., in 1984. Shortly before her 1961 graduation from college, Adams-Ender was commissioned as a second lieutenant. When Adams-Ender began her tour of duty in Germany in 1978, she was the assistant chief of nursing but became chief in less than a year. She was also promoted to colonel while there. When she was appointed in 1987 to the Office of the Attorney General as chief of the Army Nurse Corps, she had been promoted to brigadier general. Thus, Brigadier General Adams-Ender became the first black chief of the Army Nurse Corps.

## 1979      GROUNDBREAKING ARMY GENERAL

***HAZEL (WINIFRED) JOHNSON-BROWN (1927–2011)*** became the first black woman general in the U.S. Army. After graduating from Harlem University School of Nursing, she joined a veterans' hospital in Philadelphia, then joined the army in 1955. In 1960 Johnson achieved the rank of second lieutenant. Her race was never an

Hazel Johnson-Brown

issue. She progressed steadily in the army, and by the 1970s her rank of colonel made her the highest-ranking black woman in the armed forces.

## ARMY'S BRIGADIER GENERAL                  1985

*SHERIAN (GRACE) CADORIA (1940–)* was the first black woman promoted to brigadier general in the regular U.S. Army and the first black woman to command a male army battalion. In 1985 she also became the first black woman director of manpower and personnel for the Joint Chiefs of Staff. Cadoria's route to advancement in the army was unlike that of many of her women colleagues, who were able to advance through the nursing corps; she advanced through her involvement with

Sherian Cadoria

the military police. After graduating from college, she enlisted in the Women's Army Corps (WAC). She was also the first black woman to attend the army's Command and General Staff College, from which she received a diploma in 1971. She also earned a master's degree from the University of Oklahoma and a diploma from the U.S. War College, where she was again the first black woman to attend. Cadoria's rise through the ranks was accompanied by the frustrations encountered because of her race and her gender. She received many medals and commendations, including three Bronze Stars.

## 1990          AIR FORCE BRIGADIER GENERAL

*MARCELITE J(ORDAN) HARRIS (1943–2018)* became the first black woman brigadier general in the U.S. Air Force. In 1995 she became the first black woman major general. She entered the air force through Officer Training School and was the first black woman to become an

aircraft maintenance officer. In 1978, as commander of a cadet squadron at the U.S. Air Force Academy, Harris became one of the first two female air officer commanders. She was the highest-ranking woman on active duty in the air force and the highest-ranking black woman in the Department of Defense. Her many military honors include the Bronze Star, the Presidential Unit Citation, and the Vietnam Service Medal. President Barack Obama appointed her to the Board of Visitors to the United States Air Force Academy.

Marcelite J. Harris

## PERSIAN GULF WAR CASUALTY            1991

**ADRIENNE MITCHELL (1970–1991)** was the first black woman to die in combat in the Persian Gulf War.

## 1992        MARINE CORPS TRAINING OFFICER

**DENISE H. HOOVER** became the first woman to graduate from the U.S. Marine Corps Security Force Training Company in Chesapeake, Virginia. Hoover was the first woman permanently assigned to the training company's staff.

## CHANGE-MAKING NATIONAL            1994
## GUARD OFFICER

**IRENE TROWELL-HARRIS (1939–)** became the first black woman brigadier general and the highest-ranking black in the National Guard. She was also the first woman, first member of a minority group, and first nurse to head a medical clinic in the National Guard.

## 1994        PIONEERING ROTC BATTALION
## COMMANDER

**BRIGITTE LOTT (1973–2019)** was named ROTC battalion commander at Norfolk State University, becoming the first black woman in the nation to hold such a post. She was the number-one midshipman and would lead the 285-member battalion during the 1994–95 academic year.

## TREND-SETTING ROTC COMMANDER                                      1996

The first woman to be named the commanding officer of the Air Force ROTC program at North Carolina Agricultural and Technical State University in Greensboro was **CARLETTE "CJ" JONES**, a lieutenant colonel. Her duties included service as a personnel officer at the institution.

## 1996                      PIONEERING ROTC TRAINER

The first woman director of the Georgetown University Army Reserve Officer Training Corps (ROTC) program was **PAULETTE FRANCINE RUFFIN (1956–)**, a lieutenant colonel. A career officer, Ruffin began her career in the army in 1978 by attending the U.S. Army Ordnance School. She held several posts during her service, with a number of years spent at the U.S. Military Academy.

## ARLINGTON CEMETERY GUARD                            1997

The first black woman to guard the Tomb of the Unknowns at Arlington National Cemetery was **DANYELL ELAINE WILSON (1974–)**, a sergeant in the U.S. Army. She made her first walk as a tomb sentinel in January 1997. Wilson was also the first black woman and the second woman of any race to receive the "Tomb Guard Identification Badge."

## 1997                 PIONEERING MARINE COLONEL

The first black woman colonel in the U.S. Marine Corps was **GILDA JACKSON**, who received the honor in a ceremony at Marine Corps Air Station, Cherry Point, North Carolina. Jackson was an enlisted U.S. Marine before reaching the rank of sergeant.

## FIGHTER PILOT TRAINEE 1999

**SHAWNA KIMBRELL (1976–)** fought racial and gender stereotypes to become the first black woman to complete fighter pilot training in the U.S. Army. After receiving her wings this year, the F16 pilot flew her first combat sortie in 2001.

## 2000 RECORD-BREAKING ADMIRAL

Rear Admiral **LILLIAN E(LAINE) FISHBURNE (1949–)** became the first black woman admiral in the U.S. Navy. She became deputy director of fleet liaison at the Space, Information Warfare, Command and Control Directorate. She also became a naval computer and telecommunications expert.

Lillian E. Fishburne

## COAST GUARD INTELLIGENCE OFFICER 2001

The first black woman to graduate with an engineering degree from the U.S. Coast Guard Academy was Cadet First Class **ANDREA PARKER**. She was stationed onboard the CGC *Tahoma* in New Bedford, Massachusetts, as the ship's intelligence officer.

## 2001 SEARCH AND RESCUE TEAM MEMBER

The first black woman member of the U.S. Navy's search-and-rescue team was Lieutenant **SHELLY FRANK**.

## MARINE'S ULTIMATE GIFT 2002

Sergeant **JEANNETTE WINTERS (1976–2002)** became the first U.S. servicewoman of any race to die during the war on terrorism, Operation Enduring Freedom. She was also the first woman in the U.S. Marines to die in a combat zone.

# VERNICE "FLYGIRL" ARMOUR

## (1973–)

### Marine Combat Pilot

Vernice "FlyGirl" Armour became the first African American female combat pilot in 2001. She earned her wings in July 2001. She worked for the Metro Nashville (Tennessee) Police Department from 1996 to 1998, starting as a beat cop, and became the department's first female African American motorcycle officer. In 1998, she moved to the police department in Tempe, Arizona, and became its first female African American officer. She was the first African American female naval aviator in the Marine Corps and the first African American female combat pilot in the U.S. Armed Forces.

## 2003                  FIRST PRISONER OF WAR

One month after she joined Operation Iraqi Freedom, **SHOSHANA (NYREE) JOHNSON (1973–)**'s convoy was ambushed, she was taken captive in Nasiriyah, and she became the first black female prisoner of war in U.S. military history. She was a prisoner for 22 days and held along with five other members of her unit, including PFC Jessica Lynch, a white woman who was held in a different location. Johnson was freed on April 13, 2003, after a gunfight that led to her capture and a bullet wound in both ankles. She received a temporary disability honorary discharge and was awarded the Bronze Star, Purple Heart, and Prisoner of War Medal for her service in Iraq.

Shoshana Johnson

## COAST GUARD AVIATOR                                      2005

The first African American female aviator in the U.S. Coast Guard's 215-year history was **JEANINE McINTOSH-MENZE**, who received her wings on June 24 at Naval Air Station in Corpus Christi, Texas. She was assigned to fly a C-130 Hercules aircraft out of Air Station Barbers Point in Hawaii.

## 2008                    NATIONAL GUARD OFFICER

A colonel in the Maryland National Guard, **ALLYSON SOLOMON** was promoted to brigadier general and the Air Guard's assistant adjunct general. With the promotion, she became the first black to the post.

## PIONEERING REGIMENTAL                                    2009
## COMMANDER

Cadet **JACQUELINE FITCH (1987?–)** became the U.S. Coast Guard Academy's first black female regimental commander, the highest-ranking cadet in the academy. She made her debut when she led the Corps of Cadets in a parade at the academy, on its Washington Parade field.

## 2010        COAST GUARD HELICOPTER PILOT

The first African American woman helicopter pilot in the U.S. Coast Guard was **LA'SHANDA HOLMES (1985–)**. Lieutenant Jeanine McIntosh-Menze, the first black woman aviator in U.S. Coast Guard history, pinned her at a ceremony held at Naval Air Station Whiting Field, located in Milton, Florida.

## FIRST BLACK TWO-STAR GENERAL                             2011

When promoted from brigadier general to major general in the U.S. Army, **MARCIA ANDERSON (1957–)** became the army's first black female two-star general. After her promotion, she moved to the office of the chief of the U.S. Army Reserve in Washington, D.C.

## 2017        LONG GRAY LINE LEADER

***SIMONE M. ASKEW***, a native of Fairfax, Virginia, became the first black woman to lead the Long Gray Line at the U.S. Military Academy. The first captain of the 4,400-member Corps of Cadets held the highest position in the cadet chain of command, with responsibility for the overall performance of the corps.

## RANK-SHATTERING FOUR-STAR    2018
## ADMIRAL

The first woman of any race to become four-star admiral was ***MICHELLE J. HOWARD (1960–)***. She became the first woman executive officer on an American warship, the USS *Tortuga*. In March 1999 Howard was named commander of the USS *Rushmore*, becoming the first woman captain of the ship and the first black woman to command a U.S. Navy combat vessel. She was a member of one of the first coeducational classes at the U.S. Naval Academy. Howard faced gender and racial bias but also found opportunities for advancement and fair compensation. In 1992 she became the first black woman to

Michelle J Howard

reach the rank of rear admiral. Later, she was the first black woman to serve as a three-star officer in any branch of the military. Howard became the first black woman to command a ship in the U.S. Navy in 1999. She was transferred to a position in 2002 in which she worked with the Joint Chiefs of Staff. Howard has received awards throughout her career.

# Miscellaneous

History-making black women fall within many subject areas, some too detailed to place within a specific category. This demonstrates the progress, achievements, and determination that characterize these women despite the long-time bias shown against women of any race, but especially the black race. Of special interest is the success of Bessie Coleman, the first woman of her race to become an aviator and to gain an international pilot's license. She was also the first black woman "barnstormer," or stunt pilot. Her success is uncommon among women of any race. Later, major airlines hired black women as pilots for major commercial airlines in America. Black women are also hired as flight attendants. The airline industry also hired these women in administrative positions, while airports named them head of their boards of directors.

For their accomplishments, black women have received many awards and honors. Singer, vaudeville performer, and actress Hattie McDaniel was the first black Academy Award winner; Juanita Hall was the first black American to win a Tony Award; Gail Fisher was the first to receive an Emmy Award; and Isabel Wilkerson was the first black to win a Pulitzer Prize for feature writing. Black women continue to win awards in other categories, such as best supporting actress and best actress in a leading role. In the beauty and modeling category, black women have been the first of their race to appear in a mainstream fashion magazine, first to earn living entirely as a professional model, first to appear on the cover of specific magazines, and first to appear on the cover of *Sports Illustrated*'s high-profile swimsuit issue.

Beauty queens have increased in number over the years, too—from the first black Miss America (Vanessa Lynn Williams, 1983) and queens representing various states (such as Miss Ohio and Miss New York) to the first black transgender model, Tracey "Africa" Norman.

While black men had been commemorated on postage stamps, it was not until 1940 that a stamp was issued to honor a black woman. Harriet Tubman, who has been widely celebrated for her courage and determination, was the first black woman to appear on a postal service stamp.

Americans, like people of other countries, have become obsessed with royalty. In 2018, (Rachel) Meghan Markle married Prince Harry of Great Britain's royal family and became the first black American named Duchess of Sussex. In the United States, she is admiringly called "America's first black princess." Praised for her age, in 2006 Lizzie Bolden was recognized as the oldest woman of the year. When she died in Memphis in December of that year, she was 116 years old.

Initially, ships were named after kings, heroes, ideals, institutions, American places, and small insects with a potent sting, such as *Hornet* and *Wasp*. America's ship-building program addressed America's needs during World War II and called for large, mass-produced ships, known as Liberty ships. In time, they were named to honor people. The first Liberty ship named in honor of a black woman was the SS *Harriet Tubman*, launched on June 3, 1944. Black women continued to achieve in transportation, as seen in 1978 when Vallorie Harris O'Neil became the first black woman engineer for the Burlington-Northern Railroad.

Black women continue to leave an indelible mark on American history, black history, women's history, and black women's history. Their contributions were made in the United States and in many foreign countries as well.

# TREND-SHATTERING SETTLEMENT HOUSE                                                    1919

Southside Settlement House, the first for blacks with a black staff, was founded in 1918–19 by **ADA SOPHIA DENNISON McKINLEY (1868–1952)**, who recognized such a need among the thousands of blacks who migrated to Chicago during World War I in search of work. On April 1, 1949, with the help of the community, a new home was founded and renamed the Ada S. McKinley Community House in her honor. She organized the Soldiers and Sailors Club in 1919 at the facility on South Wabash that housed the program. After the war, she assisted returning soldiers and blacks who had migrated from the

South to find shelter, jobs, food, and to meet other needs. McKinley aided in settling the racial unrest that occurred on July 27, 1919 (the Chicago riots). She revitalized the South Side Community Services program and with the help of black banker Jesse Binga and others, she renamed the facility the South Side Settlement House.

# 1920                    PIONEER SOCIAL WORKER

The Katy Ferguson Home for black unwed mothers opened, the only such home at that time. ***CATHERINE "KATY" WILLIAMS FERGUSON (1779?–1854)***, for whom the home was named, was a social worker and a pioneer in the Sunday school movement. Since state law required slave masters to teach the Scripture to black children, many in the area took the children to the New York African Free School for this instruction. Ferguson became involved by teaching children in her home.

# RECORD-SETTING AVIATOR                    1921

***BESSIE COLEMAN (1892–1926)*** was the first black woman to become an aviator and to gain an international pilot's license from the Fédération Aéronautique Internationale and the first black woman "barnstormer," or stunt pilot. In 1922 she received training in France, Holland, Germany, and Switzerland. When she returned to Chicago, the *Chicago Defender* became her sponsor. On Labor Day 1922, Coleman gave her first exhibition in the United States, at Garden City, Long Island, New York. In October that year, she performed in the Chicago region and gave successful exhibitions throughout

Bessie Coleman

the Midwest. She prepared for a barnstorming show in Jacksonville, Florida, to be held on April 30, 1926, as a fundraiser for the Negro Welfare League. When Coleman and her copilot, William Wills, tried out their open-air plane in preparation for the exhibition, the equipment malfunctioned, and both died as a result.

# 1922    HISTORY-MAKING PRESERVATIONIST

***MARY (MORRIS BURNETT) TALBERT (1866–1923)*** was the first black woman to receive the NAACP's Spingarn Medal, for her efforts to preserve the home of Frederick Douglass in the Anacostia neighborhood of Washington, D.C. In 1922 the home was dedicated as the Frederick Douglass Museum. In 1920 Talbert had become the first black delegate to be seated at the International Council of Women. Talbert became an activist for women's rights and an important force in the black women's club movement. She held several posts in the National Association of Colored Women and rose in rank to become president of the group. She also became a national vice president of the NAACP.

Mary Talbert

## HISTORY-MAKING FASHION MODEL     1937

**ADRIENNE FIDELIN (1915–2004)** became the first black model to appear in a mainstream fashion magazine when her photograph was published in *Harper's Bazaar*. The spread containing the picture was captioned "The Bushongo of Africa Sends His Hats to Paris." Three white models appeared as well; however, Fidelin's picture was not integrated into their shoot. Instead, she appeared on one side with their image on the other; she wore a headdress and African jewelry.

## 1940s–50s     PIONEERING GLAMOUR GIRL MODEL

**SARA LOU HARRIS CARTER (1923–2016)**, later known as Lady Sara Lou, broke the stereotype of the black woman by being featured as a glamour girl on Lucky Strike (American Tobacco Company) cigarette posters. She also became the first black woman to model in the New York buyers' fashion show. She was a member of a girl's quartet and had a solo part in *Shuffle Along*. She appeared with singer and actress Juanita Hall (1901–1968) in the radio soap opera *The Story of Ruby Valentine*. Harris broadened career options for black women, and she saw them enter such areas as high-fashion modeling.

## AMERICAN MOTHER OF THE YEAR     1946

**EMMA CLARISSA (WILLIAMS) CLEMENT (1874–1952)** of Louisville, Kentucky, was the first black woman named "American Mother

# WILLA (BEATRICE) BROWN CHAPPELL
## (1906–1992)

### First Licensed Commercial Pilot

In 1934 Willa (Beatrice) Brown Chappell became the first black woman in the United States to hold a commercial pilot's license and the first black woman to gain officer rank (lieutenant) in the Civil Air Patrol Squadron. In 1935 she received a master mechanic's certificate. In 1937 Brown-Chappell and Cornelius R. Coffey, who was her flight instructor and later her husband, formed the National Airmen's Association of America, the first black aviators' group. In 1940, she and Coffey established the first black-owned flying school, the Coffey School of Aeronautics at Harlem Airport in southwest Chicago. (Some sources say that the school was founded in 1938 or 1939.) This was the first black-owned school certified by the Civil Aviation Authority. The school trained approximately 200 pilots within the next seven years, and the founders helped to establish standards that affect aviation today. Some of the students who graduated from the school became part of the 99th Pursuit Squadron, also known as the Tuskegee Airmen—the first black fighter squadron, located at Tuskegee Institute in Alabama. Affiliated with a flight service at Harlem Airport, she gave short entertainment jaunts for those who would pay one dollar for the ride. She taught aviation in the Works Progress Administration's Adult Education Program. In the early 1940s Brown Chappell taught aviation mechanics in the Chicago schools. The aviation school closed in 1945. In 1972, Brown Chappell became the first black member of the Federal Aviation Agency's Women's Advisory Commission.

of the Year." The Golden Rule Foundation gave her the honor on May 1, 1946. She was named "American Mother of the Year" in recognition of her qualities as the mother of children who served their country and their people and for her work as a social and community worker.

## 1950s    VISIONARY PROFESSIONAL MODEL

***DOROTHEA TOWLES (CHURCH) (1922–2006)*** became the first black woman to earn a living entirely as a professional model. She was also the first black woman to build a thriving career modeling in Paris. Her career began in Christian Dior's showroom in Europe, and in the early 1950s she walked the runways of the haute couture houses, such as those of Christian Dior, Pierre Balmain, and Italian designer Elsa Schiaparelli. She became prominent in post–World War II European fashion trends and paved the way for early black supermodels.

## BARRIER-BREAKING FLIGHT ATTENDANT                                          1958

***RUTH CAROL TAYLOR (1931–)*** became the first black flight attendant. She broke the color barrier as a means of fighting discrimination rather than due to her interest in becoming a flight attendant. For more than a year, major airlines had rejected her application; then, when she was 25, Mohawk Airlines hired her and assigned her to travel between New York and other points such as Massachusetts and Michigan.

## 1966    FASHION MODEL IN BRITISH VOGUE

The first black model to appear on the cover of a Western magazine was ***DONYALE LUNA (1945–1979)***, whose image appeared on the cover of *British Vogue* in March.

## AMERICAN PAGEANT CONTESTANT    1970

The first black contestant in a Miss America Pageant was ***CHERYL ADRIENNE BROWNE***, Miss Iowa.

# NAOMI SIMS (1948–2009)
## Record-breaking Fashion Model

Fashion model Naomi Sims became the first black woman to appear on the cover of *Ladies' Home Journal* in 1968, when the magazine featured an article on black models. Sims became the first black model on the cover of *Life* magazine the next year. In both years, International Mannequins voted her top model of the year. Two years after she began a modeling career, she appeared in practically every fashion magazine around the world. Around 1969 Sims became the nation's first black supermodel. Sims gave up her career and started a wig business, the Naomi Sims Collection. She later expanded the business to include perfume and cosmetics designed for black women and formed the company Naomi Sims Beauty Products. Sims also became an author, writing such books as *How to Be a Top Model* and *All About Hair Care for the Black Woman*.

## 1970 OHIO BEAUTY QUEEN

Legendary actress and sportscaster *JAYNE KENNEDY (1951–)* was the first black woman crowned Miss Ohio. In 1978, she became one of the first women to join the all-male contingency of television sports announcers.

## FIRST BLACK MISS WORLD 1970

The first black Miss World was *JENNIFER JOSEPHINE HOSTEN (1947–)*, who won the honor on December 3, 1970.

## 1974 MONUMENT-HONORED EDUCATOR

A monument honoring the life and contribution of *MARY McLEOD BETHUNE (1875–1955)* was built in Washington, D.C., becoming the first statue of a black erected on public land in the District. A noted educator and school founder, in 1939 she was named director of the National Youth Administration's Division of Negro Affairs and thus became the highest-ranking black woman in government.

## RECORD-SETTING SUPERMODEL          1974

The first black supermodel to appear on the cover of the American version of a major fashion magazine was **BEVERLY JOHNSON (1952–)**. The model, actress, and singer appeared in the August issue of American *Vogue* this year. In the early 1970s, she was the first black model to appear on the cover of the French magazine *Elle*. By 1992 she had appeared on the covers of some 500 magazines.

## 1978          PIONEER RAILROAD ENGINEER

**VALLORIE HARRIS O'NEIL** was the first black woman engineer for the Burlington-Northern Railroad. Harris worked in the Cicero, Illinois, yard.

## HISTORY-MAKING COMMERCIAL PILOT     1978

**JILL BROWN (1950–)** became the first black female pilot for a major commercial airline, Texas International Airlines. Her father, a U.S. Air Force instrument mechanic and building contractor, had purchased a single-engine Piper Cherokee. They used the plane to travel the United States and the Caribbean, referring to themselves as Brown's United Airline. Brown first soloed in 1967 and later earned her private pilot license. She became the first black woman accepted for pilot training in the military. After attending officers' candidate school and naval flying school, she had a short career in the military. Her primary aim was to become a pilot for a major airline. Brown later worked for a commuter airline in North Carolina, performing odd jobs and serving as copilot. She flew for Wheeler Airlines, accumulating 800 hours. Then Texas International Airlines hired her.

## 1979          PIONEER LONGSHOREMAN

**AUDREY NEAL** was the first woman of any ethnic group to become a longshoreman on the Eastern seaboard.

## *GQ'S* FEATURED MODELS                    1982

The first blacks to be featured on the cover of *GQ* magazine were **SHEILA JOHNSON** and Charles Williamson, in October.

## 1983                    FIRST BLACK MISS AMERICA

Vanessa Williams

**VANESSA LYNN WILLIAMS (1963–)**, representing New York, became the first black Miss America. She also was the first to resign the title, in 1984. Suzette Charles (1963–), the first black Miss New Jersey and the first black runner-up in the Miss America contest, took Williams's place. Williams attended Syracuse University, where she excelled in theater and music. While appearing in a college musical, Williams was asked to become a contestant in the Miss Greater Syracuse contest. She won the pageant and in 1983 was crowned Miss New York. On September 14 that year, she won the national pageant and was crowned Miss America. In July 1984, the middle of her reign, a number of provocative photographs of Williams that had been taken in the summer of 1982 surfaced. Williams then relinquished her crown. Her career in acting and singing, however, took off, and her popularity increased.

## STATE HISTORIC SITE OPENS                    1987

The first state-owned and -operated historic site honoring a black in North Carolina was the **CHARLOTTE HAWKINS BROWN MEMORIAL STATE HISTORIC SITE** in Sedalia. In 1983 the Charlotte Hawkins Brown Historical Foundation was incorporated to assist the state in establishing the site—the 40-acre former campus and 14 buildings of Palmer Memorial Institute, which Brown founded.

## 1987                    AIRPORT BOARD OF DIRECTORS CHAIR

**ERMA CHANSLER JOHNSON (1942–2015)** was the first black and the first woman to chair the Dallas/Fort Worth International Airport Board of Directors.

## CROWN-SETTING MS. SENIOR AMERICA 1989

*JOSEPHINE GENTRY-HUYGHE (1928?–)* beat out 50 contestants in Atlantic City on April 12 to become the first black Ms. Senior America. The pageant began 15 years earlier and honors outstanding women who are at least 60 years old. The talented "Josie," as she was affectionately called, performed disco dances on roller skates. She had a quiet victory, receiving no money, prizes, or media blitz. The era of her reign was significant also because, from March 30, 1990, until April 1990, black women held the titles and crowns of Ms. Senior America, Miss America, and Miss USA.

## 1990 CROWN-WINNING MISS USA

The first black Miss USA was *CAROLE ANNE-MARIE GIST (1969–)*, who was crowned in Wichita, Kansas, on March 3, 1990. The six-foot tall, 20-year-old queen from Detroit entered the contest as Miss Michigan—USA, the title she won in 1989. She was also first runner-up in the Miss Universe pageant in April 1990.

## PASSING THE CROWN 1991

The first black woman to be crowned Miss America by a reigning black queen was *MARJORIE JUDITH VINCENT (1964–)*. Vincent was the fourth black Miss America and received her crown from Debbye Turner, who was Miss America for 1990.

## 1992 PIONEER MODELING CONTRACT WINNER

Doors continued to open for black models, when *VERONICA WEBB (1965–)*, who appeared in Jungle Fever and Malcolm X, was the first black model to win an exclusive modeling contract with Revlon.

## FIRST MRS. MICHIGAN 1994

*STACEY LYNN FIELDER* was crowned Mrs. Michigan America in Detroit, becoming the first black to win the title.

# 1994      AWARD-WINNING POSTAL EMPLOYEE

**GEORGIA STRIBLING** became the first woman to earn the highest award for a suggestion from the U.S. Postal Service's St. Louis, Missouri, Accounting Center. She was awarded $35,000. After spending 21 years with the service, 19 of her ideas were implemented, and she received bonuses for 16 of her ideas.

# BIRACIAL MISS USA      1995

**CHELSI SMITH (1973–2018)** was the first biracial to be crowned Miss USA. Her prize money totaled $207,000 in cash, and she represented the United States in the Miss Universe pageant held in Windhoek, Namibia, in the spring. She planned to draw on her biracial background to teach youth of all races about the perils of racism and the importance of self-esteem.

# 1995      TREND-BREAKING AIRLINE CAPTAIN

**PATRICE CLARKE WASHINGTON (1961–)** flew United Parcel Service's DC-8 from Miami to Atlanta and became the first black woman captain to fly for the company. She joined UPS in May 1988 as a DC-8 flight engineer. She attended Embry-Riddle Aeronautical University, graduating in 1982 with a commercial pilot's certificate and a bachelor of science degree in aeronautical science. Washington was the first black woman to graduate from the school with a commercial pilot's license. She was a pilot for Trans Island Airways, a charter company in the Bahamas. Washington then served as a first officer and the first black woman pilot with Bahamasair, flying Boeing 748s and 737s. Racism and sexism followed her. UPS hired her as a flight engineer in 1988. In January 1990, UPS promoted her to first officer. She was promoted to captain in November 1994.

# CROWN-WINNING TEEN      1996

**CHANTÉ LAREE GRIFFIN (1978?–)** was elected Miss Teen of America for 1996–97, becoming the first black to hold that title. The pageant recognized America's young women and their achievements. She was crowned Miss Teen of California in 1995.

# 1997

## *SPORTS ILLUSTRATED'S* SWIMSUIT MODEL

The first black woman to appear on the cover of *Sports Illustrated*'s high-profile swimsuit issue was supermodel **TYRA BANKS (1973–)** in 1997. Banks began her modeling career in Paris, France, in 1991. She accepted an offer to model in the fall haute couture shows in Paris. There she was booked for 25 shows, then a record for a newcomer. Banks later landed several lucrative deals, including the *Sports Illustrated* assignment and a multipage advertising campaign for American designer Ralph Lauren. Cosmetics giant CoverGirl hired her, making her the second black to receive a long-term contract

Tyra Banks

with that company. Banks appeared in a number of television shows, including the NBC sitcom *The Fresh Prince of Bel-Air*. Her film credits include *Higher Learning*. Banks later promoted a line of greeting cards for Children+Families. Another line, Cards from the Heart, was created by young children and used to promote literacy among children in troubled environments.

## RECORD-SETTING UNIVERSITY QUEEN  1997

The first black to be named Miss University at the University of Mississippi was **CARISSA WELLS (1975?–)**. She had been named first runner-up in the Miss University pageant at the school when the election results were certified; however, officials realized that she was the overall winner in all of the competitions and awarded her the crown. She went on to compete in the Miss Mississippi pageant.

# 1998

## NEW MISS VIRGINIA

**NITA BOOTH (1978–)** became the first black to be named Miss Virginia. Nicole Johnson, who held the title, was named Miss America, leaving Booth to inherit the title.

## FOUR RECORD-SETTING PAGEANT WINNERS   2002

For the first time in the history of the Miss USA pageant, four of the five finalists were black. The winner was 23-year-old **SHAUNTAY**

# LIZZIE BOLDEN (1890–2006)

## Guinness Record–holding Former Slave

The world's oldest woman this year was Lizzie Bolde, according to the *Guinness Book of World Records*. When she died in Memphis in December 2006, she was 116 years old. Earlier, the daughter of former slaves was a farmworker in Fayette County, Tennessee. Only two of her seven children survived her. Other survivors included 40 grandchildren, 75 great grandchildren, 150 great-great grandchildren, 220 great-great-great grandchildren, and 75 great-great-great-great grandchildren.

*HINTON (1979–)*, Miss District of Columbia. The other finalists were 25-year-old Kelly Lloyd, Miss Indiana, second runner-up; 26-year-old Lanore VanBuren, Miss Minnesota, third runner-up; and 22-year-old Alita Hawaah Dawson, Miss Connecticut, fourth runner-up.

# 2007        SINGER GRACES FASHION MAGAZINE

The first black singer to appear on the cover of the fashion magazine *Vogue* was *JENNIFER HUDSON (1981–)*. Her image was published on the cover of *Vogue*'s March Power Issue. Previously, talk show phenom Oprah Winfrey and the Oscar-winning actress Halle Berry graced that cover.

# RECORD-SETTING FLYING ACE        2008

*KELLY ANYADIKI (1992–)*, who was then 16 years old, set a world record as the youngest black female to solo in four different aircraft. Anyadiki and another flying ace, Jonathan Strickland, were part of a program of the Tomorrow's Aeronautical Museum, which was designed to attract inner-city and minority youths to flight training.

## 2008

## FIVE-TIME MAGAZINE SWIMSUIT MODEL

Jessica White

The first black model featured in *Sports Illustrated*'s swimsuit issue for the fifth year was *JESSICA WHITE (1984–)*. When she was 16, she also became the first black model to hold two cosmetics contracts simultaneously—with Maybelline and CoverGirl. As a model, White landed campaigns with brands Chloé and the Gap. She walked runways with top designers such as Ralph Lauren and Oscar de la Renta. In 2007 she made her first appearance on the catwalk of Victoria's Secret Fashion Show. White also founded a charity called Angel Wings, based in Buffalo, which aids young girls who have been abused and women who have experienced bad situations.

## CHAMPION OF PUBLIC SPEAKING        2008

The first black woman to win a championship in public speaking was *LASHUNDA RUNDLES (1969–2012)*. When she delivered a speech called "Speak" at the Toastmasters International Speech Contest, she became the first black woman to win the title World Champion of Public Speaking.

## 2008

## NATIONAL YOUNG MOTHER OF THE YEAR

*KIMBERLY McINNIS SHELTON* was the first black to be named National Young Mother of the Year. She won the title at the American Mothers, Inc. convention held in Lincoln, Nebraska.

## FREEDOM'S VOICE AWARD WINNER        2009

An anchor on CNN, *SOLEDAD O'BRIEN (1966–)* became the first recipient of the Soledad O'Brien Freedom's Voice Award. An author, anchor, and special correspondent for CNN's *In America*, O'Brien is known for her award-winning documentaries, such as *Black in America 1 and 2, The King Assassination*, and others.

## 2009    PIONEERING WOMEN'S FLIGHT CREW

*DIANA GALLOWAY, RACHELLE JONES KERR, ROBIN ROGERS,* and *STEPHANIE GRANT* became the first all-female black flight crew. In 2009 they flew on Atlantic Southeast Airlines from Nashville to Atlanta. In February 2016, the crew was celebrated in Nashville during Black History Month. They encouraged young women and minorities to consider a career in aviation.

## APPLE BLOSSOM QUEEN                                          2009

*JAQUI RICE (1987–)* became the first black to hold the title Queen Shenandoah LXXXI (also known as the Apple Blossom Queen) of the 81st Shenandoah Apple Blossom Festival. The new queen, an aspiring singer, became the official hostess of the annual Apple Blossom Festival and presided over several events associated with the festival. The festival is affiliated with the Miss America Pageant and requires candidates to participate in competitions such as talent and gown.

## 2016                         TUBMAN APPROVED FOR PAPER CURRENCY

The abolitionist *HARRIET TUBMAN (1822–1913)* became the first African American whose image was approved to appear on U.S. paper currency and the first woman in more than 100 years to be so honored. The U.S. Treasury Department announced this decision in April. The new image would replace President Andrew Jackson on the $20 bill; his image would move to the back of the bill and get incorporated into the White House. The $5, $10, and $20 bills were scheduled for redesign over the next four years to be put into production over the next decade. The back of the $10 bill would tell the story of the women's suffrage movement, which gave women in America the right to vote in 1920. Women to be honored included Lucretia Mott, Sojourner Truth, Susan B. Anthony, Elizabeth Cady Stanton, and Alice Paul. Continuing controversy in 2019 caused a delay in the final approval until 2026. In 2021 the Treasury Department took steps to resume efforts to place Tubman's image on the $20 bill, as originally approved.

## LADY LIBERTY COIN                                          2017

The *AMERICAN LIBERTY 225th ANNIVERSARY GOLD COIN* (a $100 gold coin) depicting Lady Liberty was the first officially minted coin portraying a black woman, a departure from previous classic designs. The commemorative coin shows a woman with a crown of stars in her hair and a toga-like dress. The coin represents the first in a series of 24-karat gold coins that will feature designs depicting an allegorical Liberty in a variety of contemporary forms, including Asian Americans, Hispanic Americans, and Native Americans, among others.

## 2018     AMERICA'S FIRST BLACK PRINCESS

Meghan Markle

*(RACHEL) MEGHAN MARKLE (1981–)* married Prince Harry of Great Britain's royal family and became the first black American to be named Duchess of Sussex. In the United States, she is admiringly called "America's first black princess." Before the wedding, Queen Elizabeth conferred upon Markle the title "Meghan, Her Royal Highness the Duchess of Sussex." The wedding took place on May 19 at St. George's Chapel at Windsor, with the Most Reverend Michael Bruce Curry, Presiding Bishop and Prelate of the Episcopal Church, who lives in Chicago, officiating. The marriage of a biracial and divorced woman to British royalty sparked both racial and sexist criticism in London and opened discussion of "the role of race and racism in British culture." In 2021 the couple relinquished their royal status.

## COMMANDS COMBAT BATTALION     2018

*KAYLA FREEMAN* became the first black female pilot in the Alabama National Guard. She graduated from Fort Rucker's Army Aviation School as a second lieutenant. Freeman also became the second black woman to work in the Department of Defense to receive her wings, the first from Georgia, and the first woman in the U.S. Army to command a combat arms battalion.

## 2019     TRIPLE BEAUTY PAGEANT WINNERS

*CHESLIE KRYST (1991–)* was crowned Miss USA in May. With her win, three black women have now simultaneously claimed the crowns in three major beauty pageants—Miss America, Miss Teen USA, and

Miss USA. The Charlotte, North Carolina, native is an attorney who works on behalf of prison inmates.

## MISS TENNESSEE WINNER 2019

The first black woman to be crowned Miss Tennessee is **BRIANNA MASON (1996?–)**. She represented the state in the Miss America 2020 competition.

## 2019 PHYSICALLY CHALLENGED TRANSGENDER MODEL

**AARON PHILIP** became the first black, transgender, and physically challenged model to appear on the cover of *Paper* magazine. In its "Pride" issue, the magazine showcased Philip. She was also honored in September 2018 as the first model with her background to sign with a leading agency—Elite Model Management. Philip was born with cerebral palsy. She attributes much of her success to social media as well as the changes in the fashion industry, which is beginning to celebrate and market all body types.

# Organizations

Through their work in their own organizations, black women have focused on issues related to their families, communities, and themselves. The earliest efforts came through church groups, temperance societies, and self-help and charitable groups. The African Dorcas Association, founded in 1828, is an example of an early charitable group that black women established. The women expanded their efforts and increased their organizations in number, geographical area, and then-current issues. Some, like the National Congress of Colored Parents and Teachers, merged with white organizations, such as the White National Congress. Women also fought to remove racial barriers that prevented them from joining segregated groups. Among the organizations are those dealing with business and professional areas; charitable and civic concerns; civil rights and political issues; fraternal, social, and religious matters; and the medical and dental arenas.

Success continued when black women held high offices in state or national organizations. For example, Mary Hatwood Futrell was the first black president of the Virginia Education Association, and Elizabeth Duncan Koontz was the first black president of the National Education Association. Clara Stanton Jones was the first black president of the American Library Association. As they expanded their leadership roles, women addressed other professional or business areas. Marilyn French Hubbard founded and became first president of the National Association of Black Women Entrepreneurs, while Cheryl Boone Issacs was the first black person named president of the Academy of

Motion Picture Arts and Sciences. In addition, Paulette Brown was the first female black president of the American Bar Association.

Leadership groups like the National Association for the Advancement of Colored People (NAACP) had its first black woman board of directors chair when Margaret Bush Wilson was named to that post. Others who headed charitable and civic organizations include Gloria Dean Randle Scott, the first black president of Girl Scouts of America; Faye Wattleton, the first woman president of Planned Parenthood Federation of America; and Elaine R. Jones, first woman to head the Legal Defense Fund (LDF).

An early civil rights and political organization that touched the lives of numerous black women across the nation was the National Conference of the Colored Women of America, headed by Josephine St. Pierre Ruffin. This conference led to the formation of the National Federation of Afro-American Women, which merged into the National Association of Colored Women. Mary Church Terrell became the first president of the organization. The new organization was the first and foremost national organization of black women in the late 1800s and into the 1900s. Elaine Brown was the first black woman to become chair of the Black Panther Party; Carolyn Jefferson-Jenkins was the first black president of the National League of Women Voters; and Karen Batchelor Farmer was the first known black member of the Daughters of the American Revolution. Following recent activities, Marisa Richmond was the first transgender woman elected to public office in Tennessee and the first from any state elected a delegate to a major party convention—the Democratic National Convention.

While the American Medical Association elected its first black president, Lonnie Bristow, in 1995, nearly 25 years would pass before the group elected its first black woman president—Patrice A. Harris.

African American women's success in organizations has come with the institutions that they founded, positions held in other black organizations, and the leadership they assumed with mainstream organizations.

# PIONEERING WOMEN'S CHARITABLE 1828 GROUP

In January, 21 black women, with the advice of male ministers, met in New York to draw up plans for the *AFRICAN DORCAS ASSOCIATION*, which was officially organized in February. This was the first black women's charitable group. Its principal object was to aid young blacks in attending schools by supplying them with clothing, hats, and shoes.

## 1893                 NEW BRANCH OF THE Y

The first black branch of the **YOUNG WOMEN'S CHRISTIAN ASSOCIATION (YWCA)** was opened in Dayton, Ohio.

## HISTORY-MAKING WOMEN'S       1895
## ORGANIZATION

The **NATIONAL CONFERENCE OF THE COLORED WOMEN OF AMERICA** met in Boston, Massachusetts, in August 1895. The organizer of the conference was Josephine St. Pierre Ruffin (1842–1924), the founder of the Women's Era Club. The meeting led to the formation of the National Federation of Afro-American Women, which was merged into the National Association of Colored Women on July 21 the following year. The new organization was founded as a national coalition of black women's clubs and was the first and foremost national organization of black women at the time. Mary Church Terrell (1863–1954) became the first president of the National Association of Colored Women.

## 1897       FOUNDING LEADERS OF HISTORIC
## MISSION

**VICTORIA EARLE MATTHEWS (1861–1907)** and **MARITCHA LYONS (1848–1929)** founded the White Rose Mission, on February 11. Matthews was the organization's first superintendent. Its mission was a home for black girls and women, whose purpose was to train them for "practical self-help and right living." It operated in the Manhattan section of New York City and provided food and living quarters for Southern and West Indian migrants. Matthews became founder and first president of the Woman's Loyal Union of New York City. Lyons, an educator, writer, and lecturer, was also active in the women's club movement.

Victoria Earle Matthews

## BARRIER-BREAKING ORGANIZATION     1905
## LEADER

The first black woman on the staff of the Young Women's Christian Association (YWCA) was **EVA DEL VAKIA BOWLES (1875–1943)**.

She became the first black teacher at Chandler Normal School, an American Missionary Association institution in Lexington, Kentucky. She was named head of a project for black women that was conducted under the auspices of the YWCA. Soon it became the 137th Street Branch YWCA in New York City. With that post, Bowles became the first salaried black YWCA secretary. She was an advocate of interracial YWCAs and fought against opponents who wanted a permanent "colored department" as well as those who wanted all decisions made under white leadership.

Eva del Vakia Bowles

# 1907    YWCA'S FIRST BLACK SECRETARY

**ADDIE D. WAITES HUNTON (1875?–1943)** was the first secretary for black student affairs for the National Board of the Young Women's Christian Association (YWCA). Hunton was very active in the club movement and the women's suffrage movement. In 1889 she became the first black to graduate from the Spencerian College of Commerce in Philadelphia.

## PREMIER GREEK-LETTER SORORITY    1908

The first black Greek letter sorority was Alpha Kappa Alpha, founded at Howard University on January 15, 1908. The prime mover was **ETHEL HEDGEMAN LYLE (1887–1950)**, who became the first vice president. **LUCY SLOWE (1885–1937)** was the first president. Two other early sororities were Delta Sigma Theta (founded in 1913) and Zeta Phi Beta (1920).

# 1908    NURSING ORGANIZATION FOUNDED

The founding meeting of the National Association of Colored Graduate Nurses (NACGN) was held at St. Mark's Methodist Church in New York City. The organization, the first national organization for black nurses, aimed to meet the increasing concern of black nurses to enhance themselves professionally. **MARTHA MINERVA FRANKLIN (1870–1968)**, who was the force behind the gathering of black nurses, became the founding president. The NACGN soon attacked the practice of setting up separate black and white state boards of nursing. The association established a national headquarters in 1934, with nurse Mabel Keaton Staupers (1890–1989) as executive secretary. After obtaining full participation in the American Nurses' Association, the NACGN board voted the black organization out of existence on January 25, 1951.

## WOMEN'S AUXILIARY FOUNDED          1925

The first ladies' auxiliary of the **BROTHERHOOD OF SLEEPING CAR PORTERS** was formed as the Hesperus Club of Harlem.

## 1934          UNIA'S WOMAN LEADER

The first and only woman to serve as president general of the Universal Negro Improvement Association and African Communities League (UNIA) was **HENRIETTA VINTON DAVIS (1860–1941)**. She was a strong advocate of racial pride. She embraced the Populist Party and later the Socialist Party. She was among the UNIA's top leaders in the 1920s and 1930s.

## NATIONAL ORGANIZATION FOUNDED    1935

**MARY McLEOD BETHUNE (1875–1955)** was instrumental in founding the National Council of Negro Women on December 5, 1935—the first black organization for women and the first national coalition of black women's organizations established in the twentieth century. The organization was founded in New York City when 14 black women's organizations came together at the 137th Street. YWCA. Bethune became its first president, a post she held until 1949.

## 1942          FUNDRAISING ORGANIZATION LEADER

**MOLLIE MOON (1912–1990)** was the organizer and first president of the National Urban League Guild, a fundraising activity for the Urban

# JOSEPHINE GROVES HOLLOWAY
## (1898–1988)
### Girl Scouts Founder and Leader

Josephine Groves Holloway founded the first black Girl Scouts troop in Tennessee in 1943; she was also its first executive. In 1923 she accepted a position at the Bethlehem Center in Nashville. While there she learned about previous attempts to establish scouting at the black branch of the YMCA, Blue Triangle. Holloway was commissioned captain (Girl Scout leader) and then revived scouting for black girls in Nashville. She was forced to resign her position because she had married. Her interest in scouting continued, and between 1926 and 1933 she established another troop and encouraged others to do so. In May 1943 the Girl Scout Council approved its first black troop and made the status retroactive to 1942, when Holloway first attempted to register her troop.

League. She had wide contacts in New York's social circles and used her connections to help support the National Urban League. Moon and a group of friends held a benefit for the league in early 1942; the Victory Cocktail Party was highly successful and became a New York tradition. The black-tie ball continued each February and was renamed the Beaux-Arts Ball. Moon became the founding president of the National Council of Urban League Guilds, which functioned to raise money for the league.

## CIVIL RIGHTS ORGANIZATION FOUNDER                1946

**ELLA JOSEPHINE BAKER (1903–1986)** was elected president of the New York branch of the National Association for the Advancement of Colored People (NAACP), becoming the first woman to hold the post. Baker was a community organizer, civil rights and domestic activist, and consultant in education. She began to work with the NAACP in the early 1940s as an assistant field secretary. She resigned her position but remained active with the New York branch. After the bus boycott began in Montgomery, Alabama, in 1955, Baker concentrated on the civil rights movement and the U.S. Supreme Court's decision to end racial segregation in public accommodations. In 1957, largely through her efforts, the Southern Christian Leadership Conference (SCLC) was formed. She helped student protesters to organize the Student Nonviolent Coordinating Committee (SNCC) and became its executive secretary. She also assisted students in voter registration drives. In 1964 Baker helped to establish the Mississippi Freedom Democratic Party and gave the keynote address at its founding convention.

# 1965    SYMPHONY FOUNDATION LEADER

***LOIS TOWLES (CAESAR) (1912–1983)***, a musician and educator, was the first black to serve on the board of directors of the San Francisco Symphony Foundation. She was also the first black to serve on the board of directors of the San Francisco Symphony Association in 1969. In 1976 she became the first black and woman to serve on the Mayor's Criminal Justice Commission of San Francisco. In 1978 she became the first minority chair of the commission.

Lois Towles

## NATIONAL YMCA PRESIDENT                    1967

***HELEN CLAYTOR (1907–2005)*** was the first black president of the national Young Women's Christian Association (YWCA).

# 1968    CHANGE-MAKING EDUCATORS' GROUP

***ELIZABETH DUNCAN KOONTZ (1919–1989)*** was the first black president of the National Education Association (NEA). From 1969 to 1972, she was director of the Women's Bureau of the U.S. Department of Labor.

## FEMINIST ORGANIZATION FOUNDED    1973

The **NATIONAL BLACK FEMINIST ORGANIZATION** was founded to address the concerns of black women. Within a year, ten local chapters had been organized and met in a national conference.

## 1975    GIRL SCOUTS' NATIONAL LEADER

**GLORIA (DEAN) RANDLE SCOTT (1938–)** was the first black president of the Girl Scouts of America. She conducted workshop sessions for heads of national organizations for member countries in the Western Hemisphere of the World Association of Girl Scouts and scouts in Rio de Janeiro. Scott was the second woman president of Bennett College for Women.

## BLACK PANTHER ORGANIZATION    1975
## LEADER

**ELAINE BROWN (1943–)** moved up in ranks to become chairperson of the Black Panther Party (BPP), making her the highest-ranking woman in the party, the first black woman to hold the post, and second in command only to Huey P. Newton, who founded the party. Brown joined the BPP in 1968 and became minister of information for the Los Angeles chapter in 1969. She worked in the party's breakfast program and led voter registration drives.

## 1976    EDUCATORS GROUP PRESIDENT

**MARY HATWOOD FUTRELL (1940–)** was the first black president of the Virginia Education Association. She also served as president of the National Education Association from 1980 to 1989.

## BARRIER-BREAKING DAR MEMBER    1977

**KAREN BATCHELOR FARMER (1951–)** was the first known black member of the Daughters of the American Revolution. She traced her ancestry to William Hood, a soldier in the Revolutionary army.

# MARGARET BERENICE BUSH WILSON

## (1919–2009)

### Pioneering NAACP Official

In 1975 Margaret Berenice Bush Wilson, activist, lawyer, and civil rights leader, became the first black woman to chair the National Association for the Advancement of Colored People's Board of Directors, from 1975 to 1984. Her struggle against the racially restrictive covenants in housing contracts ended with the landmark Supreme Court decision *Shelley v. Kraemer* (1948). That same year, she became the first black woman from Missouri to run for a seat in the U.S. Congress, but she was soundly defeated. Active with the NAACP since 1956, Wilson became the first woman president of the Saint Louis branch in 1962.

## 1977      YMCA CHAPTER PRESIDENT

*FREDDA WITHERSPOON (1923?–1996)* was the first black president of the Metropolitan St. Louis Young Women's Christian Association (YWCA). She was also one of the first blacks to integrate St. Louis University.

## PLANNED PARENTHOOD'S NEW LEADER      1978

*FAYE WATTLETON (1943–)* became the first black and the first woman president of the Planned Parenthood Federation of America. She was often at the forefront of national debates over legal abortion but remained firm in her belief in women's rights and reproductive rights.

## 1979     PHARMACEUTICAL ASSOCIATION LEADER

*MARY RUNGE (1928–2014)* was the first black and first woman president of the American Pharmaceutical Association. Runge was a pharmacist in Oakland, California.

## NATIONAL YWCA DIRECTOR     1984

*GWENDOLYN CALVERT BAKER (1931–2019)* became the first black woman to be named national executive director for the Young Women's Christian Association (YWCA).

## 1985     MAJOR COMMUNITY GROUP LEADER

*ANNA F. JONES* was the first black woman to head a major community foundation, the Boston Foundation.

## HEADS OXFAM AMERICA     1986

*MARIE GADSDEN (1919–2012)* was the first black woman to chair Oxfam America. Gadsden was executive director of the Phelps-Stokes Fund and later deputy director of the National Association for Equal Opportunity in Higher Education/AID Cooperative Agreement.

## 1986     SORORITY BREAKS RACIAL BARRIER

*ALPHA KAPPA ALPHA* was the first black Greek letter sorority to have a house on the campus of the University of Alabama.

## JUNIOR LEAGUE MEMBER     1986

*LERIA LOWE JORDAN* was the first black member of the Junior League of Birmingham, Alabama.

## 1988         YMCA ASSOCIATION LEADER

**MADELINE FORD** was the first woman vice president and corporate secretary of the Young Men's Christian Association (YMCA) of Greater New York.

## HEADS NATIONAL RELIGIOUS                    1991
## CONFERENCE

**MARYANN COFFEY** was the first black, and the first woman, cochair of the National Conference of Christians and Jews.

## 1991     NATIONAL LEADER OF BUSINESS
##                                     WOMEN

**LOIS TERRELL MILLS (1958–)** was the first black national president of the American Business Women's Association. She became an industrial engineer with the Ethicon division of Johnson and Johnson in Albuquerque, New Mexico.

## LEGAL COUNSEL FOR ELECTRIC              1992
## ASSOCIATION

**EDWYNA G. ANDERSON (1930–)**, general counsel of the Duquesne Light Company, was the first black, and the first woman, president of the Pennsylvania Electric Association.

## 1992      SIERRA CLUB'S NATIONAL BOARD

**MARY ANN NELSON** was the first black elected to the national board of the Sierra Club.

## ELECTION COMMISSION PRESIDENT       1992

Attorney **ARNETTE RHINEHART HUBBARD** became the first black commissioner elected president of the Association of Election

Commissioners of Illinois. She later became a circuit court judge in Chicago.

## 1992  POLICE ASSOCIATION LEADER

**LESLIE SEYMORE** was the first woman chair of the National Black Police Association. Seymore had served on the Philadelphia police force since 1973.

## LAW ENFORCEMENT COMMISSION  1993
## PRESIDENT

**DEIRDRE HUGHES HILL (1960–)** was elected president of the Los Angeles Police Commission, becoming the youngest person and the first black woman to hold the post.

## 1993  ESL ORGANIZATION LEADER

**CORNELIA (CONNIE) WHITENER PERDREAU** was the first black elected to head Administrators and Teachers of English as a Second Language.

## NATIONAL LEADER FOR PUBLIC  1994
## RELATIONS

The first black national secretary of the Public Relations Society of America, in New York, was **DEBRA A. MILLER**. This is the world's largest group of public relations professionals.

## 1994  NEW LEADER FOR SECRETARIES

The first black president of the Professional Secretaries International was **ELNOR HICKMAN (?–2013)** of Chicago. She was elected during the 49th convention to head the world's premiere professional organization for secretaries, executive assistants, administrative assistants, and similar office professionals.

# ELAINE R. JONES (1944–)

## LDF Organization Head

In 1993 Elaine R. Jones became the first woman to head the Legal Defense Fund (LDF), a nonprofit organization that fights discrimination and civil rights violations. At one time the LDF was an arm of the National Association for the Advancement of Colored People (NAACP), but it split from the organization in 1957; the relationship between the two organizations continued in name only.

## LEGISLATIVE BLACK CAUCUS PRESIDENT     1994

The first woman president of the National Black Caucus of State Legislators was Tennessee state representative **LOIS MARIE DeBERRY (1945–2013)**, who was also Tennessee speaker *pro tempore* for the House of Representatives.

## 1994     FINANCIAL PLANNERS' LEADER

**CORNELIA W. FAIRFAX** became the first black woman president of the International Association of Financial Planners. Fairfax became a financial planner in Riverside, California.

## NEW LEADER FOR SKIERS     1995

**NAOMI BRYSON** became the first woman to head the National Brotherhood of Skiers Inc.

## 1995     BARRIER-BREAKING TOP DOCTOR

**REGINA M. BENJAMIN (1956–)** became the first black woman and only the second black named to the American Medical Association's

Board of Trustees. In 2009, President Barack Obama nominated Benjamin as surgeon general of the United States. She assumed office on November 3 and became the 18<sup>th</sup> person and the second African American woman to become "America's Doctor."

Regina M. Benjamin

## MISSISSIPPI URBAN LEAGUE PRESIDENT                                    1995

**ANNELLE LEWIS**, who was director of development at Piney Woods Country Life boarding school in Mississippi, became the first woman president of the Urban League of Metropolitan Denver.

## 1995              CALIFORNIA TEACHERS' LEADER

The first black woman to become president of the California Teachers Association was **M. LOIS TINSON (1938–2003)**, a high school teacher.

## BARRIER-BREAKING CLUB MEMBERS      1995

William and **MARSHA JEWS** became the first black members of the Baltimore Country Club in Maryland. William Jews was president and chief executive officer of Blue Cross and Blue Shield of Maryland.

## 1995              CIVIL LIBERTIES ORGANIZATION DIRECTOR

The first black woman to direct the Washington office of the American Civil Liberties Union was **LAURA MURPHY LEE**.

## LEADS ORGANIZATION FOR TV EXECUTIVES    1995

*CAROLYN KENNEDY WORFORD (1949–)* became the first black woman to chair the National Association of Television Program Executives International (NATPE), the world's largest trade association of television programming executives.

## 1995    ACCREDITING AGENCY HEAD

*MARIE V. McDEMMOND (1946–)* became the first black woman president of the Southern Association of College and University Business Officers.

## BARRIER-BREAKING EDUCATORS' ASSOCIATION LEADER    1995

The first black president of the Association of Teacher Educators was *ROSE DUHON-SELLS*.

## 1996    TRIAL LAWYERS' NEW LEADER

A trial lawyer in Washington, D.C., *SANDRA HAWKINS ROBINSON (1951–)* became the first woman and the third black president-elect of the Trial Lawyers Association of Metropolitan Washington, D.C.

## GIRL SCOUTS EXECUTIVE DIRECTOR    1996

*THERESA E. LOVELESS (1946–2020)* became the first black executive director of the Girl Scout Council of Greater St. Louis.

## 1996    HEADS REALTORS' BOARD

*GAYLE BRISCOE* was installed as president of the Greater Baltimore Board of Realtors, the nation's oldest real estate board. She was the board's first black woman president.

## LEADS STATE BOARD OF MEDICINE        1996

*KATHRYN "KATHY" GARRETT (1955–)*, a radiologist and since 1989 a partner with the Medical Center Radiology Group in Orlando, Florida, was elected chair of the 100-year-old Florida Board of Medicine, the first black to hold that post.

## 1996                       RECREATIONAL SPORTS NEW LEADER

When the National Intramural Recreational Sports Association held its 47th annual conference, *JULIETTE R. MOORE (1953–)* was elected president, becoming the first black woman elected to lead the association.

## RETIREES NATIONAL PRESIDENT          1996

*MARGARET A. DIXON (1923?–2011)* was installed in May of this year as national president of the American Association of Retired Persons (AARP), becoming the first black to hold the post.

## 1996      MUSIC SCHOOLS ACCREDITATION OFFICER

*JOYCE J. BOLDEN* became the first woman and the first minority chairperson of the Commission on Accreditation for the National Association of Schools of Music (NASM). In 1999 the NASM made her an honorary member of its board of directors, the first person of color and second woman to receive the honor.

## PHYSICIAN'S ACADEMY HEAD            1996

*AUDREY B. RHODES* became the first black and the second woman president of the South Carolina Academy of Family Physicians.

# CORNELIA (CONNIE) WHITENER PERDREAU

## Leads International Educators

The first black president of the Association of International Educators, formerly the National Association for Foreign Student Affairs, was Cornelia (Connie) Whitener Perdreau, who took the office in 1996. The association is the world's largest organization devoted to international exchange of students and scholars.

## 1997                    NATIONAL PTA PRESIDENT

*LOIS JEAN WHITE (1938–)* was elected to office in 1997, becoming the first black president of the National Parent Teacher Association.

## WOMEN'S LEGAL ADVISORY CHIEF          1997

*AUGUSTINE WRIGHT POUNDS (1936–2017)* became the first black president of the American Association of University Women's Legal Advocacy Fund.

## 1997            BARRIER-BREAKING HEAD OF JUDGES ASSOCIATION

*SHIRLEY STRICKLAND SAFFOLD* took office in 1997 as president of the American Judges Association, the first black woman to serve in an executive position.

## LEADS WOMEN'S FORUM                    1997

Retired banker **FRAN A. STREETS** became the first black president of
the International Women's Forum, an organization that promotes the
exchange of ideas and experiences of women worldwide. Among its
members were Hillary Rodham Clinton and Coretta Scott King.

## 1997    BAPTIST YOUTH CONVENTION LEADER

**DIONNE N. CURBEAM (1976–)** became the first woman president
of the National Baptist Convention of America's National Youth and
Children's Convention in New York City.

## HEADS VFW POST                         1997

The first black woman in South Carolina to become commander of a
Veterans of Foreign Wars post in that state was **MARGARITE ROBIN-
SON BLAKELY (1948?–)**.

## 1997       PRESIDENT OF PUBLIC RELATIONS
## GROUP

The first black and the second educator to be named president of the
Public Relations Society of America was **DEBRA A. MILLER**.

## POLITICAL STUDIES ORGANIZATION    1997
## OFFICER

The first woman to become vice president for research at the Joint
Center for Political and Economic Studies, a think tank in Washington, D.C., was economist **MARGARET SIMMS (1947–)**.

## 1997               THREE JUDGES IN MICHIGAN

For the first time, three black women judges in Michigan headed the
three judicial associations in the state. They were **VERA MASSEY**

# DONNA M. NORRIS (1943–)

## Psychiatric Association Leader

In 1998 Donna M. Norris, a psychiatrist, became the first black and first woman speaker at the assembly of the American Psychiatric Association in the organization's 153-year history.

---

*JONES (1943–)*, president of the Michigan Judges Association; *JEANETTE O'BANNER-OWENS (1944–2007)*, president of the Michigan District Judges Association; and *CAROLYN H. WILLIAMS*, president of the Michigan Probate Judges Association.

## HEADS ADDICTION SOCIETY                 1997

*KAREN ALLEN* became the first black president of the National Nurses Society on Addictions.

## 1998                TELECOMMUNICATIONS LEADER

The first full-time president of the New Jersey Cable Telecommunications Association, located in Trenton, was *KAREN D. ALEXANDER*.

## HEADS SCHOOL PSYCHOLOGISTS              1998

*DEBORAH CROCKETT* became the first black president of the National Association of School Psychologists, the largest professional association for school psychologists in the world.

## 1998                BROADCAST MUSIC LEADER

When her peers elected *SUSAN DAVENPORT (1967–)* as chair of the board of directors of Broadcast Music Inc. (BMI), she became the first woman and the first black woman to serve in that capacity.

## HEADS WOMEN LAWYERS GROUP          1998

**LINDA D. BERNARD** became the first black president of the 191-year-old National Association of Women Lawyers.

## 1998          PERFORMING RIGHTS GROUP ADMINISTRATOR

**JEANIE WEEMS** became the first black assistant vice president for the American Society of Composers, Artists, and Publishers (ASCAP), the world's largest performing rights society.

## LEADS HOSPITAL ASSOCIATION'S          1999 BOARD

The first black person to chair the American Hospital Association's (AHA) board of trustees was **CAROLYN B. LEWIS**.

## 1999   BAR EXAMINERS CONFERENCE CHAIR

**SARAH N. HALL** became the first black woman chair of the National Conference of Bar Examiners.

## HONORARY MUSIC BOARD MEMBER          1999

The National Association of Schools of Music elected **JOYCE BOLDEN** an honorary member of its board of directors, making her the first person of color and the second woman to receive the honor.

## 2000          RACIAL BARRIER–BREAKING SORORITY MEMBER

**CHRISTINA HOUSTON** broke the racial barrier in the University of Alabama's Greek system when she became a member of the white sorority Gamma Phi Beta in November of her freshman year.

# CAROLYN JEFFERSON-JENKINS (1952–)

## Women Voters Group President

The National League of Women Voters elected Carolyn Jefferson-Jenkins as 15th president in 1998, the first black to hold that post.

## HEADS CARDIOLOGISTS' BOARD          2000

The first woman president of the Atlanta-based Association of Black Cardiologists, for the 2000–2002 term, was *ELIZABETH O. OFILI (1956–)*.

## 2000          TENNIS ASSOCIATION EXECUTIVE

The first black woman to become executive director of the United States Tennis Association, Eastern Section, was *DENISE M. JORDAN*.

## SCHOOL BOARDS NEW LEADER          2000

*CLARICE LORRAINE CHAMBERS (1938–2010)*, an elected official and member of the clergy, became the first black woman to head the National School Boards Association. Previously she was the first black president of the Pennsylvania School Boards Association.

## 2000          YMCA BOARD PRESIDENT

The first black president of the YMCA board in Richmond, Virginia, was *KELLY C. HARRIS*.

## NAACP BOARD MEMBER          2001

*ROSLYN McCALLISTER BROCK (1965–)* became the youngest and first woman vice chair of the National Association for the Advancement of Colored People's board of directors.

## 2001 WOMEN MAYORS DIVISION HEAD

**SARA BOST (1947–)**, mayor of Irvington, New Jersey, became the first black to head the Women Mayors Division of the U.S. Conference of Mayors.

## HISTORY-MAKING LEGISLATOR 2001

State representative **HELEN GIDDINGS (1945–)**, of Dallas, Texas, was sworn in as the first black president of the National Order of Women Legislators (NOWL). At the time of her election to NOWL, Giddings had recently won her fifth consecutive term in the Texas House of Representatives.

## 2002 COUNTRY CLUB MEMBER

**BARBARA HATTON (1941–)** joined Knoxville, Tennessee's, oldest country club, the private Cherokee Country Club, becoming its first black member. An anonymous donor paid her entrance fee and monthly dues.

## PIONEER ACCREDITATION AGENCY LEADER 2005

**BELLE SMITH WHEELAN (1951–)** is the first black and first woman to serve as president of the Southern Association of Colleges and Schools, the accrediting agency for schools and colleges located in the South.

## 2007 LEADER FOR SOCIOLOGISTS

**PATRICIA HILL COLLINS (1948–)** made history at the American Sociological Association's annual meeting this year by becoming the first black woman elected president of that organization.

## AMPAS PRESIDENT 2013

**CHERYL BOONE ISAACS (1949–)** was named president of the Academy of Motion Picture Arts and Sciences (AMPAS). She was the first black person and only the third woman in the association's history to hold that position. AMPAS is popularly known for its televised annual Academy Awards ceremony in which the "Oscars" are presented for cinematic excellence.

Cheryl Boone Isaacs

## 2015    BAR ASSOCIATION'S NEW LEADER

**PAULETTE BROWN (1950–)** took office in August as the first black woman president of the American Bar Association.

## WRITERS FOUNDATION'S NEW LEADER    2016

**LISA LUCAS (1980–)** became the first black and first female executive director of the National Book Foundation. Since 1950, the foundation has given National Book Awards to deserving writers.

## 2017    PIONEER JUNIOR LEAGUE PRESIDENT

The Junior League of Nashville, Tennessee, then in its 96th year, elected its first black president, **KRYSTAL CLARK**.

## PSYCHIATRIC ASSOCIATION PRESIDENT    2018

The American Psychiatric Association, which traces its roots to 1844 and has a membership of over 37,000 physicians, elected its first black president, **ALTHA STEWART**. For the first time as well, the succession to the presidency included three women in a row.

# 2019                    YMCA PRESIDENT AND CEO

**LORIA YEADON** took over as president and CEO of the YMCA of Greater Seattle, becoming the first woman and first person of color to lead in the organization's 143-year history.

# MEDICAL ASSOCIATION ELECTS          2019
# PRESIDENT

The American Medical Association's House of Delegates elected **PATRICE A. HARRIS** as president elect at its Annual Meeting in 2018, making her the first black woman to win the office. She took office the next year. Harris previously served the AMA as a member of the Board of Trustees and has been board secretary and board chair. She continued to serve on the AMA Opioid Task Force and other AMA task forces, committees on health information technology, payment and delivery reform, and contracting.

# 2021                    BATTLE-BREAKER FOR CIVIL
#                          AND RACIAL JUSTICE

**DEBORAH ARCHER**, law school educator with expertise in civil rights and racial justice, was elected president of the American Civil Liberties Union, making her the first black president in the organization's 101-year history.

# Politics and Government

The need to create their own political agenda is central to the work of black women, primarily as a means of securing their equal rights. Their marks permeate practically every area of life. These women have long been represented in some way at local, state, and federal levels. The nation has black women first achievers as postmasters, mayors, police chiefs, heads of federal offices, boards of directors, legislators, federal judges, and members of Congress. Many times they sought office but were neither appointed nor elected, sometimes due to political or racial disparities. Several states elected black men as governor but have fallen short when it comes to black women governors. For a brief time, however, Barbara Jordan was appointed acting governor of Texas. Although Stacey Abrams was the first black woman to run for governor of Georgia, clearly racial disparities prevented her success. Despite this result, black women are prominent in the political arena and in many ways control or help shape the direction of political issues.

Black women firsts at the county or state level include Joyce Warren, the first black female judge in Arkansas and the first black to chair the state board of law examiners. Warren and many other black women are so accomplished that they hold several firsts in or beyond their major field of work. They often move up in positions, as seen in the case of Yvonne Watson Brathwaite Burke, the first black woman elected to the state assembly in California, and then the first black on the powerful Los Angeles County Board of Supervisors. She did not stop there, as she went on to become the first black U.S. representative from the West.

Well before they reached that level in major cities, black women became mayors of small towns. For example, in 1972 Ellen Walker Craig-Jones became mayor of Urbancrest, Ohio, and Hartford, Connecticut, elected its first black woman mayor in 1886, which was followed by many others through the 1980s, 1990s, and into the 2000s. Other cities included Atlanta, New Orleans, and Chicago, where Lori Lightfoot was elected as the city's first LGBTQ mayor in 2019.

The federal government has enjoyed a good share of black women firsts. In the judiciary branch, Constance Baker Motley, pioneer for justice, served judgeships at state and local levels before becoming the first black woman federal judge. The first black postmistress came in 1891, when Minnie M. Geddings Cox was appointed to that post in Indianola, Mississippi. Patricia Roberts Harris became the first black woman to serve as secretary of housing and urban development. M. Joycelyn Elders became the first black and second woman named U.S. surgeon general, while Hazel Reid O'Leary was the first black and first woman secretary of energy. Loretta Lynch was the first black woman to serve as U.S. attorney general, and Carla Hayden became the first black and first woman librarian of Congress.

The U.S. Senate added Carol E. Moseley Braun, Illinois's first black senator, after she was elected to Congress and became the first black woman U.S. senator. Unfortunately, no black woman has ever served on the U.S. Supreme Court. In the U.S. president's office, the nation saw its first black president when Barack Obama was elected to that position. This meant that his wife, Michelle Robinson Obama, promptly became the nation's first black First Lady. The pioneering developments in the office of the vice president of the United States was realized by the success of U.S. senator Kamala Devi Harris, who was selected as Joe Biden's running mate in the 2020 presidential election. The successful end of the race made Harris the first black woman vice president of the United States.

Politics and government are broad areas in which African American women set their aims high and wide, with much success in their drive. Their political agenda changes as appropriate, yet their determination to remain visible and bring about change is permanent.

## PIONEERING POSTAL OFFICIAL                1891

*MINNIE M. GEDDINGS COX (1869–1933)* was the first black postmistress in the United States. Cox was appointed to serve in the town

# CHARLOTTE E. RAY (1850–1911)

## Record-setting U.S Supreme Court Attorney

The first black woman lawyer in the United States, and the third woman admitted to law practice in the United States, was Charlotte E. Ray. As a graduate of Howard Law School (Washington, D.C.), she was automatically admitted to practice in the lower courts of the district, and on April 23, 1872, she became the first black woman admitted to practice before the Supreme Court of the District of Columbia.

of Indianola, Mississippi. President Benjamin Harrison appointed her to the post. President William McKinley reappointed her on May 22, 1897, and the appointment drew controversy from whites who wanted blacks removed from leadership positions. In 1902 she offered to resign; however, President Theodore Roosevelt refused her resignation.

## 1918       RECORD-BREAKING STATE BAR MEMBER

**GERTRUDE E. DURDEN RUSH (1880–1962)** was the first black woman admitted to the Iowa bar. From the beginning of her practice until the 1950s, she was the only black woman to practice law in Iowa. She was also a cofounder of the National Bar Association.

## PIONEERING STATE BAR MEMBER      1920

**VIOLETTE NEATLEY ANDERSON (1882–1937)** was the first black woman admitted to the Illinois bar. She became the first woman assistant prosecutor in Chicago in 1922 and on January 29, 1926, the first black woman lawyer admitted to practice before the U.S. Supreme Court.

# 1935                              CIVIL RIGHTS GODMOTHER

***DOROTHY (IRENE) HEIGHT (1912–2010)*** became the first black personnel supervisor for the Department of Welfare in New York City. Previously, she was a caseworker for the department. She was promoted to the advisory position after the Harlem riots of 1935. She also became concerned with the plight of black women who worked as domestics. In 1957 Height became president of the National Council of Negro Women, an organization that aimed to unite and uplift black women in humanitarian and social action programs. Height remained

Dorothy Height            active in civil rights activities. During the 1960s, she led the organization to become active in voter registration drives in the North and South. At her death on April 20, 2010, President Barack Obama called her "godmother of the Civil Rights Movement."

## ASSISTANT DISTRICT ATTORNEY                           1935

***EUNICE HUNTON CARTER (1899–1970)*** was the first black woman assistant district attorney for New York City. She served as the only black on Thomas E. Dewey's staff in his investigation of the rackets. Dewey named her special prosecutor for an extraordinary grand jury probe into organized crime. She was the only woman and the only black on his ten-member staff.

# 1936                              BARRIER-BREAKING FEDERAL
OFFICIAL

***MARY JANE McLEOD BETHUNE (1875–1955)***, educator, civil rights leader, advisor to presidents, and government official, was the first black woman to head a federal office. On June 24, President Franklin D. Roosevelt appointed Bethune to serve as director of the Division of Minority Affairs of the New Deal's National Youth Administration (NYA).

## ASSISTANT STATE ATTORNEY GENERAL     1937

***H. ELSIE AUSTIN (1908–2004)*** was appointed assistant state attorney general in Ohio, becoming the first black woman in the nation to hold that post.

# CRYSTAL (DREDA) BIRD FAUSET

## (1893–1965)

### First State Legislator

Elected in Pennsylvania in 1938, Crystal (Dreda) Bird Fauset was the first black woman to win a seat in a state legislature in the United States. In 1918 she began work with the YMCA in New York as the first secretary for younger black girls. Her relationship with Eleanor Roosevelt and her involvement in Franklin D. Roosevelt's election campaigns led to her position in 1941 as special consultant to the director of the Office of Civilian Defense.

## 1939 — AMERICA'S FIRST BLACK WOMAN JUDGE

In 1939 **JANE M. BOLIN (1908–2007)** became the first black woman judge in the United States when she was appointed to the Domestic Relations Court of New York City.

## FIRST DEPUTY SHERIFF — 1944

**DORIS E. SPEARS** was the first black woman deputy sheriff in the United States, taking the post in Los Angeles County.

## 1946 — DEPUTY ATTORNEY GENERAL

In January 1946 **ANNA PAULINE "PAULI" MURRAY (1910–1985)** became the first black deputy attorney general of California. Due to illness, she held the position only briefly.

## ASSISTANT ATTORNEY FOR COOK COUNTY

**1947**

*EDITH (SPURLOCK) SAMPSON (1901–1979)* became the first black woman named an assistant attorney for Cook County, Illinois

## 1949          CITY COUNCIL MEMBER

*JEAN MURRELL CAPERS (1913–2017)* was the first black woman elected to the Cleveland, Ohio, City Council.

## U.N. DELEGATE

**1950**

*EDITH (SPURLOCK) SAMPSON (1901–1979)* was named a delegate to the United Nations and became the first black woman to hold the designation.

## 1950                    STATE LEGISLATOR

*CHARLINE WHITE (1920–1959)* was the first black woman elected to the Michigan legislature.

## OFFICE-SEEKING POLITICAL ACTIVIST   1952

*CHARLOTTA A. SPEARS BASS (1874–1969)*, journalist and political activist, was the first black woman to run for vice president from a minor political party. She was the nominee of the Progressive Party.

## 1952   RECORD-SETTING ELECTED OFFICIAL

*CORA M. BROWN (1914–1972)* was the first black woman in the United States to be elected to a state senate. Since the only previous woman senator in Michigan had been appointed, she was the first woman of any race elected to the Michigan Senate. She was appointed special associate general counsel of the U.S. Post Office Department

# BESSIE ALLISON BUCHANAN

## (1902–1980)

### State Legislator

Bessie Allison Buchanan was, in 1954, the first black woman elected to the New York legislature. She was active in social welfare and civil rights issues. From 1963 to 1967, she served on the New York State Human Rights Commission, the first black woman to serve on the seven-member commission.

on August 15, 1957, becoming the first black woman member of the department's legal staff.

## POLITICAL COMMITTEE MEMBER          1952

*SARAH ROBERTA CHURCH (1914–1995)* became the first black woman elected to the Tennessee Republican State Committee.

## 1954          NEW YORK CITY CABINET MEMBER

*ANNA ARNOLD HEDGEMAN (1899–1990)* was the first black woman member of the cabinet of a New York City mayor. In 1922 she was the first African American graduate of Hamline University (St. Paul, Minnesota). She was a major organizer of the March on Washington in 1963.

## HISTORY-MAKING ATTORNEY          1955

*JEWEL STRADFORD LAFONTANT (1922–1997)* was the first black woman named assistant U.S. attorney for the Northern Illinois district. President Dwight D. Eisenhower appointed her to the post. In 1973 Lafontant became the first black woman deputy U.S. solicitor general.

## 1957                    STATE OFFICE HOLDER

*MADALINE A. WILLIAMS (1894–1968)* was the first black woman to
serve in the New Jersey state assembly.

## PIONEERING STATE LEGISLATOR          1958

*FLOY CLEMENTS (1891–1973)* was the first black woman elected to
the Illinois legislature.

## 1958                              MIAMI VOTER

*BLANCHE CALLOWAY (1902–1973)* was the first black woman to
vote in Florida.

## RACIAL BARRIER-BREAKING          1958
## POLITICIANS

*IRMA DIXON (1911–1965)* and *VERDA FREEMAN WELCOME
(1907–1990)* were the first black women elected to the Maryland
House of Delegates. The two represented bitterly opposed factions in
the Democratic Party. In 1962 Welcome became the first black woman
elected to the state senate.

## 1959                              CITY OFFICIAL

*ALICE PRISCILLA STATEMAN HANNIBAL (1916–1994)* became the
first woman and the first black elected to the Board of Aldermen of
Kinston, North Carolina.

## PREMIERE STATE JUDGE                1959

*JUANITA KIDD STOUT (1919–1998)* was the first woman judge in
Pennsylvania. Stout was appointed to the Philadelphia Municipal
Court in September and won election to a ten-year term in November

of 1959. On March 3, 1998, she became the first black woman to serve on any state supreme court.

## 1959                      ALASKA'S FIRST BLACK ATTORNEY

*MAHALA ASHLEY DICKERSON (1912–2007)* was admitted to the state bar and became the first black attorney in Alaska. Previously, she was admitted to the state bar in Alabama.

## PIONEERING STATE LEGISLATOR          1960

*BLANCHE PRESTON McSMITH (1920–2006)* was Alaska's first black state legislator.

## 1961                      MUNICIPAL COURT JUDGE

*VAINO HASSAN SPENCER (1920–2016)* was the first black municipal court judge in California. She served on the Los Angeles Municipal Court. She was also the first black president of the National Association of Women Judges.

## HISTORY-MAKING MENTAL HEALTH          1962
## LEADER

*MILDRED MITCHELL-BATEMAN (1922–2012)* was the first woman in the United States to head a state mental health department; she was also the first black to have a cabinet rank in West Virginia government.

## 1962                      STATE REPRESENTATIVE

*DEVERNE LEE CALLOWAY (1916–1993)* was the first black woman to be elected to state office in Missouri, when she became a member of the state house of representatives.

# EDITH (SPURLOCK) SAMPSON
## (1901–1979)

Municipal Court Judge

In 1962 Edith (Spurlock) Sampson became the first black woman elected judge on the municipal court. In 1925 she graduated from John Marshall Law School in Chicago with an LL.B. degree. Sampson was the first woman to receive an LL.M. degree from Loyola University. In 1934 she was admitted to practice before the Supreme Court. Sampson was also the first black appointed to serve on the U.S. delegation to the United Nations in 1950.

## STATE SENATOR                                                        1964

**CONSTANCE (BAKER) MOTLEY (1921–2005)** was the first black woman to win a seat in the New York state senate on December 10. Before becoming the first black woman federal judge in 1966, Motley was the first woman New York City borough head in 1965.

## 1964          DEPUTY ASSISTANT OFFICER

**CHARLOTTE MOTON HUBBARD (1911–1994)** was the first black woman deputy assistant secretary of state for public affairs. President Lyndon Johnson named her to the post—the highest permanent position held by a woman at that time. She helped eliminate racial discrimination against black soldiers in the Vietnam War.

## RECORD-SHATTERING AMBASSADOR    1965

*PATRICIA ROBERTS HARRIS (1924–1985)*, lawyer and diplomat, was the first black woman ambassador appointed to an overseas post and the first black woman to hold diplomatic rank. Harris was appointed ambassador to Luxembourg, and later she was named an alternate delegate to the United Nations. In 1971 she was elected to head the credentials committee at a meeting of the Democratic National Committee—the first black to chair the committee.

## 1965    MANHATTAN BOROUGH PRESIDENT

*CONSTANCE BAKER MOTLEY (1921–2005)* was the first black woman president of the Borough of Manhattan in New York City.

## POSTAL OFFICIAL                                    1966

*GERTRUDE SIMS CAMPBELL (1942?–2020)* was the first black woman hired in the post office in Greenville, Mississippi.

## 1966         VISIONARY FEDERAL JUDGE

Constance Baker Motley

*CONSTANCE BAKER MOTLEY (1921–2005)*, who received national acclaim for her civil rights work, became the first black woman federal judge and the highest-paid black woman in government. Motley worked with the NAACP as legal assistant and associate counsel and won many difficult civil rights cases—her most famous victory was the case of James Meredith against the University of Mississippi. Working with the NAACP Legal Defense Fund, she and other attorneys represented the demonstrators in the sit-in movement, including Martin Luther King Jr. and Fred Shuttlesworth.

## CITY COUNCIL MEMBER                        1967

*VICTORINE QUILLE ADAMS (1912–2006)* became the first black woman elected to the city council in Baltimore, Maryland. In 1946 she began a drive to elect blacks to political positions in the city.

# 1967                                    TEXAS SENATOR

***BARBARA (CHARLINE) JORDAN (1936–1996)*** was the first black to sit in the Texas senate since 1883. In 1972 she became president *pro tempore* of the senate, the first black woman to preside over a legislative body in the United States, and the first acting black governor of the state. In 2001 the City Council of Austin approved a statue to Jordan to be placed in the Austin-Bergstrom International Airport at the Barbara Jordan Passenger Terminal by 2002.

Barbara Jordan

## HONORED "LADY FROM FULTON"        1967

***GRACE TOWNS HAMILTON (1907–1992)*** was the first black woman in Georgia's legislature and became known as "the Lady from Fulton." Hamilton was active in social work and from 1943 to 1960 was executive director of the Atlanta Urban League.

# 1967                    CIVIL SERVICE COMMISSIONER
# PRESIDENT

***ERSA HINES POSTON (1921–2009)*** was the first black president of the New York State Civil Service Commission.

## STATE ASSEMBLYWOMAN                    1967

***YVONNE (WATSON BRATHWAITE) BURKE (1932–)*** was the first black woman elected to the California state assembly. In 1993 she became the first black on the powerful Los Angeles County Board of Supervisors and was later named chair of that five-member team.

Yvonne Burke

## 1967                             STATE LEGISLATOR

*DOROTHY LAVINIA "DR. D" BROWN (1919–2004)* was the first black woman to serve in the Tennessee legislature. Elected from the Fifth District in 1966, she took office the next year and for two years served in the lower house.

## STATE REPRESENTATIVE             1968

*HANNAH DIGGS ATKINS (1923–2010)* was the first black woman elected to the Oklahoma House of Representatives. The appointment was the first time a black had occupied a cabinet position in the state.

## 1968             FIRST BLACK WOMAN U.S. REPRESENTATIVE

*SHIRLEY ANITA ST. HILL CHISHOLM (1924–2005)* was the first black woman elected to the House of Representatives. In 1964 she was elected to the New York state legislature. In 1993 she served as U.S. ambassador to Jamaica.

## GENDER-BREAKING FEDERAL       1968 OFFICIAL

*BARBARA M. WATSON (1918–1983)* was the first black and the first woman to serve as an assistant secretary of state. She served as administrator of the Bureau of Security and Consular Affairs, and later, she was ambassador to Malaysia. In the latter post, she was the ranking American official in Malaysia with responsibility for all U.S. mission operations.

## 1969                                OHIO JUDGE

*LILLIAN W. BURKE (1915–2012)*, of Cleveland, was the first black woman elected to the Ohio bench. She was a judge in the municipal court.

# GEORGIA M. DAVIS POWERS
## (1923–2016)

### Passionate Civil Rights Advocate and Senator

Georgia M. Davis Powers, a Louisville businesswoman and civil rights worker, was the first black, and the first woman, elected (in 1968) to the Kentucky State Senate. In 1964 Powers was an organizer of the Allied Organization for Civil Rights. The next year, she helped organize the Kentucky Christian Leadership Conference, and she participated in the Selma-to-Montgomery March. She marched for open housing in Louisville and joined Martin Luther King Jr. in the march in Memphis to support sanitation workers. She was a local organizer for the Poor People's Campaign held in Washington, D.C.

## PRISON SUPERINTENDENT                          1969

The nation's first black superintendent of a woman's prison was **JESSIE L. BEHAGEN**, who was appointed to that post. She took charge of Rikers Island in New York, where over 500 inmates were housed.

## 1969                                          STATE JUDGE

**EDITH JACQUELINE INGRAM-GRANT (1942–2020)** was the first black woman judge in Georgia when she took that position on the Hancock County Court of Ordinary. In 1973 she became judge in that county's probate court.

## STATE ASSEMBLY MEMBER                          1970

**HENRIETTA JOHNSON (1914?–1997)** became the first black woman elected to the general assembly in Delaware.

# 1970        STATE LEGISLATOR

*GWEN(DOLYN SAWYER) CHERRY (1923–1979)* was the first black woman in the state legislature of Florida.

Gwen Cherry

## CHICAGO ALDERMAN        1971

*ANNA RIGGS LANGFORD (1917–2008)* was the first black woman elected alderman in Chicago.

# 1971        POLITICAL CAUCUS MEMBER

*(CYNTHIA) DELORES NOTTAGE TUCKER (1927–2005)* became the first black woman cabinet member in Pennsylvania when she was appointed secretary of state. Tucker was a founding member of the National Women's Political Caucus and cofounder of the Black Women's Political Caucus.

## PUBLIC SERVICE COMMISSIONER        1971

*CARMEL CARRINGTON MARR (1921–2015)* became the first woman to serve on the New York State Public Service Commission when she was named its commissioner. From 1953 to 1971, Marr served as a lawyer on the staff of the United Nations.

# 1971        CITY COUNCIL MEMBER

*ETHEL D. ALLEN (1929–1981)*, a physician, politician, and civil rights activist, became the first black woman Republican council member of

Philadelphia, Pennsylvania. In the 1975 election, she became the first black councilwoman elected to an at-large seat on the council.

## CORRECTIONS ADMINISTRATOR 1971

***DORA B. SOMERVILLE (1920–1994)*** was the first black woman to hold the position of correctional programs administrator for the Illinois Department of Corrections. Previously, she was the first woman member of the Illinois Parole and Pardon Board.

## 1971 NEBRASKA'S FIRST BLACK JUDGE

***ELIZABETH DAVIS PITTMAN (1921–1998)*** became the first woman judge and the first black judge in Nebraska. When the municipal courts in Omaha and Lincoln merged into the county system in 1985, Pittman became a county judge.

## STATE LEGISLATOR 1971

***DOROTHY MAE (DeLAVALLADE) TAYLOR (1928–2000)*** was the first black woman elected to the Louisiana legislature. In 1986 she was elected the first councilwoman-at-large of New Orleans and was also the first woman to serve as acting mayor of the city.

## 1971 STATE SENATOR

***WYNONA LIPMAN (1923–1999)*** became the first black woman elected to the state senate of New Jersey. Lipman championed the causes of women, minorities, children, and small businesses.

## COUNTY COMMISSIONER 1971

In November 1971, ***ELIZABETH BIAS COFIELD (1920–2009)*** was the first black, and the first woman, elected to the Wake County, North Carolina, Board of Commissioners.

**1972**                    **PRESIDENTIAL HOPEFUL**

*SHIRLEY (ANITA) CHISHOLM (1924–2005)* became the first black from one of the major parties to run for U.S. president. She sought to become the nominee of the Democratic Party.

Shirley Chisholm

## HISTORY-MAKING POLITICIAN          1972

*YVONNE WATSON BRATHWAITE BURKE (1932–)* was the first black congresswoman from the West. She was victorious in a 1966 campaign to become the first black California assemblywoman. She was the first black woman vice chair of the Democratic National Convention in 1972.

**1972**                    **U.S. CONSTITUTIONALIST**

*BARBARA (CHARLINE) JORDAN (1936–1996)* was the first Southern black woman elected to the U.S. House. She gained recognition from a nationwide television audience as the House Judiciary committee considered articles of impeachment against President Richard Nixon. She was elected to the Texas state legislature in 1965. Her reputation as one of the twentieth century's great orators was sustained by her keynote address to the 1976 Democratic Convention.

## TRAILBLAZING MUNICIPALITY MAYOR   1972

*ELLEN WALKER CRAIG-JONES (1906–2000)* was the first black woman elected mayor of a U.S. municipality, serving as mayor of Urbancrest, Ohio, from 1972 to 1975.

## 1973 — FIRST MAYOR IN OKLAHOMA

On April 16, 1973, **LELIA SMITH FOLEY (1942–)** was elected mayor of Taft, Oklahoma, a city of about 500, and has been called the first black woman mayor in the United States as well as the first black woman mayor in Oklahoma.

## CHANGE-MAKING POLITICIAN — 1973

Cardiss Collins

**CARDISS (HORTENSE ROBERTSON) COLLINS (1931–2013)** was the first black congresswoman from Illinois and the fourth black woman to serve in Congress. In 1975 she became the first black to chair the House Government Operations Subcommittee on Manpower and Housing. Collins was the first black whip-at-large (1975). She served 23 years in the House, becoming its longest-serving black woman.

## 1973 — FIRST METROPOLITAN CITY MAYOR

The first black woman to govern a metropolitan city as mayor was **DORIS ANN DAVIS (1935?–)** of Compton, California. She was one of several black woman mayors in the United States around this time.

## STATE LEGISLATOR — 1974

**GERALDINE TRAVIS (1931–)** was the first black elected to the Montana legislature.

## 1975 — APPELLATE COURT JUDGE

The first black woman appointed judge of the District of Columbia Appellate Court was **JULIA P. COOPER (1920–2014)**. She was the highest-ranking woman in the federal courts.

## POLICE DEPARTMENT SPECIAL TEAM MEMBER 1976

**MARY HALL** was the first woman of any race on the Special Weapons and Tactics (SWAT) Team of the Atlanta Police Department. At the time, she was 22 years old.

## 1976 KEYNOTE CONVENTION SPEAKER

**BARBARA CHARLINE JORDAN (1936–1996)** delivered a powerful keynote address at the Democratic National Convention in New York City, becoming the first black woman selected to present the keynote address.

## FBI AGENT 1976

**JOHNNIE MAE M. GIBSON (1949–)** was the first black woman agent with the Federal Bureau of Investigation (FBI).

## 1977 DEPUTY MAYOR

**LUCILLE MASON ROSE (1920–1987)** was the first black woman named deputy mayor of New York City. Mayor John Lindsay in 1966 named her assistant commissioner and later first deputy commissioner for the Manpower and Career Development Agency.

## GLASS CEILING–BREAKING MAYOR 1977

**UNITA BLACKWELL (1933–2019)**, of Mayersville, was the first black woman mayor in Mississippi. She was a leading figure in the civil rights struggle and in the organization of the Mississippi Freedom Democratic Party in 1964. She became the first woman president of the National Conference of Black Mayors in 1990.

## 1977 CIVIL SERVICE COMMISSIONER

**ETHEL S. BARNETT (1928–2020)** was the first black woman member of Pennsylvania's Civil Service Commission.

## ASSISTANT ATTORNEY GENERAL          1977

*SHIRLEY CREENARD STEELE* was the first black woman assistant attorney general of Iowa.

## 1977                              HEADS 4-H ACTIVITIES

*CLAUDIA H. PAYNE (1936–2019)* was the first black to head 4-H home economics activities in Maryland.

## REGIONAL HOUSING DIRECTOR          1977

*EMMA DANIELS McFARLIN (1921–2021)* was the first black woman to head the western region of the U.S. Department of Housing and Urban Development.

## 1977      FIRST SECRETARY OF AGRICULTURE

*JOAN S(COTT) WALLACE (1930–2018)* was the first black and the third woman to serve as assistant secretary for administration in the Department of Agriculture. Among her significant accomplishments while in office were programs designed to address the plight of black farmers. She helped recruit blacks to serve the USDA and held national forums to inform black farmers of assistance programs that were available to them.

Joan S. Wallace

## STATE SENATOR                        1977

*GWEN B. GILES (1932–1986)* was the first black woman elected to Missouri's state senate.

## 1977                              ALABAMA LEGISLATOR

A businesswoman who became interested in politics while visiting a coffee shop, *LOUPHENIA THOMAS (1918–2001)* became the first black woman elected to the Alabama legislature.

# FIRST U.S. CABINET SECRETARY        1977

**PATRICIA R(OBERTS) HARRIS (1924–1985)**
became the first black woman to serve as a Cabinet
secretary. Appointed by President Jimmy Carter, she
was secretary of housing and urban development. In
1980 she was named secretary of health, education,
and welfare, which later became the Department of
Health and Human Services. She was the first black
woman dean of Howard University's law school.

Patricia R. Harris

# 1978        COUNT BOARD SUPERVISOR

**YVONNE WATSON BRATHWAITE BURKE (1932–)** was the first
black member of the Los Angeles County Board of Supervisors.

# PIONEER STATE TROOPER        1978

**ALETHA MORGAN** was the first black woman trooper in South Carolina's state highway patrol.

# 1978        CALIFORNIA'S CHANGE-MAKING POLITICIAN

**DIANE (EDITH) WATSON (1933–)** was the first
black woman elected to the California state senate.
She later became ambassador to Micronesia. In 2001
Watson was sworn in as the fifteenth black woman
member of the U.S. House of Representatives.

Diane Watson

## CHANGE-MAKING STATE OFFICIAL    1978

*VEL(VALEA HORTENSE) R(ODGERS) PHILLIPS (1924–2018)* was the first woman, and the first black, to be elected to a statewide constitutional office, secretary of state for Wisconsin. Her law degree from the University of Wisconsin in 1951 was also a first. She was the first black elected to the Milwaukee Common Council (1956–71), the first black elected to serve on the National Convention Committee of either party in 1958, and the first black woman judge in the state in 1972.

Vel R. Phillips

## 1978    HUMAN RESOURCES OFFICER

*JEAN LOUISE HARRIS (1931–2001)* became the first black secretary of human resources for the state of Virginia. In 1955 she received her medical degree from the Medical College of Virginia, where she was the first black graduate.

## MEDICAL BOARD LEADER    1978

*FLORENCE STROUD (1933–2007)* was the first black, the first woman, and the first nonphysician to head the California Board of Medical Quality.

## 1978    PEACE CORPS LEADER

*CAROLYN ROBERTSON PAYTON (1925–2001)* was the first woman and black to head the Peace Corps.

## EMPLOYMENT ADMINISTRATOR    1979

*AGALIECE MILLER (1911?–1996)* became the first woman and the first black administrator of the Illinois Department of Labor's Bureau of Employment Security.

## 1979                                   BRIDGE-EXPERT JUDGE

**AMALYA LYLE KEARSE (1937–)** became the first woman justice in the 2nd Circuit Court. President Jimmy Carter appointed her to the Court of Appeals for New York City. She was the first black woman partner in the Wall Street law firm Hughes, Hubbard, and Reed. Kearse also became known as one of the country's most talented bridge players. She wrote Bridge Conventions Complete and edited the third edition of the Official Encyclopedia of Bridge. She translated and edited *Bridge Analysis* and won major national titles in 1971 and 1972.

## FEDERAL DISTRICT JUDGE                              1979

**JOYCE LONDON ALEXANDER (1949–)** was the first black American federal judge in the District of Massachusetts. She subsequently was named chief judge of that court. She was also the first black woman chief judge in any court in Massachusetts.

## 1979    EASTERN DISTRICT FEDERAL JUDGE

President Jimmy Carter appointed **ANNA DIGGS TAYLOR (1932–2017)** to the federal court for the Eastern District of Michigan (based in Detroit). She was sworn in on November 15, becoming the first black woman in the state to receive such a post.

## FLORIDA CONGRESSWOMAN                              1979

**CARRIE P. MEEK (1926–)** was the first black woman to represent Florida in Congress. She was a Florida state senator and as a legislator sponsored more than 30 major bills.

Carrie P. Meek

## 1979       DISTRICT COURT JUDGE

The first black and the first woman to be appointed to the U.S. District Court for New Jersey was **ANNE E. THOMPSON (1934–)**. She also served as chief judge for the District of New Jersey from 1984 to 2001.

## HUMAN RIGHTS ADMINISTRATOR     1980

**JOYCE TUCKER (1948–)** was the first black woman to serve in the state cabinet, as director of the Department of Human Rights in Illinois.

## 1980       STATE LEGISLATOR

The first black American elected to the Wyoming legislature was **HARRIET ELIZABETH BYRD (1926–2015)**. Byrd served in the legislature as a representative of the 44th District, and in 1988 she became a state senator, serving for four years. While in office, she sponsored a bill to establish a state holiday for Martin Luther King Jr.'s birthday. In 1991, the legislature agreed to call the celebration Martin Luther King Jr./Wyoming Equality Day instead.

## CONNECTICUT STATE LEGISLATOR     1980

**CARRIE SAXON PERRY (1931–2018)** was the first black woman elected to Connecticut's legislature.

## 1981       POLICE COMMANDER

**BILLIE ANN WILLIS** was the first woman of any race to become a police precinct commander in Detroit.

## LABOR SPECIALIST     1981

**LILLIAN ROBERTS (1928–)** was the first black woman to head the New York State Department of Labor.

# 1981              PROTECTION BOARD CHAIR

**GLORIA E. A. TOOTE (1931–2017)**, attorney and entrepreneur, was the first black chair of the Merit System Protection Board (formerly the Civil Service Commission).

# COMMISSION ON AGING              1981
# ADMINISTRATOR

**LENNIE-MARIE PICKENS TOLLIVER (1928–)** was appointed to be the commissioner of the Administration on Aging, the first black to hold that post.

# 1982              CITY FINANCE DEPARTMENT
# HEAD

**BELLA MARSHALL (1950–2012)** became the first woman to head the finance department for Detroit.

# NEW YORK CITY FIREFIGHTER              1982

**JOANN M. JACOBS (1951–)** was the first black woman firefighter in New York City.

# 1982              PASADENA MAYOR

On May 6, 1982, **LORETTA THOMPSON GLICKMAN (1945–2001)**, of Pasadena, California, became the first woman mayor of a city of more than 100,000.

# STATE SENATOR              1982

**CARRIE MEEK (1926–)** was the first black state senator in Florida since Reconstruction. She served in the state house for three years.

# 1982                              OPA LOCKA MAYOR

**HELEN MILLER (1925?–1996)** became the first black woman mayor of Opa Locka, Florida.

# STATE TROOPER                                    1982

**CYNTHIA REESE**, a resident of Riviera Beach, Florida, was the first black woman state trooper.

# 1982            GENERAL SESSIONS JUDGE

**BERNICE BOUIE DONALD (1951–)** was the first elected black woman general sessions court judge in Tennessee. She served in Shelby County. In 1988 Donald became the first black woman to serve on a U.S. bankruptcy court.

# HOUSING DIRECTOR                          1982

**JANET PURNELL (1936–2008)** was the first black, and the first woman, executive director of the Akron, Ohio, Metropolitan Housing Authority.

# 1983                      SENATE PEACEMAKER

**TRUDI MICHELLE MORRISON (1950–)**, attorney and presidential aide, was the first black woman deputy sergeant-at-arms of the Senate.

# SUPERIOR COURT CLERK                      1983

**CHERYL HOLLAND** was the first black in North Carolina to hold the position of clerk of the superior court in Gates County.

# 1983                       CIRCUIT COURT JUDGE

**EVELYN MARIE BAKER** was the first black woman circuit court judge in Missouri. She was the third woman, and the second black, to be a judge in Saint Louis.

## FEDERAL RELATIONS ADMINISTRATOR      1983

**BARBARA J. MAHONE**, automobile executive, was the first black woman to chair the U.S. Federal Labor Relations Authority.

## 1983     TRANSPORTATION ADMINISTRATOR

**CARMEN (ELIZABETH PAWLEY) TURNER (1931–1992)** was the first black woman to head a major public transportation network. Turner was named as general manager of the Washington, D.C., transit authority. In mid-December 1990, Turner became the first black undersecretary at the Smithsonian Institution.

## FEDERAL JUDGE      1984

**ANN CLAIRE WILLIAMS (1949–)** was the first black woman nominated to the federal bench in Chicago.

Ann Claire Williams

## 1984      SECRETARY OF STATE

**MYRA ATWELL McDANIEL (1932–2010)** was appointed secretary of state in Texas, the first black to hold that post.

## SECURITIES COMMISSION ADMINISTRATOR      1984

**AULANA LOUISE PETERS (1941–)**, attorney, was the first black woman appointed to the Securities and Exchange Commission.

## 1984                                                          STATE JUDGE

*JOAN BERNARD ARMSTRONG (1941–2018)* became the first black woman state judge when she was appointed to the state court of appeal. She served as New Orleans Parish Juvenile Court judge from 1974 to 1984.

## TAX COLLECTOR                                                          1984

*JACKIE WALKER* was the first black woman tax collector in Dallas County, Alabama.

## 1984                                          VITAL RECORDS REGISTRAR

*JULIA DAVIDSON-RANDALL (1942–)*, of Maryland, was the first black woman state registrar of vital records in the United States.

## STATE SENATOR                                                          1984

*YVONNE B(OND) MILLER (1934–2012)* was the first black woman member of Virginia's general assembly. In 1988 Miller became a member of the state senate.

Yvonne B. Miller

## 1985                                          DEPUTY CHIEF OF POLICE

*JOYCE F. LELAND (1941–)* was the first woman deputy police chief in Washington, D.C. Leland had been on the force for 20 years and rose through the ranks to become deputy chief.

## POLITICAL PARTY TREASURER          1985

**SHARON PRATT (DIXON KELLY) (1944–)** was the first black (and woman) treasurer of the Democratic National Committee.

Sharon Pratt

## 1985          STATE COMMITTEE CHAIR

**GLORIA BUTLER (1941–)** was the first black and first woman to chair Georgia's Campaign and Financial Disclosure Commission.

## STATE LEGISLATOR          1985

**ALYCE GRIFFIN CLARKE (1939–)** was the first black woman member of the Mississippi House of Representatives.

## 1985          SUPERIOR COURT JUDGE

**THELMA WYATT-CUMMINGS MOORE (1945–)** was the first black woman appointed judge in the State Court of Fulton County, Georgia. In 1998 she became the first black woman judge on Fulton County's Superior Court.

## NEWPORT NEWS MAYOR          1986

**JESSIE M. RATTLEY (1929–2001)** was the first black and first woman mayor of Newport News, Virginia. In 1970 Rattley was the first black and the first woman elected to the city council.

## 1986                           LITTLE ROCK MAYOR

*LOTTIE H. SHACKELFORD (1941–)* was the first woman mayor of Little Rock, Arkansas. Shackelford had served for eight years on the city's board of directors.

## CITY ATTORNEY                                    1986

*JAYNE WILLIAMS (1948?–)* was the first black woman city attorney in the state of California when she was appointed to the post in Oakland.

## 1986                    CIVIL SERVICE COMMISSION
## ADMINISTRATOR

*THERESE L. MITCHELL* was the first black chair of Pennsylvania's Civil Service Commission.

## PIONEERING STATE BAR MEMBER          1986

*IDA MAE LEGGETT* was the first African American admitted to the bar in Idaho. In 1992, she was appointed trial court judge in the city of Lewiston, the first of her race appointed to the bench in that state.

## 1986                              PRESIDING JUDGE

*MAXINE F. THOMAS (1947–1998)* was the first black woman presiding judge in the Los Angeles Municipal Court.

## OKLAHOMA STATE SENATOR                 1986

*VICKI MILES-LAGRANGE (1953–)* was the first black woman elected to the Oklahoma state senate.

# 1986 STATE LEGISLATOR

*LUCILLE SIMMONS WHIPPER (1928–2010)* was the first black woman member of the state legislature from Charleston County, South Carolina. Whipper was also the first president of the Avery Institute of Afro-American History and Culture.

# HARTFORD MAYOR 1987

As mayor of Hartford, Connecticut, *CARRIE SAXON PERRY (1931–2018)* was the first black woman mayor of a major northeastern city.

# 1987 PUBLIC HEALTH COMMISSIONER

*DEBORAH BOUTIN PROTHROW-STITH (1954–)* became the first woman and the youngest commissioner of public health for the Commonwealth of Massachusetts.

# SPEAKER PRO TEMPORE 1987

*LOIS MARIE DeBERRY (1945–2013)* was the first black woman speaker *pro tempore* of the Tennessee House. DeBerry was first elected to the House in 1972.

# 1987 CIRCUIT COURT CLERK

*ROSIE S. SIMMONS* was the first black elected in a countywide election since Reconstruction when she was elected to the position of Bolivar County, Mississippi, circuit clerk.

# STATE COMPENSATION COMMISSIONER 1987

*BEVERLY WADE HOGAN (1951–)* was the first black and the first woman commissioner of Mississippi's Workers' Compensation Commission.

## 1988                    CITY COUNCIL MEMBER

***CORA PINSON (1934–1994)*** was the first black city council member in Olympia, Washington, and the first black woman elected to any city post in the state.

## LAW ENFORCEMENT COMMANDER          1988

***JACQUELINE MURRAY*** was the first black woman commander on the Chicago police force.

## 1988               CIRCUIT CHANCERY JUDGES

***KATHLEEN BELL, JESSE L. KEARNEY (1950–)***, and ***JOYCE WIL-LIAMS WARREN (1949–)*** were the first blacks appointed to circuit chancery judgeships to oversee Arkansas's newly established juvenile division. Warren was the first black woman judge in Pulaski County, and Bell was the first black in the First Judicial District.

## PRESIDENTIAL HOPEFUL                    1988

***LENORA FULANI (1950–)*** was the first black woman to qualify for federal matching funds in a presidential election and the first black (and woman) to appear on the presidential ballot in all 50 states. She was also the only black woman Marxist psychologist to run for president. Fulani was running on the National Alliance Party ticket.

Lenora Fulani

## 1988       BOARD OF LAW EXAMINERS CHAIR

***JOYCE WILLIAMS WARREN (1949–)*** was the first black to chair Arkansas's state board of law examiners. Warren became a county judge in 1983 and was the first black female judge in the state. She became a state judge in 1989. The next year, Warren became the first black ever elected to a state-level trial court judgeship in the state. She was the first black president of the Arkansas Judicial Council in 2010. Warren was elected chair of the Arkansas Judicial Discipline and Disability Commission in 1913, the first female to serve in that capacity.

## MANHATTAN CITY ADMINISTRATOR    1989

*C. VIRGINIA FIELDS (1945–)* became the first black woman elected to the city council from Manhattan. In 1997 she was elected New York City's Manhattan Borough president and then was inaugurated president for her second term in January 2002.

## 1989    HOUSE OF CORRECTIONS WARDEN

*JANICE WHITE* was the first woman warden of the Manhattan House of Corrections in New York City, often called the "Tombs," and at the time the only woman warden in the New York penal system.

## MAYOR                                                        1989

*JESSIE BANKS* was the first black mayor of Tchula, Mississippi. Banks had been elected the first black alderman of the city in 1977.

## 1989    FIRST LADY'S SECRETARY

The first black to serve as press secretary for a First Lady of the United States was *ANNA PEREZ (1951–)*. She provided assistance to Barbara Bush from 1989 to 1993.

## NATIONAL SECURITY    1989
## ADMINISTRATOR

President George H. W. Bush appointed *CONDOLEEZZA "CONDI" RICE (1954–)* as director of Soviet and East European Affairs on

# AUDREY (FORBES) MANLEY

## (1934–)

Physician

Named to the post in 1989, Audrey (Forbes) Manley was the first black female assistant secretary in the U.S. Health and Human Services Department. After graduating from Meharry Medical College and completing a residency at Cook County Children's Hospital in Chicago, she became the first black woman appointed chief resident. From 1995 to 1997, she was surgeon general under President Bill Clinton. On July 1, 1997, Manley accepted the presidency of Spelman College in Atlanta, becoming the college's first alumna president.

the National Security Council, making her the first black woman to hold that post.

## 1989      MEDIA RELATIONS DIRECTOR

**KRISTIN CLARK TAYLOR (1959–)** became the first black director of media relations for President George H. W. Bush's White House staff.

## SOCIAL SECURITY COMMISSIONER    1989

**GWENDOLYN STEWART KING (1941–)** was the first black woman to serve as commissioner of social security.

## 1989     PERSONNEL MANAGEMENT ADMINISTRATOR

***CONSTANCE BERRY NEWMAN (1935–)*** was the first black administrator of the Office of Personnel Management. In 1992 Newman was
named undersecretary of the Smithsonian Institution.

## CITY ATTORNEY             1990

***IRIS J. JONES (1952–)*** became the first black woman city attorney of
Austin, Texas.

## 1990             CITY COUNCIL MEMBER

Juanita Millender-McDonald

***JUANITA MILLENDER-McDONALD (1938–
2007)*** was elected to the city council of Carson
City, California, becoming the first black woman
to sit on the council. She was appointed mayor *pro
tempore* during her second year in office. In 1984
she took her daughter to the Democratic National
Convention as a delegate; they were the first mother-daughter team to serve as delegates to a political
party's national convention. In 1992 she was elected
to the California state legislature representing the
55th Assembly District, the first woman to represent that district. In 1996 she was elected to the
U.S. House of Representatives, filling the unexpired term of a former
representative who resigned from office. She won the seat in the full
election seven months later.

## BOUNDARY-BREAKING MAYOR     1990

The first black woman to be elected mayor of a major American city
(Washington, D.C.) was ***SHARON PRATT (DIXON KELLY) (1944–)***.
She served one term in Washington, D.C.

## 1990             COUNTY JUDGE

***CYNTHIA A. BALDWIN (1945–)*** was the first black woman elected to
the Allegheny County, Pennsylvania, bench, for a ten-year term. Baldwin was also the first black woman installed as president of the Penn
State Alumni Association.

## POPULAR TELEVISION JUDGE                          1990

*GLENDA HATCHETT (1951–)* was appointed judge of Fulton County Juvenile Court, becoming Georgia's first black chief presiding judge of its state court. She stepped down in 1999 and later starred on the syndicated television series *Judge Hatchett.*

Glenda Hatchett

## 1990                          COUNTY TAX ASSESSOR

*NELDA WELLS SPEARS (1946–2018)* became the first black woman in Texas to be elected county tax assessor-collector (in a Travis County special election). In 1992, she won a full term.

## SUPERIOR COURT JUDGE                              1990

*ZINORA M. MITCHELL (1957–)* and Michael L. Rankin were the first husband and wife to serve together on the Superior Court of the District of Columbia.

## 1990                                      COUNTY JUDGE

The first black woman elected to a judgeship in Queens County, New York, was *PATRICIA POLSON SATTERFIELD (1942–).*

## STATE POLITICAL PARTY LEADER                      1990

*LOTTIE H. SHACKELFORD (1941–)* was the first black chair of Arkansas's Democratic Party. At the time of her selection, she was serving on the Arkansas Regional Minority Council. She was also the first woman elected mayor of Little Rock in 1987.

# 1991        CITY COUNCIL MEMBER

*RITA WALTERS (1930–2020)* was the first black woman to serve on the Los Angeles City Council.

# STATE ATTORNEY GENERAL      1991

*PAMELA LYNN CARTER (1949–)* was the first black woman in the United States to be elected state attorney general and the first woman to be elected to the position in Indiana. Carter was the second black elected to a statewide office.

# 1991        CIRCUIT COURT JUDGE

Appointed to her post as associate circuit judge of the 21$^{st}$ Judicial Circuit in St. Louis in March, *SANDRA FARRAGUT-HEMPHILL* became the first black to serve on the circuit court bench in St. Louis County, Missouri. In 1998 she was elected the first black president of the Missouri Association of Probate and Associate Circuit Judges.

# KENTUCKY'S FIRST BLACK JUDGE     1991

*JANICE R. MARTIN (1956?–)* was the first elected black woman judge in Kentucky. She has been in private law practice and head of the Juvenile Division of the Jefferson County Attorney's Office.

# 1991        POLITICAL PARTY LEADER

*VERA HALL (1937–)*, a member of the Baltimore City Council, was the first black woman chair of the state's Democratic Party.

# SPEAKER PRO TEMPORE      1991

*WILHELMINA R(UTH) DELCO (1929–)* served ten years in the Texas legislature and this year she was appointed speaker *pro tempore*. This

Wilhelmina R. Delco

made her the first woman and the second black to hold the second highest position in the Texas House of Representatives. Her political career began in 1968, when she became the first black elected to the Austin Independent School District Board of Trustees.

## 1991            TENNESSEE STATE SENATOR

**THELMA MARIE HARPER (1940–2021)** was the first black woman elected to the Tennessee state senate.

## BARRIER-BREAKING SUPREME            1992
## COURT JUDGE

The first woman and the second black to serve on the Georgia Supreme Court was **LEAH WARD SEARS (1955–)**. She was first appointed to the seat, but in the same year she won a permanent seat in a statewide election. Sears served as a trial lawyer and a judge on the Atlanta Traffic Court, and in 1988 was the youngest person in Georgia to sit on the Fulton County Superior Court.

Leah Ward Sears

## 1992            APPELLATE COURT JUDGE

**M. YVETTE MILLER (1955–)** became the first woman director and judge of the appellate division of the State Board of Worker's Compensation in Georgia.

# U.S. REPRESENTATIVES                    1992

**EVA M. CLAYTON (1934–)** and Melvin Watt (1945–) were the first black representatives from North Carolina in the twentieth century. Clayton was also the first black woman to represent the state.

# 1992                    U.S. CONGRESSWOMEN

Corinne Brown

**CORINNE BROWN (1946–)**, representing the 3rd Congressional District, and **CARRIE MEEK (1926–)**, representing the 17th Congressional District, became the first black women elected to Congress from Florida since Reconstruction.

# RACE-BASED POLITICAL PROTESTOR    1992

**CYNTHIA (ANN) McKINNEY (1955–)** was the first black woman elected to the U.S. House from Georgia. McKinney was victorious in a new congressional district mandated by the 1990 census. During her second term in Congress, the U.S. Supreme Court ruled that the boundaries for the new district in Georgia that she represented were drawn solely on the basis of race. That meant that the boundaries for the 11th District were unconstitutional. Although that district was subsequently redrawn and eliminated many black voters, she won reelection in the white majority district.

Cynthia McKinney

# 1992                    NEW SHERIFF IN TOWN

**JACQUELYN "JACKIE" H. BARRETT (1950–)** was the first black woman to be elected sheriff, winning the Fulton County, Georgia, post. Barrett had 16 years of experience in law enforcement; as sheriff, she supervised more than 700 employees. Her election in 1992 signaled a major change in the image of a typical law enforcement officer in the South. Under her administration, the sheriff's office provided security for the state majority leader and the 1996 Summer Olympics.

## SENATOR TAKES FIRST SEAT                                    1992

*CAROL (ELIZABETH) MOSELEY BRAUN (1947–)* was the nation's first black woman senator. She served one term beginning in the 103rd Congress, representing Illinois. She was also Illinois's first black senator. In 1995 she became the first woman named to a full term on the powerful Senate Finance Committee.

Carol Moseley Braun

## 1992                          SAN FRANCISCO ASSESSOR

*DORIS M. WARD (?–2018)* was sworn in as assessor of the city and county of San Francisco, becoming the first black elected to that post in California.

## NEW SHERIFF IN VIRGINIA                                    1993

*MICHELLE BURTON MITCHELL (1963–)* became the first black woman to serve as sheriff in Virginia, holding the post in Richmond.

## 1993                          BARRIER-BREAKING ENERGY
## LEADER

*HAZEL R(EID) O'LEARY (1937–)* was the first black and the first woman secretary of energy. During President Jimmy Carter's administration, O'Leary became chief of the Department of Energy's Economic

Regulatory Administration. When she opened documents related to the government's human radiation treatments during the 1940s and 1950s, she caused a stir among many women who had received the treatments. President Bill Clinton named her U.S. secretary of energy from 1993 to 1997. O'Leary returned to her alma mater, Fisk University, as president from 2004 to 2012.

Hazel R. O'Leary

# EVANSTON MAYOR                           1993

**LORRAINE H. MORTON (1918–2018)** was the first black, and the first Democrat, elected mayor of Evanston, Illinois.

# 1993          MASSACHUSETTS STATE JUDGE

The first black appointed to the Probate and Family Court of Massachusetts was **JUDITH NELSON DILDAY (1943–)**, who received a lifetime position. In 1989 Dilday became a founding partner of Burnham, Hines & Dilday, the only law firm in Boston owned by black women. She was the first black president of the Women's Bar Association in 1990–91.

# U.S. CONGRESSWOMAN                        1993

The first black and the first woman elected to Congress from North Texas was **EDDIE BERNICE JOHNSON (1935–)**. She ran for a seat in the Texas house in 1972 and won in a landslide to become the first black woman from Dallas elected to public office.

Eddie Bernice Johnson

# (MINNIE) JOYCELYN ELDERS

## (1933–)

### America's Pioneering Top Doctor

In 1993 (Minnie) Joycelyn Elders became the first black and the second woman named U.S. surgeon general. She was also the first woman and the first black to hold the position of Arkansas health director. Her outspoken views on drugs, guns, human sexuality, birth control, and similar issues stirred controversy with conservatives.

## 1993                    WHITE HOUSE LIAISON

**ALEXIS M. HERMAN (1947–)** became the first black woman to direct a White House liaison program. From 1993 to 1997 Herman was director of the White House Office of Public Liaison as well as an assistant to President Bill Clinton.

## FEDERAL BUSINESS ADMINISTRATOR                    1993

**JEANETTE L. BROWN** left her post as director of the Office of Procurement and Grants Management, U.S. Small Business Administration, in Washington, D.C., to become director of the Office of Acquisition Management, U.S. Environmental Protection Agency. She was the first black and the first woman to hold the position.

## 1993       WHITE HOUSE PHOTOGRAPHER

*SHARON FARMER (1951–)* was the first black woman to serve as White House photographer, covering President Bill Clinton and the first family, and she became the first black and first woman to direct the White House photography office.

## CITY COUNCIL MEMBER       1994

*KATHY COLE (1947?–)* became the first council member in San Jose, California, to be voted out of office for racial remarks and gestures that Latinos, Asians, and gays considered offensive. She made the remarks at an African American leadership conference in May. Cole represented the Evergreen District, whose residents were one-third Asian American and one-quarter Hispanic.

## 1994       GARY, INDIANA, JUDGE

*KAREN MARIE FREEMAN-WILSON (1960–)* became the first black woman judge of the Gary, Indiana, City Court.

## PIONEERING MAYOR       1994

*JEAN LOUISE HARRIS (1931–2010)* was elected mayor of Eden Prairie, Minnesota, becoming the first black and the first woman mayor of this suburban town.

## 1994       POLICE CAPTAIN

*JOYCE STEPHENS* was promoted from lieutenant to captain on the police force in New York City, becoming the first black woman to attain that rank.

## POLICE FORCE CHIEF       1994

The first black woman to lead the police force in a major metropolitan city in the United States was *BEVERLY JOYCE BAILEY HARVARD (1950–)*, in Atlanta.

## 1994                    DELAWARE STATE SENATOR

**MARGARET R. HENRY (1944–)** became Delaware's first black woman state senator.

## COUNTY CHIEF OF STAFF                    1994

**KAREN ELAINE WEBSTER (1960–)** became the first woman chief of staff for the Fulton County, Georgia, commissioner.

## 1994          CONGRESSIONAL COMMITTEE MEMBER

**LORETTA COLLINS ARGRETT (1937–)** became the first black woman in the history of the Justice Department to hold a position that required Senate confirmation. She was the first black member of the Joint Committee on Taxation of the U.S. Congress.

## FEDERAL JUDGE                    1994

**VANESSA D(IANE) GILMORE (1956–)** was sworn in as a federal district judge in Texas, becoming the only black and the youngest sitting judge in that post in the state.

Vanessa D. Gilmore

## 1994                    MINNEAPOLIS MAYOR

The first black and the first woman mayor of Minneapolis took office this year. **SHARON SAYLES BELTON (1951–)**, a former welfare mother and women's rights advocate, was elected in 1993 and won a second term in 1997, capturing 55 percent of the vote of a largely white population.

Sharon Sayles Belton

## STATE SUPREME COURT JUDGE          1994

**BERNETTE JOSHUA JOHNSON (1943–)** became the first black woman to sit on the Louisiana Supreme Court. Previously, Johnson was chief justice for the Civil District Court.

## 1994    ASSISTANT SECRETARY OF COMMERCE

**LAURI FITZ-PEGADO** was approved as assistant secretary of commerce and director general of the Foreign Commercial Service. She is the first black to hold the post.

## INFORMATION AGENCY INSPECTOR          1994

The first black to become inspector general for the United States Information Agency was lawyer **MARIAN C. BENNETT**.

## 1994                    PERSONNEL DIRECTOR

**EVELYN M. WHITE** was named director of personnel for the U.S. Department of Agriculture, the first black woman to hold the post.

## PROMINENT STATE OFFICE HOLDER          1994

**VICTORIA "VIKKI" BUCKLEY (1947–1999)** rose from the welfare rolls to become the first black woman in Colorado to hold a statewide office and the first black woman to become Colorado's secretary of state. She was also the highest-ranking Republican woman in a state-wide office.

## 1994 BUREAU OF MINES ADMINISTRATOR

The first black person nominated as director of the U.S. Bureau of Mines in its 84-year history was *RHEA L. GRAHAM (1952–)*, a senior geologist with a private engineering firm in Albuquerque, New Mexico. Action on her nomination was blocked in the closing hours of the Senate.

## POLICE OFFICER 1995

The first black woman officer on the police force of Gonzales, Texas, was *JOYCE PATTERSON*.

## 1995 CHIEF OF DETECTIVES

*HELENA ASHBY* was appointed chief of detectives for the Los Angeles County Sheriff's Department, becoming the highest-ranking woman and the first woman to hold the position.

## COUNT COURT JUDGE 1995

*CLAUDIA J. JORDAN* was sworn in as a judge of the Denver County Court, making her the first black woman judge in the city.

## 1995 POLICE CAPTAIN

*JANET K. SMITH* became the first black woman captain in the Police Department of New Castle County, Delaware.

## POLITICAL COMMITTEE DIRECTOR 1995

*MINYON MOORE (1958–)* became the first black woman to serve as political director for the National Democratic Committee. In 1997 she became the first black deputy political director in the White House.

# 1995                                          STATE POLICE MAJOR

The Pennsylvania State Police promoted *VIRGINIA L. SMITH (1946–)* to the rank of major, making her the first woman in the department's 89-year history to hold that rank. Two years earlier, she also became the first black woman to reach the rank of captain.

# BOARD OF ELECTIONS                           1995
# ADMINISTRATOR

*SYBIL CARTER HADLEY* became the first woman chairperson and chief registrar of the Fulton County Board of Elections and Registration in Atlanta, Georgia.

# 1995                                          CIRCUIT COURT JUDGE

*DONNA HILL STATON (1957–)* became the first black circuit court judge in Howard County, Maryland. In 1997 she became the state's first black deputy attorney general.

# MARKETING DIRECTOR                           1995

The first senior director of marketing for the National Aquarium in Baltimore was *DENISE LONDON*. Earlier she was the first woman patrol officer in Camden County, New Jersey.

# 1995                                          MAYOR

*LAMETTA K. WYNN (1933–2021)* was elected mayor of Clinton, Iowa, becoming the city and state's first black mayor.

# COUNTY COMMISSIONER                          1995

*YVONNE ATKINSON GATES (1956–)* was elected chair of the Clark County Commission in Las Vegas, Nevada, becoming the first black woman to hold that position.

# KATHRYN "KATHY" WATERS
## Pioneering Transportation Director

In 1995 Kathryn "Kathy" Waters became the first black and the first woman in Maryland to manage a commuter rail service in Baltimore. After serving as acting manager of Maryland's MARC commuter rail system's Office of Transit Operation, she was named manager.

## 1995                                    PRESS SECRETARY

*DIANNA D. ROSBOROUGH* was named press secretary to Maryland governor Parris Glendening. A radio and television traffic reporter in Baltimore, she was the first black to hold that post.

## CIRCUIT JUDGE                                              1995

*JANNIE LEWIS (1958?–)*, sworn in as a circuit judge in Mississippi, became the first black judge in two of the counties in her district.

## 1995                                              INS JUDGE

*RENETTA SMITH (1960?–2007)*, a former trial attorney for the U.S. Immigration and Naturalization Service in Chicago, became the first black and the only woman judge with the INS in that city.

## MINORITY BUSINESS DIRECTOR                          1995

The first woman director of the Minority Business Development Agency at the Department of Commerce was *JOAN PARROTT-FON-SECA*.

# SHIRLEY ANN JACKSON (1946–)

## Nuclear Power Regulator

The first black woman to chair the Nuclear Regulatory Commission (NRC) was Shirley Ann Jackson. In 1995 she was placed in charge of regulating the safety of the country's 110 nuclear power plants.

## 1995    STATE DEPARTMENT INSPECTOR

*JACQUELYN L. WILLIAMS-BRIDGERS (1956–)* became the first black and the first woman inspector general of the State Department.

## CITY BUSINESS OFFICIAL                    1995

The first black woman executive director of the Equal Business Opportunity Commission in Columbus, Ohio, was *GWENDOLYN H. ROGERS*.

## 1995                          FEDERAL JUDGE

The first woman and the first black federal administrative law judge in Mississippi was *COVETTE ROONEY*. In 1996 Rooney became the first black woman administrative law judge at the Occupational Safety and Health Review Commission (OSHRC).

## POLICE DIVISION CHIEF                     1995

Lieutenant *ARMEDIA GORDON* became the first black division chief of special operations for the Denver (Colorado) Police Department.

## 1995    FBI INFORMATION RESOURCES DIRECTOR

**CAROLYN G. MORRIS (1939?–)** was promoted to assistant director of information resources for the FBI, becoming the highest-ranking black woman in the bureau's history.

## CITY OFFICIAL                                    1996

The first woman commission of the Chicago Department of Water was **JUDITH CAROL RICE (1957–)**.

## 1996    FROM SERGEANT TO LIEUTENANT

**JANET PINA (1951–2018)** became the first woman in Philadelphia, Pennsylvania, promoted to lieutenant in the sheriff's department. Previously she was the first woman promoted to sergeant.

## CITY ADMINISTRATOR                              1996

**STEPHANIE PALMER (1952–)** became the first woman executive director of the New York City Mission Society.

## 1996                                         MAYOR

**VIOLA THOMAS** became the first black mayor of Fairfield, New Jersey.

## POLICE OFFICER IN LINE OF DUTY       1996

**LAURETHA VAIRD (1952–1996)**, of Philadelphia, Pennsylvania, became the first black woman police officer killed in the line of duty when she responded to a silent alarm at PNC Bank's Feltonville Branch.

## 1996              ST. LOUIS COMPTROLLER

The first woman elected comptroller in St. Louis was **DARLENE GREEN**. She was also the first woman elected to the city's Board of Estimate and Apportionment, which controls the city's budget.

# ITTA BENA MAYOR                    1996

**THELMA COLLINS (1945?–)**, a ninth-grade school teacher, was elected mayor of Itta Bena, Mississippi, becoming the first black and the first woman to hold the post.

# 1996    POLITICAL COMMITTEE PRESS SECRETARY

The Democratic National Committee hired media consultant **DELMA-RIE COBB** as press secretary, making her the first black in that post. She was assigned to handle the Chicago media for the 1996 convention and to serve as spokesperson for the convention's chief executive officer.

# POLITICAL COMMITTEE PRESS SECRETARY                     1996

**JANICE ROGERS BROWN (1949–)**, a political conservative and judge, was appointed to the California Supreme Court, making her the first black woman to serve on the highest court in the state.

# 1996    CHIEF JUDGE IN MASSACHUSETTS

**JOYCE LONDON ALEXANDER (1949–)** became the first black woman chief judge in Massachusetts and the first black chief federal magistrate in the nation.

# INS OPERATIONS DIRECTOR                    1996

**CAROL JENIFER** was the first black woman to direct operations of an Immigration and Naturalization Service office.

# 1996    DISTRICT COURT FEDERAL MASTER

The first black woman to become special master for the District Court in the U.S. Virgin Islands was **DARLENE GRANT**.

# DONNA (MARIE) CHRISTIAN-CHRISTENSEN (1945–)

## Physician Elected to Congress

Donna (Marie) Christian-Christensen (1945–) became the first woman physician elected to Congress in 1996. Although she represented the Virgin Islands and was a nonvoting member of Congress, she was the first woman to represent a U.S. possession in Congress.

## ST. LOUIS COMPTROLLER                              1996

The first woman elected comptroller in St. Louis was **DARLENE GREEN**. She was also the first woman elected to the city's Board of Estimate and Apportionment.

## 1996          PIONEERING CONGRESSWOMAN

*JULIA (MAY) CARSON (1937–2007)* was the first woman of any race elected to Congress from Indianapolis, Indiana.

Julia Carson

## SHERIFF RISES IN RANK                    1996

**LISA A. GREEN**, a juvenile detective, was promoted to lieutenant in the sheriff's office of Charleston, South Carolina, becoming the first black officer to receive that rank.

## 1997                              POLICE OFFICER

**JAWANA SMITH** became the first black police officer in the 64-year history of the Bexley, Ohio, police department.

## SCHOOL SUPERINTENDENT                    1997

The first woman superintendent of the 63,000-student district of the Columbus, Ohio, Public Schools was **ROSA A. SMITH**.

## 1997                          CITY COUNCIL MEMBER

**ELLA HOLMES HINES (1958–)** became the first woman of any race elected to the City Council in Gulfport, Mississippi.

## CITY COUNCIL MEMBER                      1997

**BETSY STOCKARD (1946–2015)** became the first black woman to serve on the city council of Decatur, Illinois.

## 1997                              CITY MANAGER

**ANITA R. FAVORS (1951–)** was named city manager of Tallahassee, Florida, becoming the first woman and the first black to hold the post. With her appointment, she became one of only three black women who managed cities with populations of over 100,000.

## FOOD STAMP ADMINISTRATOR                 1997

The first black food-stamp chief was **SHIRLEY ROBINSON WATKINS (1938–)**, who was named undersecretary for the U.S. Department of Agriculture's Food, Nutrition and Consumer Services agency.

# 1997                  MOUNTED POLICE OFFICER

The city's first black woman to serve as a mounted police officer in Chicago was **DAWN PETER (1966?–)**.

# ACTING CHIEF OF POLICE                                    1997

**SONYA T. PROCTOR (1954?–)** became the first black woman acting chief of police for the District of Columbia.

# 1997            PRESIDENT'S INAUGURAL
# COMMITTEE CO-CHAIR

**ANN DIBBLE JORDAN (1934–)** became the first black woman to serve in the command role as cochair for the inauguration of a U.S. president. As she prepared for the second-term inauguration of President Bill Clinton, she spearheaded the theme of diversity, utilizing minorities and women in each planned activity.

# PUBLIC SERVICE COMMISSIONER                    1997

At 33, **JULIA L. JOHNSON (1963–)** became the youngest elected chair of the Florida Public Service Commission (PSC) and in 1993 the first black woman to serve on the commission.

# 1997      RECORD-SETTING DISTRICT JUDGE

**NORMA HOLLOWAY JOHNSON (1932–2011)** became the first black woman chief federal district judge for the District of Columbia. She became known worldwide when she presided over the grand jury that considered allegations against President Bill Clinton tied to his relationship with White House intern Monica Lewinsky.

# TRAINING FACILITY DIRECTOR                    1997

Ambassador **RUTH A. DAVIS (1943–)** became the first director of the Foreign Service Institute, the top training facility for U.S. diplomats. Later this year, she was promoted to career minister, becoming the first black woman to hold the top rank.

# PATRICIA "PATTI" G. SMITH (1947–2016)

## Space Transportation Leader

Patricia "Patti" G. Smith was named head of the Commercial Space Transportation section of the Federal Aviation Administration in 1997, becoming the first black woman to lead a line of business in FAA history. She managed private space launches, including private communication satellites and private scientific space research experiments.

## 1997    INFORMATION AGENCY COUNSELOR

**HARRIET L. ELAM-THOMAS (1941–)** became the first black agency counselor of the U.S. Information Agency, and the highest-ranking American woman in all three of the U.S. diplomatic missions in Belgium.

## POLICE CHIEF                                      1998

The first black woman police chief in Pritchard and one of three women police chiefs in Alabama was **GWENDOLYN BOYD**. She was a member of the police force in Miami for 24 years. After moving to Pritchard, she became a major, then moved up in command.

## 1998                    PARK ADMINISTRATOR

**CAROLYN WILLIAMS MEZA** became the first woman to hold the top job of general superintendent at the Chicago Park District.

## POLICE CAPTAIN                                      1998

**BARBARA GEORGE** was sworn into office, becoming the first black woman police captain of Newark, New Jersey.

# ALEXIS M. HERMAN (1947–)

## Pioneer Labor Department Administrator

In 1997 Alexis M. Herman (1947–) became the first black secretary of the Department of Labor. President Bill Clinton nominated Herman, who was already serving as his director of public liaison. She was also director of the Women's Bureau in the U.S. Department of Labor.

## 1998                              COUNTY PROSECUTOR

**PATRICIA HURT** was sworn in as Essex County, New Jersey, prosecutor, becoming the first black and the first woman to hold the post. When she took office, she was the only black prosecutor in the state.

## OCCUPATIONAL SAFETY                              1998
## COMMISSIONER

**THOMASINA VENESE ROGERS (1951–)** became the first black commissioner for the U.S. Occupational Safety and Health Review Commission.

## 1998            CREDIT UNION ADMINISTRATOR

**CAROLYN D. JORDAN (1941–)** became the first black executive director of the National Credit Union Administration, an independent federal agency that supervises and insures 97 percent of the 12,000 federally insured credit unions.

## FEDERAL MAGISTRATE                              1998

**SUSAN D. DAVIS WIGENTON (1962–)** became the first black federal magistrate for New Jersey as well as the state's youngest judge on the federal bench.

## 1998 — COMMISSIONER OF CORRECTIONS

*ALICE F. POLLARD* became the first woman commissioner of corrections in St. Louis

## MARINE EXCHANGE LEADER — 1998

*WILMA D. POWELL* became the first woman president of the Marine Exchange of Los Angeles–Long Beach Harbor. The exchange is a mutual benefit trade organization that documents the tonnage of ship movement through the two harbors.

## 1998 — PIONEERING POSTMASTER

*GERTRUDE SIMS CAMPBELL (1942?–2020)* moved up in positions she held in the Greenville, Mississippi, post office, and in 1998 the former supervisor in customer services was named the new postmaster in Starkville. With the promotion, she became the highest-ranking woman postmaster in the state.

## POLICE DISTRICT COMMANDER — 1998

*CATHY L. LANIER (1967–)* was placed in the command slot in the Fourth District, becoming the first black woman commander of any of the seven police districts in the District of Columbia.

## 1999 — FIRST BLACK MAYOR

The Trenton, North Carolina, Town Council, by unanimous vote, elected *SYLVIA WILLIS* as mayor, making her the first black to hold office.

## FIRST BLACK MAYOR — 1999

The first black woman mayor of East St. Louis, Illinois, and the second-youngest mayor of the city was *DEBRA A. POWELL (1964–)*. She was elected to office on April 13, when she was 35 years old.

## 1999        CITY COUNCIL MEMBER

*LYNETTE BOGGS McDONALD (1963–)* was sworn in as a member of the Las Vegas, Nevada, city council, becoming the first woman and the first black to serve on the council.

## NOAA ADMINISTRATOR        1999

Rear Admiral *EVELYN (JUANITA) FIELDS (1949–)* became the first woman and the first black director of the National Oceanic and Atmospheric Administration (NOAA) Commissioned Corps and NOAA Corps Operations, located in Washington, D.C.

Evelyn Fields

## 1999        CHIEF EXECUTIVE COUNSEL

*PENNY BROWN REYNOLDS* was named chief executive counsel in the office of Georgia governor Roy Barnes. She was the first black to hold the position.

## MOTHER-DAUGHTER LEGISLATORS        1999

*AMBER BOYKINS (1969–)* and her mother, *BILLIE BOYKINS (1945–2010)*, became the only mother-daughter combination to serve in the Missouri legislature in the history of the Missouri House of Representatives. From 1978 to 1982, Billie Boykins served in the house and, at the time, was the youngest black woman legislator.

**1999** PIONEERING AMBASSADOR

Sylvia Stanfield

***SYLVIA (GAYE) STANFIELD (1943–)*** became the first black woman ambassador to Brunei. She also became one of the highest-ranking blacks in the diplomatic service.

## HISTORIC PRESIDENTIAL CAMPAIGN MANAGER    1999

***DONNA L(EASE) BRAZILE (1959–)*** was placed in charge of day-to-day operations for presidential candidate Al Gore, becoming the first black woman to manage a major presidential campaign. She has managed four presidential campaigns, working for Jesse Jackson in 1984 in his unsuccessful bid for the Democratic nomination, and in 1988 for Jackson, Richard Gephardt, and Michael Dukakis. In 1984 Brazile was national director of the twentieth anniversary of the March on Washington.

Donna L. Brazile

**1999** COUNTY SOLICITOR GENERAL

***GWENDOLYN R. KEYES*** became the first black, the first woman, and, at 30 years old, the youngest person elected to the post of solicitor general of DeKalb County, Georgia.

## PORT BOARD CHAIR    1999

The first black woman to chair the Port of San Diego (CA) Board was ***PATRICIA A. McQUATER (1951–)***.

## 1999        MARSHAL SERVICE EXECUTIVE

**BROADINE M. BROWN** was named management chief at the U.S. Marshals Service in Arlington, Virginia, becoming the first black to reach the executive level.

## CONVENTION BUREAU        2000
## ADMINISTRATOR,

**WANDA COLLIER-WILSON** became the first person to head the Convention and Visitor's Bureau in Jackson, Mississippi, and the first person promoted to the top position within the bureau.

## 2000        FIRE DEPARTMENT CAPTAIN

A 13-year veteran of the Los Angeles, California, County Fire Department, **VERONIE STEELE-SMALL** became the first black woman in the department to be promoted to captain.

## PORT ADMINISTRATOR        2000

**KAREN V. CLOPTON** became chief of operations for the Port of San Francisco, the first black woman to hold the position. She was the first black woman president of the San Francisco Civil Service Commission.

## 2000        CIVIL RIGHTS POLITICIAN

The first black woman to become director of the New Jersey Division on Civil Rights in Trenton was **O. LISA DABREU**.

## FEDERAL JUDGE        2000

The first black woman judge for the Court of Appeals, ninth circuit, was confirmed, making **JOHNNIE RAWLINSON (1952–)** the first black woman ever to serve on the court. The ninth circuit covers nine states in the West and includes Hawaii and Alaska.

## 2000      FIRST BLACK FEMALE REPUBLICAN MAYOR

*YVONNE BROWN (1952–2012)* was elected mayor of Tchula, Mississippi, becoming the first black Republican woman mayor in the state.

## MAYOR OF HAMPTON      2000

*MAMIE (EVELYN) LOCKE (1954–)* was elected mayor of Hampton, Virginia, becoming the first black to hold the position. In 1994, the council selected Locke to be vice mayor and supported her campaign to be elected mayor.

## 2000      FEDERAL JUDGE

Former Common Pleas Court judge *PETRESE B. TUCKER (1951–)* was confirmed by the Senate, becoming the first black woman federal judge in Philadelphia.

## FBI TRAINING EXECUTIVE      2000

*CASSANDRA M. CHANDLER (1958?–)* was named assistant director for training for the FBI, becoming the first black woman at the agency to hold the rank of assistant director. She also became the agency's top black woman.

## 2000      REGIONAL DIRECTOR FOR TECHNOLOGY

*FLORA MURPHY SHAFFER* was promoted from regional director of information technology for the U.S. General Services Administration (GSA), located in Chicago, to grade 15, reaching the highest level in the government's pay system. She was the first black in the Great Lakes region to reach that rank.

## DEPUTY POLICE CHIEF      2000

A 20-year veteran with the Birmingham (AL) Police Department, *ANNETTA W. NUNN (1958–)* became the first black woman deputy chief. She commanded the patrol division.

## 2001

# FIRST BLACK WOMAN MAYOR
# OF DAYTON

Former state majority leader **RHINE (LANA) McLIN (1948–)** was elected mayor of Dayton, Ohio, becoming the first woman of any race to win that position. She was also the first black woman elected to the Ohio State Senate and the first African American woman to serve as Ohio senate minority leader. In late 2005, she became the first black woman to serve as head of the Ohio Democratic Party.

Rhine McLin

# MAYOR OF CAMDEN                           2001

**GWENDOLYN A. FAISON (1925–2021)** became the first woman mayor of Camden, New Jersey.

## 2001

# HISTORY-MAKING MAYOR
# OF ATLANTA

A first-time candidate, **SHIRLEY (CLARKE) FRANKLIN (1945–)** won the mayoral election on November 6 to become the first woman to be elected mayor of Atlanta and the only black woman then leading a major southern city.

Shirley Franklin

# POLICE CHIEF                               2001

Police department veteran **MARY BOUNDS (1947–)** was sworn in as Cleveland, Ohio's police chief, becoming the city's first woman to hold that post.

# CONDOLEEZZA "CONDI" RICE

## (1954–)

## Security Council Head

Condoleezza "Condi" Rice was named head of the National Security Council in 2001 during the George W. Bush administration. She took office this year, becoming the first woman to hold that post. Four years later she became the first black woman secretary of state, a position she held from 2005 to 2009. Rice taught political science at Stanford University, where she was also a member of the Center for International Security and Arms Control. After serving President George H. W. Bush's administration as director of Soviet and European Affairs on the National Security Council in 1989–91, she returned to Stanford and became provost—the number two job at Stanford. She was the youngest and the first black chief academic and budget officer at the school. Rice became national security consultant in the George W. Bush campaign, and then took her new position when Bush became president.

# 2001 LAW ENFORCEMENT ADMINISTRATOR

The first black woman to become captain with the Los Angeles Police Department was **ANN E. YOUNG**, a 19-year veteran with the department.

# PUBLIC WORKS ADMINISTRATOR 2001

**VALERIE L. SHAW** was elected president of the Los Angeles Board of Public Works, the city's only full-time policy-making commission. Shaw was the first black woman to hold that post.

# 2001            FOREIGN SERVICES DIRECTOR

When **RUTH A. DAVIS (1943–)** was sworn in as director general of the U.S. Foreign Services and director of human services for the U.S. Department of State, Secretary of State Colin Powell read the oath of office. This was the first time in history that a black secretary of state administered the oath to a black foreign services officer. Davis also became the first black woman to reach that high level in the Department of State.

# REGIONAL STATISTICS OFFICER            2001

The first black to head the Department of Labor's regional statistics office was **SHEILA WATKINS**, a career employee for 18 years.

# 2001            HOUSE OF DELEGATES MEMBER

The first foreign-born woman, the first female veteran, and the first black woman elected to Virginia's House of Delegates was **WINSOME SEARS (1964–)**.

# CITY ADMINISTRATOR            2002

**HELEN M. MARSHALL (1929–2017)** took office on January 1, becoming the first black woman elected as New York City's Queens Borough president.

# 2002            FIRE DEPARTMENT CAPTAIN

The first black woman appointed captain of the Charlotte (NC) Fire Department was **SYLIVIA SMITH-PHIFER (1969?–)**.

# FIREFIGHTING ADMINISTRATOR            2002

**ELLA McNAIR** was promoted to lieutenant in a ceremony at the New York City Fire Department's Brooklyn headquarters, becoming the first black woman to hold that rank in the department. In 1982 she was a member of the first class of firefighters to include women.

## 2002        BLACK LEGISLATIVE CAUCUS DELEGATE

*WINSOME EARLE SEARS (1964–)* became the first GOP woman delegate to Virginia's Black Legislative Caucus.

## STATE SECRETARY OF EDUCATION     2002

*BELLE SMITH WHEELAN (1951–)* was sworn in as secretary of education to Virginia governor Mark Warner's cabinet on January 13, making her the first black woman to serve in this capacity.

## 2005        BARRIER-BREAKING SECRETARY OF STATE

*CONDOLEEZZA RICE (1954–)* was named secretary of state in the George W. Bush administration, becoming the first black woman to hold that post.

## PIONEERING CHIEF OF POLICE     2007

*JACQUELINE SEABROOKS (1981?–)*, a veteran in law enforcement and former captain of the Santa Monica (California) Police Department, became this city's first woman chief of police.

## 2007        STATE REGULATORY AUTHORITY BOARD MEMBER

The first black woman named to a three-year term on the Tennessee Regulatory Authority Board was *MARY W. FREEMAN (1966–)*.

## TOURISM DIRECTOR     2007

The first black to serve as assistant director of tourism for the state of Ohio was *ALICIA REECE (1971–)*.

## 2007                           FIRE CHIEF DEPUTY

**TERESA EVERETT** became the first black woman to be named deputy fire chief for the Rochester, New York, Fire Department.


## INFORMATION OFFICER                          2007

**MELODIE MAYBERRY-STEWART (1948–)** became the first black female chief information officer of the state of New York. Stewart enjoyed a number of firsts. She was the first CTO and CIO for Cleveland, Ohio, in 2002. She was also the first black woman to earn a doctorate from the Peter F. Drucker Graduate School of Executive Management (Claremont Graduate University in California).


## 2007    HOUSE OF REPRESENTATIVES CLERK

The first black to serve as clerk of the House of Representatives was **LORRAINE C. MILLER (1948–)**. She was also senior advisor to Speaker of the House Nancy Pelosi.


## MAYOR OF BALTIMORE                          2008

The first black woman to be elected mayor of Baltimore was **SHEILA (ANN) DIXON (1953–)**. She had served as interim mayor since January 2007 and won the mayoral election with 88 percent of the vote.

Sheila Dixon


## 2008                           CITY COUNCIL MEMBER

**ANITA PRICE** was elected to the Roanoke (VA) City Council and became the city's first black woman to hold that post.

## SHAQUANDA COTTON (1991–)

### Teen Inmate Freed

The first juvenile inmate ordered freed by a special master appointed to investigate the sentences of many youth held in Texas juvenile prisons was 15-year-old Shaquanda Cotton. In 2007 Texas governor Rick Perry ordered the statewide investigation to determine whether the prison terms for many youths might have been unfairly extended. The teen, a ninth grader when sentenced, was convicted of "assault on a public servant" after shoving a school hall monitor at Paris (TX) High School. She was sentenced to prison for up to seven years.

## STATE ASSEMBLY SPEAKER                     2008

Los Angeles lawmaker **KAREN RUTH BASS (1953–)** became the first black woman, the first Democratic woman, and the 67th person elected speaker of the California State Assembly. Her post is recognized as the second most powerful position in the state's government. In 2004, Bass was elected to the 80-member chamber. She was elected to the U.S. House of Representatives in 2011.

## 2008          TREND-SETTING CHIEF SUPREME COURT JUSTICE

Justice **PEGGY A(NN) QUINCE (1948–)** became the first black woman to be chief justice of the Florida Supreme Court or any branch of the state's government. Her appointment to the 2nd Court of Appeals in 1993 made her the first black woman to serve in any appellate court in Florida.

Peggy A. Quince

## MARYLAND CONGRESSWOMAN

## 2008

The first black woman elected to represent Maryland in Congress was **DONNA EDWARDS (1958–)**, who won a special election in the state's 4th Congressional District. She lost when she ran for the congressional seat in 2006, then ran for a full term in November 2008 and won.

Donna Edwards

## 2008

## TRANSGENDER PUBLIC OFFICE HOLDER

**MARISA RICHMOND** became the first transgender woman elected to public office in Tennessee and the first black transgender woman from any state to be elected a delegate to a major party convention. She was a delegate to the 2008 and 2012 Democratic National Conventions. Richmond is a staunch advocate for human rights (particularly for women), the transgender community, and communities of color. She is president of the Tennessee Transgender Coalition and has served on the Board of Directors of the Tennessee Equality Project & Board of Advisors of National Center for Transgender Equality.

## STATE ATTORNEY GENERAL

## 2010

**KAMALA (DEVI) HARRIS (1964–)** became the first black woman elected as California attorney general. Harris was deputy district attorney in Alameda County (1990–98) and in August 2000 became managing attorney of the Career Criminal Unit, Office of the San Francisco District Attorney. *Ebony* magazine and the *New York Times* named her one of 17 most likely to become the nation's first female president.

## 2010

## ASSOCIATE COUNTY JUDGE

**ROMONDA D. BELCHER** became the first African American woman to be a Polk County District associate judge in Iowa.

# MICHELLE (ROBINSON) OBAMA
## (1964–)

### First Lady

When Barack Obama took office as president of the United States in 2009, Michelle (Robinson) Obama became the first black First Lady of the United States. Her special concerns included the plight of military families, childhood obesity, and promoting healthier eating habits. She quickly became a fashion trendsetter as she selected styles from affordable dress lines to high-end fashion designers. In 2018 she published her memoir, *Becoming*, which quickly became a best-seller. She remains a highly admired supporter of racial justice.

## FEDERAL JUDGE IN INDIANA                                       2010

The U.S. Senate confirmed Marion Superior Court Judge **TANYA WALTON PRATT (1959–)** to a lifetime appointment as a federal judge of the Southern District of Indiana. This action made Pratt the first black federal judge in Indiana.

## 2010              ALABAMA CONGRESSWOMAN

**TERRI A. SEWELL (1965–)** became the first black woman Alabama has sent to Congress.

## STATE LEGISLATOR                                               2011

The fall 2010 midterm elections put many Republicans in political power, among them unprecedented numbers of blacks, including

Florida lieutenant governor–elect **JENNIFER CARROLL (1959–)**, the first black woman and the first woman elected to that post. She took office on January 4, 2011. In 2003 she won a special election, becoming the first black woman Republican elected to Florida's legislature.

## 2011 STATE SUPREME COURT JUSTICE

**YVETTE McGEE BROWN (1960–)** became the first black woman justice on the Supreme Court of Ohio.

## COUNTY CONSTITUTIONAL OFFICER 2012

Davidson County, Tennessee, clerk **BRENDA WYNN**, a Democrat, was appointed to the position in August, and in November she handily topped two opponents to retain her post. The successful election made her the first black woman to win an election for a constitutional office in the county.

## 2013 MAYOR OF COMPTON

Aja Brown

Elected to office when she was only 32 years old, **AJA BROWN (1982–)** was the youngest person to become mayor of Compton, California.

## FCC ACTING HEAD 2013

**MIGNON L. CLYBURN (1962–)** became the first and only female to be named acting chair of the Federal Communications Commission (FCC), following her appointment by President Barack Obama.

## 2013      PIONEERING NATIONAL PRINTER

President Barack Obama nominated **DAVITA E. VANCE-COOKS** **(1957?–)** as public printer on May 9. She was confirmed on August 1, becoming the first black and first woman to head the Government Printing Office and the 27th public printer.

## REPUBLICAN ELECTED TO CONGRESS    2014

**MIA LOVE (1975–)** became the first black Republican woman elected to a seat in the House. Representing Utah, she gained national attention after addressing the Republican National Convention.

Mia Love

## 2015      BANKRUPTCY JUDGE

On September 24, **STACEY MEISEL** became the first black bankruptcy judge in the District of New Jersey.

## BARRIER-BREAKING FEDERAL    2015 PROSECUTOR

**LORETTA E. LYNCH (1959–)** became the 83rd U.S. attorney general, and the first black woman to hold that office, on April 27, 2015. She took this position at a contentious time, as tensions grew between police and minority communities nationwide.

## 2016      TOP LIBRARIAN

President Barack Obama nominated **CARLA (DIANE) HAYDEN** **(1952–)** to become the 14th librarian of Congress. On September 14,

2016, Hayden was sworn in and began her first ten-year term, becoming the first black person to hold that position. Hayden was president of the American Library Association in 2003 and 2004.

Carla Hayden

# TREND-SETTING TECHNOLOGY RECRUITER                  2016

TaskRabbit became the first company to sign on to a Congressional Black Caucus initiative to recruit more African Americans in technology from Silicon Valley's hiring practices. **STACY BROWN-PHILPOT (1975–)**, who had served as the company's chief operating officer, was promoted to CEO of TaskRabbit, one of Silicon Valley's tech start-ups and part of a small group of black women company heads in Silicon Valley.

# 2018                                      POLITICAL LEADER

Tennessee House Democrats selected a new leadership for its next legislative session and chose **KAREN CAMPER (1958–)** as House minority leader, making her the first black person in this role.

# PIONEERING MAYOR                                     2018

**LATOYA CANTRELL (1972–)** rose from membership on the city council to become the first woman of any race to serve as mayor of New Orleans. She won with 60 percent of the votes.

LaToya Cantrell

# STACEY (YVONNE) ABRAMS

## (1973–)

## Gubernatorial Candidate

In 2018 Stacey (Yvonne) Abrams became the first African American female nominee for governor of Georgia. Her political journey began in 2007, when she was elected to the Georgia House of Representatives from the 84th district and continued in 2011 when she became minority leader of the House and in 2013 when she was elected to the House representing the 89th district. In 2013 Abrams launched the New Georgia Project, which registered over 200,000 people to vote two years later. At the 2020 Democratic Convention, she was one of 17 speakers who jointly delivered the keynote address. Abrams boosted Democratic voters in Georgia, resulting in a victory in the state for Joe Biden in the 2020 U.S. presidential elections. She also successfully boosted black voters to support two black candidates for the U.S. Senate. In 2021 she was nominated for a Nobel Peace Prize for her activism supporting voter rights.

## 2018      TRAILBLAZING MAYOR

**NIKUYAH WALKER (1980–)**, an independent candidate, became the first black woman mayor of Charlottesville, Virginia. She took office just months after white nationalist rallies plunged the city into international attention. The city was a meeting place for a white supremacist rally that left one dead and several injured.

## COUNTY CRIMINAL COURT JUDGE            2018

Democrat **AUDREY FAYE MOOREHEAD (1968–)** was elected to office on November 6, becoming the first woman to be a judge of Dallas County Criminal Court #3, of Dallas, Texas. When elected, she had just completed her term on the Board of Directors of the State Bar of Texas (2015–2018) and was the only black woman on the board.

## 2018            TRAILBLAZING "BLACK GIRL MAGIC" JUDGES

Black female judicial candidates in Harris County, which includes Houston, Texas, won their races by double digits. Seventeen black women lawyers, ranging in age from 31 to the early 60s, ran for judge during midterm elections, campaigning together under the slogan "**BLACK GIRL MAGIC**," and they all won. The slogan has been used to celebrate the success of black women.

## CHIEF PUBLIC DEFENDER            2018

**MARTESHA JOHNSON (1983?–)** was sworn in as the Metropolitan Chief Public Defender in Nashville, Tennessee, August, becoming the first black to hold that post.

## 2018            BARRIER-BREAKING MAYOR

**LONDON BREED (1974–)** became the first black woman mayor of San Francisco. Raised by her grandmother in a decrepit public housing project located in what was once the heart of San Francisco's black neighborhood, she persevered through a difficult childhood and community. Both of her siblings were drug addicts, and her younger sister died of a drug overdose.

London Breed

## PIONEERING U.S. CONGRESSWOMAN 2018

*AYANNA PRESSLEY (1974–)* upended ten-term representative Michael Capuano to become the first black woman nominated for Congress in Massachusetts. A Democrat, she had a successful run for office and during the midterm elections became the first black woman to represent her state in Congress. In 2009, she was also the first black woman elected to the Boston city council.

Ayanna Pressley

## 2018 CONNECTICUT CONGRESSWOMAN

Democrat *JAHANA HAYES (1973–)* defeated a Republican candidate to become Connecticut's first black woman in Congress.

## PIONEERING STATE COURT JUDGE 2018

*RONDA COLVIN-LEARY (1971–)*, who became a state court judge, was the first black person elected to any countywide post in Gwinnett County, Georgia, and the first black to win an election for state court.

## 2019 RECORD-SETTING SUPREME COURT JUSTICE

*CHERI BEASLEY (1966–)* was sworn into office on March 7, becoming the first black woman chief justice of the North Carolina Supreme Court.

## BARRIER-BREAKING CHICAGO MAYOR 2019

*LORI LIGHTFOOT (1962–)* handily defeated another black woman candidate, Toni Preckwinkle (1947–), to become Chicago's first black and first openly gay mayor. She joined seven other black women serving as mayors of major cities in the United States.

# KAMALA (DEVI) HARRIS
## (1964–)

## U.S. Vice President

Kamala (Devi) Harris, U.S. senator from California and the daughter of immigrant parents, became the first black woman and the first South Asian American elected vice president of the United States in 2020. She was also the first of her ethnic background selected as vice presidential running mate on a major party's presidential ticket. While her selection came when the nation was grappling with racism and the COVID-19 virus, Harris declared in her acceptance speech before the Democratic Convention in August that "there is no vaccine for racism," leaving this task for the people to resolve. The Biden-Harris ticket skyrocketed among voters, and when the presidential elections ended, President Donald Trump and many of his Republican supporters refused to accept the results, claiming that the election was rigged. Lawsuits, some reaching as far as the U.S. Supreme Court, resulted in the rejection of Trump's claim. While the false claim continued, Harris still rose in popularity among the American public and worldwide.

# Religion

The African influence in America was seen early in the black family structure, in funeral practices, and later in church organizations. As independent black churches were founded, most of the organizers had no place for leadership positions for women. After early leader Richard Allen organized Bethel Methodist Church in Philadelphia in 1794, he sanctioned the inclusion of women in the ministry and authorized Jarena Lee to be an exhorter in the church.

Women of righteous discontent emerged and became vital leaders of the community, sometimes serving as traveling evangelists. Little is known about Elizabeth (whose last name is also unknown), a formerly enslaved woman from Maryland, whose ministry began in 1796. She spoke of many female preachers she had known and was accused of preaching without a license. Women became faith healers; for example, in the 1860s and 1870s, Sarah Freeman Mix, who had been healed of tuberculosis, became the nation's first recorded black healing evangelist. In 1894 Julia E. A. Foote, of the African Methodist Episcopal Zion Church, became the first woman ordained a deacon and, six years later, an elder.

After being denied access to the pulpit for many years, women finally emerged as leaders. They included Sojourner Truth, Zilpha Elaw, and Jarena Lee. Rebecca Cox established the first largely black Shaker family (or the United Society of Believers in Christ's Second

Coming) in Philadelphia. Lucy (Madden) Smith founded the inter-racial All Nations Pentecostal Church in Chicago, becoming the first woman in the city to transform the roving congregation into an established church. In 1977 Pauli Murray, lawyer, poet, scholar, author, educator, administrator, and civil rights and women's movement activist, became the first woman ordained a priest in the Episcopal Church.

Since 1984 the nation has seen the first black women bishops—Leontine T. C. Kelly in the United Methodist Church, Barbara Clementine Harris in the Anglican Church, Vashti McKenzie in the African Methodist Episcopal Church, and Teresa Elaine Jefferson-Snorton in the Christian Methodist Episcopal Church. While black women had long been members of the Jewish faith, in 2009 Alysa Stanton became the first African American woman ordained a rabbi in Jewish history. She began her new post in North Carolina. As women continued to demand equality in the 1970s, many joined the feminist movement and followed a trend called woman's theology. The term was derived from the "womanist" theory of black writer Alice Walker, who believed that the experiences of black women and white women are different. Some writers say that it resembles black theology, or the hope and liberation of women or of black people.

Black women rose above a submerged role in the black church; now they hold many leadership positions. Women preachers are easily found, as these churches depart from the early claim that they should hold subordinate roles and remain silent in the church.

## RELIGIOUS INSTRUCTION FOR NUNS    1730

The **URSULINE NUNS** of New Orleans, Louisiana, undertook efforts to instruct black Catholics; their efforts persisted until 1824. Catholic instruction for blacks was practically nonexistent in most places, and white Catholics were only somewhat better served.

## 1764                    PIONEERING SLAVE CHURCH
## FOUNDER

A slave named **ANNE SWEITZER** (Aunt Annie) was one of the founding members of the first Methodist society in the colonies, organized in Frederick County, Maryland. Blacks were members of Methodist groups from the beginning; for example, they belonged to Saint George's Methodist Church in Philadelphia, which dates to 1767, and in 1776 a black servant named Betty would be a charter member of the John Street meeting, the first society in New York City.

## PIONEERING PREACHER 1817

*JARENA LEE (1783–1864)* was the first woman to preach in the African Methodist Episcopal (AME) Church. After hearing Richard Allen preach, she experienced conversion and later felt a call to preach. Although never formally licensed to speak by the church, Lee began an extraordinary career as an evangelist. She began her work as leader of a predominantly female praying and singing band, later becoming an evangelist. Lee and other women made a considerable impact on religious life and the growth of their denomination.

Jarena Lee

## 1824 VISIONARY RELIGIOUS GROUP

The first attempt to build a community of black nuns was the formation of an auxiliary group to the *SISTERS OF LORETTO* in Loretto, Kentucky. This group consisted of three free black women whose names were not recorded. The attempt did not outlive the stay of the sponsoring priest, who soon left for Missouri.

## VISIONARY RELIGIOUS ORDER 1829

On July 2, the first permanent order of black Catholic nuns, the *OBLATE SISTERS OF PROVIDENCE*, was founded in Baltimore, Maryland. This teaching order was formally recognized October 2, 1831. The sisters opened the first Catholic school for girls in 1843. The school survives today as the Child Development Center and Reading and Math Center, established in 1972.

## 1859 RELIGIOUS DENOMINATION FOUNDER

*REBECCA COX JACKSON (1795–1871)* established the first largely black Shaker family in Philadelphia. A religious visionary, Jackson became an itinerant preacher and spiritual autobiographer. She joined praying bands influenced by the Holiness movement within the Methodist church.

## PIONEERING HEALING EVANGELIST                      1860s–70s

*SARAH FREEMAN (MRS. EDWARD) MIX (1832–1884)*, who had been healed of tuberculosis, became the nation's first recorded black healing evangelist around this time. Mix was so well respected for her accomplishments that doctors sent their patients to her for prayer.

## 1888              FIRST OVERSEAS MISSIONARY

The first woman missionary of the African Methodist Episcopal Church appointed to a foreign field was *SARAH E. GORHAM (1832–1894)*.

## PASSIONATE DEACON                                 1894

*JULIA A. J. FOOTE (1823–1901)*, of the African Methodist Episcopal (AME) Zion Church, became the first woman ordained a deacon on May 20, 1894. Bishop Alexander Walters ordained two black women elders in the AME Zion Church—*MARY J. SMALL (1850–1845)* in 1898 and Foote in 1900. They became the first women of any race in the Methodist denomination to achieve the full rights that ordination as an elder provided.

## 1898                              PIONEERING ELDER

*MARY J. SMALL (1850–1945)* became the first Methodist woman to be ordained an elder. Her status infuriated some of the male clergy, who thought it inappropriate for women to hold such status. She was an officer in the Women's Home and Foreign Missionary Society and also belonged to the Women's Christian Temperance Union. She was licensed as an evangelist and missionary in 1892.

## COMMISSIONED DEACON                          1901

*ANNA HALL (1870–1964)* was commissioned this year, becoming the first black graduate deaconess of the African Methodist Episcopal Church. She went to Liberia and remained for 24 years, working as evangelist, dentist, nurse, teacher, and in other capacities. In 1952 the Liberian Church named a mission station in her honor.

## 1904   RELIGIOUS ORGANIZATION FOUNDER

*MARY LARK HILL* sought to bridge the gap between women in all denominations and to encourage and advance women preachers. About 1904 she founded an organization known as the First Church of the Women's E. W. of A., or Queen Esther Mission, located in Chicago. Most of the officers and members were women preachers who were now united in their efforts to spread the gospel.

## FIRST COGIC WOMEN'S DEPARTMENT   1911

Mother *LIZZIE WOODS ROBINSON (1860–1945)* was the first to organize a women's department in the Church of God in Christ. She was born a slave in Phillips County, Arkansas, and learned to read the Bible by the time she was eight years old.

## 1916            CHANGING-MAKING GOSPEL
## RADIO PREACHER

*LUCY (TURNER) SMITH (1874–1952)* founded the interracial All Nations Pentecostal Church in Chicago, becoming the first woman in the city to transform the roving congregation into an established church. She was said to be known as the "preacher to the disinherited class." In 1925 Elder Smith, as she became known, first broadcast her Sunday night services over radio station WSBC; later, station WIND aired her services on Sundays and Wednesdays. She was the first black religious leader to broadcast services on the air. In 1933 she became a pioneer in black gospel radio, exposing her ministry over the air to wider audiences. She was the first in the city to mix gospel programming with appeals for the poor.

# NANNIE HELEN BURROUGHS

## (1879–1961)

Pioneering Elder

Nannie Helen Burroughs first proposed Women's Day celebrations in churches in Memphis, Tennessee, in September 1907. When she presented a resolution for Woman's Day (as it was first called), she was dubbed an "upstart" and the day was criticized as only tokenism for women. The purpose of this national observance day was to stimulate women's interest in local churches to raise money for foreign missions—then the primary interest of the Woman's Convention. At first, women were not allowed in the pulpit on Women's Day celebrations, but Women's Day observations in churches now provide women an opportunity to lead the worship service and deliver sermons.

## PENTECOSTAL CHURCH LEADER                    1924

**IDA BELL ROBINSON (1891–1946)** founded what became the first sizeable black Pentecostal denomination headed by a woman. The new body, Mount Sinai Holy Church of America, was chartered in Philadelphia this year. The affiliate of the United Holy Church was fertile ground for Robinson, who began to attract people to her small congregation. Robinson was concerned about the church's restriction on female ordination, especially since she had so many women parishioners and they demanded a more active role in the church. She left the United Holy Church and established a denomination to "loosen (women) from the bondage of male domination."

# 1936                              ORDAINED ELDER

**LAURA J. LANGE (1879–1948)** was the first woman ordained a local elder in the Methodist Episcopal Church, by the Lexington Conference. Lange had been made a deacon in 1926. It would not be until 1956 that a black woman would be ordained an elder and admitted into full connection in an annual conference. This woman was **SALLIE A. CRENSHAW (1900–1986)**.

# RELIGIOUS GUEST SPEAKER                              1968

**CORETTA SCOTT KING (1927–2006)** was the first woman of any race to preach at Saint Paul's Cathedral in London, England.

# 1971      CHURCH WOMEN'S ORGANIZATION

**CLARIE COLLINS HARVEY (1916–1995)** became the first black to head Church Women United. Harvey was a Mississippi businesswoman, a civil rights activist, and a church worker.

# FIRST ORDAINED PRESBYTERIAN              1974
# WOMAN

**KATIE GENEVA CANNON (1950–2018**) was ordained on April 23, becoming the first black woman ordained in the Presbyterian Church.

# 1976        NATIONAL CHURCH MODERATOR

**THELMA DAVIDSON ADAIR (1920–)** became the first black woman moderator of the United Presbyterian Church.

# FIRST WOMAN PRIEST                                    1977

On January 8, 1977, *(ANNA) PAULINE "PAULI"*
*MURRAY (1910–1985)* became the first woman
ordained a priest in the Protestant Episcopal
Church. Murray was active in movements to foster
racial and gender equality in the United States. In
fall 1938, for example, she sought admission to the
graduate school at the University of North Carolina
but was denied admission due to her race. Her
efforts became public news nationwide and were the
first of their kind to receive wide attention. In 1978
the university offered to award Murray an honorary
degree; she refused the degree because the univer-

Pauli Murray

sity system failed to implement an appropriate plan
to desegregate its 16 campuses. Murray's interest in civil rights was
demonstrated also in March 1940 when she and a friend, Adelene
McBean, were arrested in Virginia for refusing to move to the back
of a Greyhound bus into a broken seat. While in jail for three days,
the women drafted a "Statement of Fact." In 1946 vindication came
for the two women in the *Morgan v. Virginia* case, which declared the
state's Jim Crow statute invalid. In January 1946, Murray became the
first black deputy attorney general of California. In 1965 she received
the Doctor of Juridical Science from Yale University's law school, the
first person to receive this degree from Yale. Murray became active in
women's rights. She was ordained an Episcopal priest on January 8,
1977, at the National Cathedral in Washington, D.C., the first black
woman ordained a priest in the church's 200-year history.


# 1982                                    PRIEST IN FLORIDA

*WINNIE McKENZIE BOLLE (1924–)* was the first black, and the first
woman, priest in the Diocese of Southeast Florida.


# PRIEST IN NEW JERSEY                                    1982

*GAYLE ELIZABETH HARRIS (1951–)* was the first black woman priest
in the Diocese of Newark, New Jersey.

## 1982                PRIEST IN NEW YORK CITY

**SANDRA ANTOINETTE WILSON** became the first woman priest of the Protestant Episcopal Church in the New York City Archdiocese on January 25, 1982.

## RELIGIOUS CONVENTION LEADER      1982

**CYNTHIA LYNETTE HALE (1952–)** became the first woman president of the predominantly black National Convocation of the Christian Church (Disciples of Christ). Hale was chaplain at the Federal Correctional Institute in Butner, Alabama, and others in Colorado and North Carolina, becoming the first female chaplain to serve in all-male correctional institutions.

## 1983                  WOMEN ORDAINED

The **SOUTH CAROLINA BAPTIST EDUCATIONAL AND MISSIONARY CONVENTION** authorized the ordination of women. This was the first state organization in the National Baptist Convention to do so.

## RELIGIOUS COUNCIL OFFICIAL        1983

**DEBORAH CANNON PARTRIDGE WOLFE (1916–2004)** was the first Baptist woman president of the Clergy Council of Cranford, New Jersey.

## 1983                  BAPTIST PREACHER

As pastor of Mariner's Temple Baptist Church in New York City, **SUZAN DENISE JOHNSON (1957–)** was the first black, and the first female, pastor in the American Baptist Churches USA.

# YVONNE REED CHAPPELLE (SEON)

## (1937–)

### Ordained Church Woman

In 1981 Yvonne Reed Chappelle, also known as Yvonne Seon and "Mama Inga," became the first black woman ordained in the Unitarian Universalist Church. During the 1960s, she spent two years in the Congo. While there, she was secretary to the High Commission on the Inga Dam, one of the first positions as a foreign affairs officer in the Office of International Conferences. When the Fourteenth General Assembly of UNESCO met in Paris, she was the first African American selected as secretary of the delegation, the chief administrative officer.

## VISIONARY RELIGIOUS LEADER                    1984

*LEONTINE T(URPEAU CURRENT) KELLY (1920–2012)*, trailblazer, spiritual mother, and champion of women of color in leadership, became the first woman bishop of a major denomination, the United Methodist Church. She was consecrated on July 20, 1984. In addition, she was the first woman of any race to preach on the program *National Radio Pulpit* of the National Council of Churches and the first black woman to preside at a General Conference of the church.

## 1986                    INTERFAITH COUNCIL

*CHRISTINE E. TRIGG (1928–2016)* was the first woman president of the New Jersey Council of Churches. Trigg was a member of the Clinton Memorial African Methodist Episcopal Zion Church in Newark, New Jersey.

## LOCAL CHURCH MODERATOR                    1989

*SARA BROWN CORDERY (1920–2007)* was the first black woman moderator of the Presbytery of Baltimore. From 1991 to 1994, she was moderator of the Presbyterian Women Churchwide, becoming the first black woman to hold that post.

## 1989                                            PIONEERING BISHOP

**BARBARA CLEMENTINE HARRIS (1930–2020)** became the first woman Anglican bishop in the world. On February 12, she was consecrated suffragan bishop in the Diocese of Massachusetts. She was ordained to the diaconate in 1979 and served as deacon-in-training at the Church of the Advocate. She was ordained to the priesthood in 1980.

## CHURCH LEADER                                                  1989

**JOAN SALMON CAMPBELL (1938–2019)** was the first black woman and only the sixth woman to head the Presbyterian Church (USA).

## 1990                                                PARISH LEADER

The first black nun to head a parish in the United States was **SISTER CORA BILLINGS (1939–)**, in Richmond, Virginia. In 1999 she was diocesan director for Black Catholics.

## RELIGIOUS DENOMINATION LEADER          1995

**G. ELAINE SMITH** was elected president of the American Baptist Churches USA, becoming the first black woman to hold that position.

## 1996          BOUNDARY-BREAKING CHURCH LEADER

**HARRIET TUCKER WATKINS (1945–2015)** was ordained in the Peachtree Baptist Church in Atlanta; this was the first time the church had ordained a woman. This year she also became assistant pastor of the predominantly white church. A dozen Confederate soldiers are buried in the church cemetery. Tucker held membership in the

Southern Baptist Convention—an organization that is overwhelmingly white in membership.

## FIRST WOMAN PRIEST                                  1997

**ANNA MARTIN HENDERSON (1942–2015)** was named vicar at St. Anselm's Episcopal Church in Nashville, Tennessee, becoming the first black woman priest at the church and the only black priest among 80 in the Middle Tennessee diocese. She was also the only black woman and the fifth black among more than 200 Episcopal priests in the state.

## 2000    CHURCH DISTRICT SUPERINTENDENT

**BETTYE LEWIS** was named a district superintendent for the Tennessee Conference, becoming the first black woman to hold this position.

## HISTORY-MAKING *RABBI*                              2009

**ALYSA STANTON (1963–)** became the first African American woman ordained a rabbi in Jewish history. She was formally ordained on June 6 by Rabbi David Ellenson, president of Hebrew Union College–Jewish Institute of Religion in Cincinnati, where Stanton completed several years of rabbinical training. She began her new post at Congregation Bayt Shalom in Greeneville, North Carolina, on August 1. Her synagogue is affiliated with the Reform and Conservative movements. Her appointment made her the first black woman rabbi to lead a majority white congregation; about 60 families comprise the congregation.

Alysa Stanton

## 2010                              CME CHURCH BISHOP

**TERESA E. JEFFERSON-SNORTON (1955–)** became the 59th bishop and the first female bishop elected in the Christian Methodist Episcopal (CME) Church on June 30 in Mobile, Alabama. Her assignment was as presiding bishop of the new Eleven Episcopal District, which

# VASHTI MURPHY McKENZIE

## (1947–)

Glass Ceiling–breaking Bishops

On July 11, 2000, Vashti Murphy McKenzie became the first woman elected bishop in the African Methodist Episcopal (AME) Church. McKenzie became bishop of the 18th Episcopal District in southeast Africa that includes Lesotho, Botswana, Swaziland, and Mozambique. In 1997 *Ebony* magazine named McKenzie one of its "Fifteen Greatest African-American Preachers" and placed her at the top of the list.

included 11 countries in Central, Southern, and East Africa. She later was assigned to the Fifth Episcopal District, which includes Alabama and Florida.

## HISTORY-MAKING BISHOP                    2016

In a historic election, **SHARMA LEWIS (1963–)** of the North Georgia Conference became the first black female bishop elected in the Southeastern Jurisdiction and the first black woman elected bishop in the denomination since 2000. Lewis had many other firsts in her ministry: she was the first female senior pastor and first black pastor of Powers Ferry United Methodist Church; the first woman to serve as senior minister of Wesley Chapel United Methodist Church; and the first woman to serve as district superintendent of the Atlanta-Decatur-Oxford District. She was also the first woman to receive the G. Ross Freeman Leadership Award given by the United Methodist Men—an award for engaging men in ministry.

# Science and Medicine

Many changes in science and medicine have come through the contributions of black women. The history of Africans in medicine shows that as enslaved people, they lived in unsanitary conditions, were concerned about their health, and used homeland knowledge of herbs, barks, and other items found in everyday life to create cures. Herb or root healers dispensed medicine for the treatment of the enslaved and their masters. In addition to the self-trained practitioners during the slavery period, some early black physicians were also self-taught while others were trained by apprenticeship. Despite these developments, black women's involvement in medical developments was slow to come.

Racial disparities denied blacks access to mainstream medical facilities, formal training, and recognitions of their inventions. They responded by developing their own facilities, medical schools, and hospitals, and finally they obtained patents for their inventions. Finally, we see evidence of black women's involvement in science, medicine, and inventions.

In 1864, Rebecca Davis Lee Crumpler, a student at New England Female Medical College, became the first black woman awarded a medical degree in the United States. Women achieved in dentistry as well. Ida Gray Nelson Rollins was the first black woman to earn a doctor of dental surgery degree in the United States. L. Eudora Ashburne Evans, who was educated at historically black Howard University's medical school, was the first black woman to graduate from the school. Howard was also the first historically black college or university (HBCU) to establish a medical school. It was not until 1951 that Harvard University's medical school graduated a black woman, Mildred Fay Jefferson.

The first two black women to graduate from veterinary schools and to receive the doctorate in veterinary medicine were Jane Hinton and Alfreda Johnson Webb. Both graduated in 1949. Webb received her degree from Tuskegee University, the only HBCU to establish a veterinary school specifically to train black veterinarians.

Black women achievers in science and space included three women pioneers—Mary Jackson, Katherine Johnson, and Dorothy Vaughan, who were the first black women to perform complex calculations that led to Americans' venture into space. When the space program finally acknowledged their contributions, they were called "hidden figures." Mae C. Jemison, the first black woman astronaut, boarded the space shuttle *Endeavor* in 1992 as science mission specialist on the historic eight-day flight.

First black women inventors include Sarah Elisabeth Goode, who patented a folding cabinet bed in 1885; she is said to be the first known black woman to secure a patent. Sarah Boone invented the collapsible ironing board. Gladys (Brown) West, another "hidden figure" in black women's history, has been credited with inventing the global positioning system (GPS). Patricia E. Bath discovered and invented Laserphaco Probe, a new device for cataract surgery, and became the first black woman doctor to receive a patent for medical purposes. The importance of black hair care stimulated Marjorie Stewart Joyner to patent a permanent waving machine for hairstyling. With this machine, she became one of the first black women to receive a patent for an invention.

Black women continue to become pioneers in science and medicine. As evidence of this, Valerie Montgomery Rice is the first female president and dean of the medical school at historically black Morehouse College. The recent success of Kizzmekia "Kizzy" Corbett, the lead scientist in COVID-19 vaccine research for the Moderna/National Institutes of Health joint program, is credited for developing a vaccine to combat the virus and save thousands of lives worldwide.

# ARMY NURSE                                              1863

***SUSIE KING TAYLOR (1848–1912)*** was the first black army nurse in U.S. history, serving with the First Regiment of the South Carolina

Volunteers. While she first served as a laundress who cared for uniforms, bandages, and other supplies, she soon began assisting military surgeons by caring for the sick.

# 1864 PIONEERING PHYSICIAN

**REBECCA DAVIS LEE CRUMPLER (1831–1895)** was the first black woman awarded a medical degree in the United States. She completed the four-year medical program at the New England Female Medical College in Boston, and on March 11, 1864, she was awarded the doctress of medicine degree. When the Civil War ended, Crumpler returned to her Richmond hometown to work with the Freedmen's Bureau, providing health care and treatment to newly freed blacks who had no medical provisions. After returning to Boston in 1869, she may have continued her practice; whatever the case, there is no indication that she was in active practice after 1883. In honor of her pioneer work in the medical profession, the first medical society for black women was founded and named the Rebecca Lee Society.

# BOUNDARY-BREAKING MEDICAL DOCTOR 1870

**SUSAN (MARIA) McKINNEY STEWARD (1847–1918)** was the first black woman to graduate from a New York state medical school. After graduating from New York Medical College for Women on March 23, 1870, she practiced in Brooklyn for more than 20 years. In 1873 she became the first black woman doctor to be formally certified. Steward worked to enhance the cause of women in medicine and was a founder of the Women's Loyal Union of New York and Brooklyn. In 1881 she cofounded the Women's Hospital and Dispensary in Brooklyn. In 1882 she served on the medical staff of the New York Hospital for Women.

Susan McKinney Steward

# 1872 PIONEERING MEDICAL DOCTOR

**REBECCA J. COLE (1846–1922)** was the first black woman to establish a medical practice in Pennsylvania. Cole became the first black graduate of the Female Medical College of Pennsylvania in 1867. From 1872 to 1881, she was resident physician at New York Infirmary for Women and Children, a health care facility that women physicians owned and operated. She and another woman physician, Charlotte Abbey, began Women's Directory Center in Philadelphia, providing medical and legal services to Philadelphia's destitute women and children.

## PIONEERING BLACK GRADUATE NURSE 1879

**MARY ELIZABETH MAHONEY (1845–1926)** became the first black graduate nurse in the United States. She was 33 years old in 1878 when she entered the New England Hospital for Women and Children to begin a 16-month course in nursing. Mahoney was a strong supporter of the women's suffrage movement and became one of the first women in her city to register to vote in 1921, at the age of 76.

## 1885          TIRELESS CHAMPION INVENTOR

Sarah E. Goode

The first known black woman inventor is **SARAH E(LISABETH) GOODE (1855–1905)**, who patented a folding cabinet bed on July 14, 1885. Since ethnic identity is not part of a patent application, it is impossible to be sure of absolute priority. Another black woman might be the first, since Ellen F. Eglin (1836–1916) of Washington, D.C., invented a clothes wringer before April 1890. While no patent was issued in her name, Eglin sold the idea to an agent. At the beginning of the twentieth century, Miriam E. Benjamin (1861–1947) of Massachusetts, who patented a gong signal system for summoning attendants on July 17, 1888, was believed to be the first; her invention was adopted by the U.S. House of Representatives to summon pages.

## FIRST BLACK NURSING SCHOOL          1886

**SPELMAN SEMINARY** (now Spelman College) in Atlanta, Georgia, began the first nursing school for black women. Blacks were forced to organize schools of their own for the training of nurses, and the number of African American graduate nurses steadily rose. Spelman's nursing school flourished until 1921.

## 1890                PIONEERING DENTIST

**IDA (GRAY NELSON) ROLLINS (1867–1953)** became the first black woman to earn a doctorate in dental surgery in the United States. She graduated from the University of Michigan in June. After graduation, she established a dental practice in Cincinnati and served all races and ages and both women and men. She moved to Chicago and opened an office there. She appears to have been the first black woman to establish a dental practice in Chicago.

## PIONEERING MEDICAL DOCTOR       1891

**HALLE TANNER DILLON JOHNSON (1864–1901)** became the first black woman to practice medicine in Alabama and also the first woman ever admitted on examination to practice medicine in that state. She also became the first black physician to do so. She established a Nurses' Training School and Lafayette Dispensary at Tuskegee.

## 1892    RECORD-BREAKING PATENT-HOLDER

**SARAH BOONE (1832–1904)** was the first person to receive a patent for an ironing board. Her invention was a narrow board with a padded cover and collapsible legs, an improvement over the existing boards that were placed across chairs for support.

## COLORADO'S FIRST BLACK WOMAN     1902
## PHYSICIAN

**JUSTINA L(AURENA) FORD (1871–1952)** became the first black woman licensed to practice medicine in Colorado. She was also the first black woman physician to practice in the Rocky Mountain West. She settled in Denver around 1902, received her state license, and established a medical practice. At first neither Ford nor black patients had access to the Denver General Hospital; consequently, Ford delivered health care to homes in Denver and the surrounding area. Only 15 percent of her patients were black. Because she delivered over 7,000 babies, she became known as the "Baby Doctor."

Justina L. Ford

## 1909                          PIONEERING DENTIST

***GERTRUDE ELIZABETH CURTIS McPHERSON (1880–1973)*** became the first black woman to pass the New York State Board of Dentistry. She began her practice in 1909.

## BLACK MEDICAL SCHOOL GRADUATE    1912

***L. EUDORA ASHBURNE EVANS (1887?–1992)*** became the first black woman to graduate from historically black Howard University Medical School and the first black woman licensed to practice general medicine in Virginia.

## 1915                     HISTORIC MEDICAL FACILITY

Walden Hospital, the first and only black-owned and -operated hospital in Chattanooga, Tennessee, was dedicated on July 30. ***EMMA ROCHELLE WHEELER (1882–1957)***, a trailblazing physician, was founder and operator.

## RED CROSS NURSE                              1916

The first black nurse to enroll officially in the Red Cross nursing service was ***FRANCES ELLIOTT DAVIS (1883–1965)***.

# 1916          TREND-SETTING PHARMACIST

***ELLA P. STEWART (1893–1987)*** was the first black woman graduate of the University of Pittsburgh School of Pharmacy. She was also the first black woman to pass the Pennsylvania State Board of Pharmacy.

# PIONEERING SCIENCE WRITER          1924

***ROGER ARLINER YOUNG (1899–1964)*** published her first scientific paper, "On the Excretory Apparatus in the Paramecium," in the September 12, 1924, issue of *Science*, making her the first black woman to research and publish professionally in the field of science. A zoologist, she became a research assistant for eminent scholar Ernest Everett Just (1883–1941).

# 1926          HARLEM'S PIONEERING INTERN

***MAY EDWARD CHINN (1896–1980)*** was the first black woman to intern at Harlem Hospital. She was also the first black woman to practice medicine in Harlem, the first to receive admitting privileges at Harlem Hospital, the first woman physician to ride with Harlem Hospital's ambulance crews on emergency calls, and the first black woman to graduate from the University of Bellevue Medical Center.

# RECORD-SETTING SCIENTIST          1935

***ROGER ARLINER YOUNG (1899–1964)*** received a doctorate in zoology, becoming the first black woman to do so. She conducted research with biologist Ernest Everett Just and in 1924 published her first article in *Science*, making her the first black woman in her field to conduct research and publish the findings professionally.

# 1936          NURSING ADMINISTRATOR

***ESTELLE MASSEY OSBORNE (1901–1981)*** was the first black director of nursing at City Hospital No. 2 (now the Homer G. Phillips Hospital Training School). She had been the first black nursing instructor at Harlem Hospital School of Nursing and later the first educational

# MARJORIE STEWART JOYNER

## (1896–1994)

### Inventor

Marjorie Stewart Joyner was the first black to patent a permanent waving machine for hairstyling and, in 1928, became one of the first black women to receive a patent for an invention. She later developed a hair-straightening comb. Joyner was an employee of Madame C. J. Walker, to whose company the patent was assigned. She eventually became national supervisor of the Walker organization's chain of beauty schools. In 1916 Joyner opened her own salon.

director of nursing at Freedmen's Hospital School of Nursing (now the Howard University College of Nursing). In 1943 as the first black consultant on the staff of any national organization (in this case, the National Nursing Council for War Service), she more than doubled the number of white nursing schools to admit blacks. In 1948 Osborne was the first recipient of a master's degree in nursing education from Teachers College of Columbia University. She was the first black member of the nursing faculty at New York University, and she also became the first black to hold office in the American Nurses Association.

## HISTORY-MAKING SURGEON IN THE SOUTH                                  1948

**DOROTHY LAVINIA "DR. D" BROWN (1919–2004)** was the first black woman appointed to a residency as a general surgeon in the South. Born in Philadelphia to a young unwed mother, Brown lived in an orphanage from age five months to age 13. Reunited with her mother for a brief period, she was then hired out as a domestic. With the support of the Women's Division of Christian Service of the Methodist Church in Troy, New York, Brown received a scholarship for study at the Methodist-

Dorothy Lavinia "Dr. D" Brown

affiliated Bennett College for Women in Greensboro, North Carolina. She graduated in 1948 with an M.D. and interned at Harlem Hospital in New York City. Brown then took a residency in general surgery at George Hubbard Hospital in Nashville, Tennessee. Later, when she was 40 years old and unmarried, she became the first single black woman in Tennessee to adopt a child.

## 1949          PIONEERING VETERINARIANS

The first two black women to graduate from veterinary school and to receive the doctorate in veterinary medicine degree were *JANE HINTON (1919–2003)* and *ALFREDA JOHNSON WEBB (1923–1992)*.

## FORGOTTEN SCIENTISTS                    1950s

*MARY JACKSON (1921–2005), KATHERINE JOHNSON (1918–2020),* and *DOROTHY VAUGHAN (1910–2008)* became part of the National Advisory Committee for Aeronautics (NACA), the precursor to the National Aeronautics and Space Administration (NASA). These three human "computers," known as the "West Computers," were the first black women to perform complex calculations that led to Americans venturing into space. Their calculations plotted the path for Alan Shepard's historic and record-setting journey into space in 1961, and they allowed other space heroes like Neil Armstrong and John Glenn to have successful space flights, too. Until 2016, when their work with NASA was published in the book *Hidden Figures*, their work remained obscured from the public. In 2016 the Oscar-nominated film *Hidden Figures,* based on the book of the same title, was released and brought the women and their work the widespread attention that they deserved. All mathematicians, the women did the same work as their white counterparts in the NASA Langley Research Center in Hampton, Virginia, yet, due to racial discrimination, they were paid less and were relegated to separate dining facilities and bathrooms.

Mary Jackson

Katherine Johnson

Their education paralleled that of the white women, yet they were required to retake courses that they had already passed in college, and they were never considered for promotion within NACA. Johnson graduated *summa cum laude* from historically black West Virginia State University. She was the only woman among the three students who desegregated West Virginia University's graduate school. In 1952 NACA hired her for its space program. Johnson's team was assigned "to trace out in extreme detail Freedom 7's exact path from lift off to splashdown." The project was highly successful and led NASA to aim for the nation's first orbital mission. In 2015 President Barack Obama presented her with the Presidential Medal of Freedom. NASA honored her in 2017 by naming a new research building after her. By this time, Johnson was the only living member of her team. Vaughan graduated from historically black Wilberforce University in 1919. An expert FORTRAN programmer, she joined Langley Memorial Aeronautical Laboratory in 1943; in 1949 she became NACA's first black supervisor in the all-black "West Computing" unit and was a steadfast advocate for women in her unit. The third woman in the group, Jackson, joined NACA in 1951, and in 1958 she became NASA's first black female engineer. She took a demotion and filled the position of federal women's program manager at Langley. There she impacted the hiring and promotion of the next generation of NASA female mathematicians, engineers, and scientists.

Dorothy Vaughan

## 1950      PROMINENT FELLOW IN SURGERY ORGANIZATION

**HELEN OCTAVIA DICKENS (1909–2001)** became the first black woman admitted as a fellow of the American College of Surgeons. Dickens was long recognized in the medical profession and in academia for her research on intensive medical, psychological, educational, and social services intervention with socially deprived pregnant teenagers and their families.

## RACIAL BARRIER-BREAKING                1951
## MEDICAL STUDENT

The first black woman to graduate from Harvard University's Medical School was **MILDRED FAY JEFFERSON (1927–2010)**.

# 1955        BOUNDARY-BREAKING PHARMACOLOGIST

***DOLORES COOPER SHOCKLEY (1930–2020)*** became the first black woman to receive a doctorate in pharmacology from Purdue University.

## DENTAL SCHOOL EDUCATOR        1967

***JULIANN STEPHANIE BLUITT (FOSTER) (1938–2019)*** became the first black to teach full-time in Northwestern University's Dental School. She accepted that post at a time when the dental school decided to upgrade its dental hygiene program to departmental status and needed to strengthen its faculty.

# 1967    PIONEERING MEDICAL SCHOOL DEAN

Jane Cooke Wright

***JANE COOKE WRIGHT (1919–2013)*** was America's first black woman associate dean of a major medical school, New York Medical College. She received her medical degree from New York Medical College in 1945. She had appointments at Harlem Hospital and its Cancer Research Foundation and began teaching at New York Medical School in 1955. In July 1967 she became associate dean and professor of surgery at her alma mater. In 1971 she became the first woman elected president of the New York Cancer Society.

## NURSING SCHOOL DEAN        1969

***ANNA BAILEY COLES (1925–2015)*** became the founding dean of Howard University's College of Nursing. The school was formed when a 1967 act of Congress called for the transfer of Freedmen's Hospital School of Nursing to Howard. Freedmen's admitted its last class in 1970 and graduated its last class in 1973. Altogether, 1,700 nurses had graduated from the school.

## 1970s–1980s      TRAILBLAZING INVENTOR

**GLADYS (BROWN) WEST (1930–)**, "a hidden figure" in black women's history, has been credited with inventing the global positioning system (GPS). West was finally recognized for her work on December 6, 2018, when the U.S. Air Force honored her at the Pentagon and inducted her into the Air Force Space and Missile Pioneers Hall of Fame.

Gladys West

## TEACHING HOSPITAL DIRECTOR      1971

The first black woman to head a major teaching hospital was **FLORENCE SMALL GAYNOR (1920–1993)**. She became the new executive director of the Sydenham Hospital in the Harlem section of New York City.

## 1973      ZOO VETERINARIAN

**ROSALIE A. REED (1945–)** became the first woman veterinarian employed by the Los Angeles Zoo—the nation's third largest zoo. She was also the first woman veterinarian at a major American zoo.

## NIH NURSING CHIEF      1973

The first black nurse to become chief of the Nursing Department at the National Institutes of Health in Washington, D.C., was **VERNICE FERGUSON (1928–2012)**.

## 1975      DENTAL SCHOOL DEAN

The first woman to become dean of a dental school in the United States was **JEANNE FRANCES CRAIG SINKFORD (1933–)**. She chaired the prosthodontics department at Howard University, becoming the first woman in the country to administer such a unit. Sinkford served as associate dean from 1967 to 1974, and on July 1, 1975, she broke racial and gender barriers when she was appointed dean. Her induction into the International College of Dentists made her the first American woman dentist to receive this honor.

## TRAILBLAZING ALTERNATE ASTRONAUT                    1976

The first woman scientist trained to be an astronaut was **PATRICIA S(UZANNE) COWINGS (1948–)**. An alternate in the early astronaut period, she preceded Sally Ride's appointment but never had a chance to fly. The Spacelab Mission Development-3 was a joint effort between the Johnson Space Center and the Ames Research Center. It was the first simulation of a life-sciences-dedicated space shuttle mission. Cowings and Richard Grindeland were the backup payload specialists for the program; they were in intense training for nearly two years. Cowings became a research psychologist with the National Aeronautical and Space Administration (NASA).

Patricia S. Cowings

## 1977          SMITHSONIAN MUSEUM ADMINISTRATOR

**MARGARET SANTIAGO (1931–2018)** was the first black to become registrar of a major scientific museum, the Smithsonian's National Museum of Natural History.

## RACIAL BARRIER–BREAKING OPTOMETRIST                    1978

The first black woman optometrist in Mississippi was **LINDA DIANNE JOHNSON (1954–)**, director of optometry for the Jackson-Hinds Comprehensive Health Center in Jackson. In 1997 she was elected president of the National Optometric Association.

## 1982          WOMEN'S HEALTH CONFERENCE

The National Black Women's Health Project (NBWHP) held the first national conference on black women's health issues. The NBWHP was founded under the leadership of **BYLLYE Y. AVERY (1937–)**. It aimed to mobilize black women to take charge of their lives and also improve their health. Avery also cofounded the Women's Health Center in Gainesville, Florida, to provide an alternative birthing place for women in the city.

## PIONEERING NEUROSURGEON          1984

**ALEXIA IRENE CANADY (1950–)** was the first black woman neurosurgeon in the United States. In 1977 she became the first woman, and the first black, neurosurgical resident at the University of Minnesota.

## 1984          REHABILITATION CENTER ADMINISTRATOR

**JANE MORGAN LYONS (1928–2013)** was the first black woman to serve as chief executive officer of Sea View Hospital Rehabilitation Center and Home in Staten Island, New York.

## FIRST KNOWN MULTIPLE BIRTHS          1984

The nation's first known black quintuplets were born. The Gaither quintuplets—Joshua Frank Johnson, Brandon Burrus, **ASHLEE CHARLENE, RENEE BROOKS,** and **RHEALYN FRANCES**—were born four weeks premature to Sidney and Suzanne Gaither. The quintuplets were conceived without the use of fertility drugs.

## 1986          RECORD-SETTING INVENTOR

**PATRICIA E. BATH (1942–2019)** discovered and invented the Laserphaco Probe, a new device for cataract surgery. She was also the first black woman doctor to receive a patent for a medical purpose. An ophthalmologist and laser scientist, Bath advocated for blindness prevention, treatment, and cure. Later, she held four patents. In 1974 Bath

Patricia E. Bath

became the first woman ophthalmologist appointed to the faculty of the University of California at Los Angeles School of Medicine's Jules Stein Eye Institute. In 1983 she was the first woman to chair an ophthalmology residency program in the United States.

## MEDICAL SCHOOL DEAN                                1993

**BARBARA ROSS-LEE (194?–)**, a practicing family physician, naval officer, and medical educator, was named dean of Michigan State University's College of Osteopathic Medicine in East Lansing, Michigan. She took the position on August 1, to become the first black woman to head a medical school in the United States.

## 1994                      MEDICAL BOARD MEMBER

**VALERIE WALKER** became a member of the Missouri Board of Registration for the Healing Arts, the first black woman to serve in this capacity.

## CHANGE-MAKING BLACK MEDICAL          1997
## SCHOOL DEAN

The first woman dean of the School of Medicine at Meharry Medical College in Nashville, Tennessee, was **ANNA CHERRIE EPPS (1930–2017)**. She held the post from July 1, 1997, until 2002. In 1999 she became senior vice president of academic affairs, the first woman to hold that post.

## 1997                      FIRST BLACK SEXTUPLETS

**JACQUELINE** and Linden **THOMPSON**, of Washington, D.C., gave birth to the first black sextuplets in the United States. Although one

## MAE (CAROLE) JEMISON

### (1956–)

Record-shattering Astronaut

Mae (Carole) Jemison was named the first black woman astronaut in 1987. On September 12, 1992, she boarded the space shuttle *Endeavor* as science mission specialist on the historic eight-day flight. Jemison left the National Aeronautics and Space Administration (NASA) in 1993 and founded a private firm, the Jemison Group. The firm specializes in projects that integrate science issues into the design, development, and implementation of technologies. She also became professor of environmental studies at Dartmouth College and directs the Jemison Institute for Advancing Technology in Developing Countries. After receiving her medical degree from Cornell Medical School in 1981, she worked as a staff physician for the Peace Corps for two and a half years in Sierra Leone.

daughter was stillborn, there were five girls and one boy. Born at Georgetown University Medical Center, they were delivered by cesarean section and each weighed between two pounds and two pounds, six ounces. The surviving children had no health problems.

## FIRST BLACK SURVIVING SEXTUPLETS   1997

Doctors **PAULA R. MAHONE** and **KAREN L. DRAKE** made medical history when they delivered the first sextuplets born alive in the United States at the Iowa Methodist Medical Center in Des Moines, Iowa. Highly respected in the field of perinatology, the women were concerned that some of the embryos might not survive and were excited when they did.

## 1997                                EXPERIMENTAL PATIENT

The first person in the United States to undergo experimental laser heart surgery was **DOROTHY WALKER (1940?–)**. The procedure, performed at Northwestern Memorial Hospital, is less painful and requires a shorter recovery time than previous methods.

## NURSING SCHOOL EDUCATOR                        1998

*FANNIE GASTON-JOHANSSON (1938–)* became the first black female full professor with tenure at Johns Hopkins University School of Nursing. Gaston-Johansson held the Elsie M. Lawler Endowed Chair and directed international and extramural affairs at the nursing school, retiring in 2014.

## 2000          EXPERIMENTAL HEART PATIENT

The first person to have a new type of miniature heart pump successfully implanted temporarily was *LOIS SPILLER (1948?–)*. On approval of the U.S. Food and Drug Administration, her physicians inserted the battery-operated heart pump, the Jarvik 2000 left ventricular device.

## EXPERIMENTAL ROBOT PATIENT                    2000

*KIMBERLY BRIGGS* made medical history after a robot removed her gallbladder at Henrico Doctors' Hospital in Richmond, Virginia. This was the first operation in the United States performed by the da Vinci Surgical System, a recently approved system.

## 2019    EXPERIMENTAL SICKLE CELL PATIENT

*VICTORIA GRAY (1985–)* was the first patient identified publicly for being in a study testing the use of CRISPR to treat sickle cell disease.

The success of the landmark treatment for sickle cell disease may remain unknown for some time.

# HISTORY-MAKING SURGEON GENERAL  2019

*NADINE BURKE HARRIS (1975–)* was named California's first black surgeon general.

# 2020        HISTORY-MAKING IMMUNOLOGIST

Kizzmekia "Kizzy" Corbett

*KIZZMEKIA "KIZZY" (SHANTA) CORBETT (1986–)*, a viral immunologist, was the first black woman to lead coronavirus vaccine research, resulting in an approved vaccine to stop the virus. In March 2020, her team began first-stage trials of a COVID-19 vaccine, the first of its kind in the world. Corbett became the lead scientist and research fellow with the National Institutes of Health in a joint program with the biotechnology company Moderna to develop a vaccine to prevent infection with the virus that causes COVID-19. By late January 2020, health care workers began vaccinating specific groups throughout the nation, then moved to other groups to help vaccinate America. Corbett joined the NIH Vaccine Research Center in 2014 as a postdoctoral fellow. Two other types of coronaviruses had caused widespread outbreaks that were now under control. The success in controlling those viruses helped to set the path for controlling spread of the newly emerged virus. Anthony Fauci, the infectious disease expert and chief medical advisor to President Joe Biden, confirmed Corbett's pioneering achievement by reporting, "The first thing you might want to say to my African American brothers and sisters is that the vaccine that you're going to be taking was developed by an African American woman." Regrettably, skepticism came from some members of the black community who remembered the history of racism in medical research and health care on the part of the federal government in programs like the Tuskegee syphilis experiment on black people conducted from 1932 to 1972.

# Sports

As Africans came to America, men and women came not empty-handed but rather with skills and abilities that entertained their masters and gave them some self-pleasures. Some of the athletic contests that the enslaved entered were connected to religious ceremonies. Such contests were sometimes rites of passage, and other times simply entertainment for onlookers. Women rarely had an opportunity to demonstrate their talents, and when they did, they were engaged in folk games, dance, and a few athletic events.

Boxing has long been a popular sport and is said to have had a more profound effect on the lives of African Americans than any other sport. Although women's boxing was a growing sport in the late 1800s that was about as popular as men's boxing, its heyday was reached in the 1910s and 1920s before falling into disfavor in the United States. The sport for women resurfaced in the 1970s, however, and began to boom by the 1990s. Black women started obtaining licenses to box in 1975, but it was not until recent times that black women boxers became popular with fans of the sport. They included pioneers Laila Ali and Jacqui Frazier-Lyde, daughters of two great black boxing greats—Muhammad Ali and Joe Frazier. Free and enslaved blacks also engaged in the sport of horseracing, and the best jockeys and horse trainers were black. In the late 1800s, the first jockey of any race to win the Kentucky Derby was black. Black jockeys were replaced by white jockeys or men of another race, but not women.

Barrier-breaking black women were gradually seen in other sports activities, including baseball, tennis, golf, track and field, skating, and swimming. Women became players, coaches, referees, sports administrators, and sports announcers. Both college sports and Title IX of the Civil Rights Act had a major impact on the development of women's sports by removing gender and racial biases in that field. In 1953 Mamie "Peanut" Johnson became the only woman to pitch in baseball's Negro leagues. On the college scene, legendary C. Vivian Stringer excelled as a women's basketball coach and became the first to advance to the Final Four from two different colleges. Black women have excelled in professional basketball by becoming star players, coaches, and team owners.

We also see black women distinguishing themselves in golf. In 1935 Ora Washington was the first black woman to win seven consecutive titles in the American Tennis Association. In 1956 Althea Gibson became the first black to win a major tennis title when she won the women's singles in the French Open and the next year the Wimbledon, and the first black to win a major U.S. national championship. The Williams sisters—Serena and Venus—brought international attention to the game by becoming firsts together and individually. The team was the first to succeed in the U.S. Open in New York and the first to win Olympic gold in doubles at the 2000 Olympic Games. They are the first sister duo in which each has won a Grand Slam championship.

Sports administration reached a new high when Anita Lucette DeFranz became the first black elected to the Olympic Committee's executive board. Black women sports stars continue to excel in Olympic Games by winning medals, beginning in 1948, when Alice Coachman Davis was the first black woman Olympic gold medal winner in track and field and the only American to win gold in the Olympics. Notable among Olympic winners is Wilma Glodean Rudolph, an early polio survivor who became the first woman to win three gold medals in a single Olympics. Rudolph and the Tigerbelles of Tennessee State University brought international acclaim to black women in Olympic Games.

Gymnast Simone Biles brought distinguished performance to gymnastics. In 2016 she was the first American to win Olympic gold in the vault competition, becoming the first gymnast—male or female—to do so, and the first to win four gold medals in a single Olympics. Her career successes enabled Biles to become the world's greatest gymnast. Black women set records in the 2020 Olympics, too, including Allyson Felix, who won her 11th gold medal and was named the most decorated track and field athlete in Olympic history.

The future of African American women firsts in sports is being determined by younger stars who have emerged, among them Cori "Coco" Gauff, the youngest competitor to qualify at the All England Club in the professional era. She upset five-time Wimbledon singles champion Venus Williams.

## AMERICAN TENNIS ASSOCIATION WINNER                    1917

*LUCY DIGGS SLOWE (1885–1937)* of Baltimore and Tally Holmes of Washington, D.C. won the women's and men's singles, respectively, to become the first players to win the all-black American Tennis Association (ATA) championships. The matches, the first ATA Nationals, were held in August this year at Druid Hill Park in Baltimore. Slowe also became the first black woman national champion in any sport.

Lucy Slowe

## 1932    PIONEERING OLYMPIC COMPETITORS

The first black women selected for Olympic competition were *LOUISE STOKES (1913–1978)* and *TIDYE PICKETT (1914–1986)*. They qualified in the 100-meter race for showpiece games held in Los Angeles. Two white athletes replaced them, but later on Stokes qualified for the 1936 Olympics.

## PIONEERING TENNIS CHAMPION                    1935

The first black woman to win seven consecutive titles in the American Tennis Association (ATA) was *ORA (MAE) WASHINGTON (1898?–1971)*. She began her career in 1924. During 12 undefeated years, she used her blazing pace to upset many of the ATA's top-seeded stars. She remained undefeated until 1936, when she became ill during play and lost the match, but she regained the championship in 1937.

Ora Washington

Originals! Black Women Breaking Barriers

## 1937   HBCU TRACK AND FIELD CHAMPIONS

The women's track team of **TUSKEGEE INSTITUTE** (now University) was the first black team to win the National AAU women's track and field championship. Coached by Christine Evans Petty, Lulu Hymes sparked the team by winning the long jump, taking second place in the 50-meter dash, and helping the 400-meter relay team place second.

## OLYMPIC MEDAL WINNER                1948

**AUDREY "MICKEY" PATTERSON-TYLER (1926–1996)** became the first black woman from the United States to win a bronze medal. Competing in the Olympic Games in London, she placed third in the 200-meter race.

## 1948                OLYMPIC GOLD MEDALIST

**ALICE COACHMAN (DAVIS) (1923–2014)** was the first black woman Olympic gold medal winner in track and field and the only American woman to win a gold medal in the 1948 Olympics in London. She took the gold for the high jump and set an Olympic record that held until two Olympiads later.

## "BIG MO" JOINS AAU                    1953

The first black American woman to make the national Amateur Athletic Union (AAU) women's basketball team was **MISSOURI "BIG MO" ARLEDGE (1935–2020)** of Philander Smith College in Arkansas. In 1955 she also became the first black woman All-American basketball player.

## 1953                NEGRO LEAGUES PITCHER

**MAMIE "PEANUT" JOHNSON (1935–2017)** was the only woman to pitch in baseball's Negro leagues. The 5-foot-4-inch athlete weighed less than 120 pounds but had a strong right arm and a competitive spirit. Her nickname came from an opposing player who said that she looked no bigger than a peanut when she took the mound. She played with the Indianapolis Clowns but had a brief professional career that ended before she was 20 years old. In 1992 the film *A League of Their Own* accurately portrayed the All-American Girls Professional Baseball League as composed of all white women. No black women were allowed tryouts.

## BARRIER-BREAKING NEGRO LEAGUE PLAYER                        1953

Second baseman ***MARCENIA LYLE (TONI) STONE (1921–1996)*** joined the Negro League's Indianapolis Clowns as the first woman to play as a regular on a big-league professional baseball team.

## 1956          BARRIER-BREAKING GOLF PLAYER

The first black American to play in an integrated women's amateur golf championship was ***ANN GREGORY (1912–1990)***.

## BARRIER-BREAKING TENNIS WINNER          1956

***ALTHEA GIBSON (1927–2003)*** became the first black to win a major tennis title when she won the women's singles in the French Open on May 26. She won the Wimbledon championship the next year on July 6, 1957, when she also captured the women's singles, becoming the first black to win these honors. Gibson defended her Wimbledon championship successfully in 1958. She became the first black to win a major U.S. national championship on September 8, 1957, when she defeated Louise Brough at Forest Hills to win the women's singles.

Althea Gibson

## 1956   PIONEERING OLYMPIC GAMES COACH

***NELL CECILIA JACKSON (1929–1988)*** was head coach of the U.S. women's track and field team for the Olympic Games held in Melbourne, Australia, becoming the first black person to serve as head coach of an Olympic team. In 1972 she was head coach again, for the Olympic Games held in Munich, Germany.

# WILMA (GLODEAN) RUDOLPH

## (1940–1994)

Record-setting Olympic Gold Medalist

Wilma (Glodean) Rudolph overcame great odds in 1960 to become the first woman to win three track gold medals in a single Olympics. When she was four years old, she was diagnosed with polio, which left her paralyzed in the left leg and unable to walk well until age ten. While a student at Tennessee State University in Nashville, Rudolph was a member of the famed Tigerbelles and became well known for her running technique and scissoring stride. She ran in the 100-meter, 200-meter, and relay, becoming also the first black woman winner of the 200-meter. After taking a bronze medal as a member of the women's 4 × 100-meter relay team at the Melbourne Olympics in 1956, Rudolph became the first black woman to win the Sullivan Award (1961). Rudolph was one of five athletes and the only track star honored in June 1993 at the first annual National Sports Awards held in Washington, D.C. Rudolph grew up in Clarksville, Tennessee, and for years had to endure weekly visits to Nashville for therapy and daily massages at home. She wore a steel brace from the time she was five years old until she was 11 and did not enter school until she was seven years old, when she was allowed to enter at the second-grade level. By the time she entered seventh grade, she was ready to begin her sports odyssey, and she began by playing basketball. As a sophomore, Rudolph ran in five different events in 20 races and won all of them. Then she lost every event at a meet held at Tuskegee Institute (Alabama). Shortly after the meet, she went to Tennessee State's summer track camp, and when the team went to the National AAU meet in Philadelphia, Rudolph won all of the nine events she entered. From there it was on to the 1956 Olympics.

## CHANGE-MAKING PROFESSIONAL GOLFER                                         1964

**ALTHEA GIBSON (1927–2003)** became the first black woman to play on the Ladies' Professional Golf Association tour. She is best known, however, for her achievements in professional tennis.

## 1968                    OLYMPIC TRACK AND FIELD COMPETITOR

**WYOMIA TYUS (1945–)**, the most successful U.S. woman track and field Olympic athlete, was the first athlete, male or female, to win an Olympic sprint title twice. She won a gold medal for the 100-meter run at the 1964 Olympics in Tokyo and a silver medal for the 4 × 100-meter relay at the same event. In 1968 she won the gold medal for the 100-meter run and the 4 × 100-meter relay in Mexico City. She set an Olympic and world record in the 100-meter run (the second time she had set a world record in the event) and helped set an Olympic and world record of 42.8 seconds in the latter event.

Wyomia Tyus

## OLYMPIC GOLD MEDAL WINNER                                      1968

**MADELINE MANNING (1948–)** was the first black woman to win a gold medal for the 800-meter race in the Olympics with an Olympic record time of 2 minutes and 0.9 seconds. In the 1972 games in Munich, she won a silver for the women's 4 × 400-meter relay.

## 1969              NATIONAL FENCING CHAMPION

When she was only 17 years old and still in high school, **RUTH WHITE (1951–)** became the youngest woman and the first black American to win a national fencing championship. She held four national titles. In 1972 she was a member of the U.S. Olympic team.

## FIRST LACROSSE TEAM COMPETITOR     1969

The first black American women to compete on the U.S. National Lacrosse team was *TINA SLOAN-GREEN (1944–).*

## 1969          OLYMPIC COMMITTEE BOARD MEMBER

The first black American to sit on the U.S. Olympic Committee's board of directors was *NELL CECILIA JACKSON (1929–1988)*. In 1977 Jackson was inducted into the Black Athletes Hall of Fame in recognition of her achievements as track star and sports administrator.

## FIRST BLACK WOMAN JOCKEY          1971

*CHERYL WHITE (1953–2019)* became the first black woman jockey on June 15, at Thistledown Racetrack in Cleveland, Ohio. She was the first black woman to ride on a U.S. commercial track.

## 1972   FIRST COMPETITOR IN FIVE OLYMPICS

In 1972 *WILLYE BROWN WHITE [WHYTE] (1939–2007)* became the first black woman to compete in five Olympic events. She won a silver medal for the long jump in 1956 and another silver for the 400-meter relay in 1964. White won the AAU long jump title ten times and the indoor once. A native of Greenwood, Mississippi, she was the first black inducted into the Mississippi Hall of Fame in 1982.

## NATIONAL DART CHAMPION          1972

*ADELE NUTTER*, the only black woman in dart championship play this year, became the first black U.S. dart champion. She was a founder and charter member of the American Dart Organization.

# 1977     JUNIOR OLYMPIC GYMNASTICS COMPETITOR

***DONNA LYNN MOSLEY (1964?–)*** became the first black American to compete in the U.S. Gymnastics Federation Junior Olympic Nations, at age 13.

# NBA DRAFTEE     1977

***LOUISA HARRIS (1955–)*** became the first black American woman drafted by a National Basketball Association team.

# 1980     BOXING COMMISSIONER

The first black woman commissioner of the Michigan State Boxing Commission was ***HIAWATHA KNIGHT (1929–2014)***.

# MAJOR BASEBALL ADMINISTRATOR     1980

***SHARON RICHARDSON JONES*** was named director of outreach activities for the Oakland Athletics, becoming the first black woman in major league baseball administration.

# 1981     GYMNASTICS CHAMPION

The first black woman to win the United States Gymnastics Championship was ***DIANNE DURHAM (1968–2021)***, who won the title for two consecutive years. The first internationally ranked black American female gymnast, she seemed a sure medalist for the 1984 Olympics but injured herself just before the competition.

# PARADE BASKETBALL TEAM MEMBER     1984

***CHERYL D. MILLER (1964–)*** was the first player, male or female, to be named to the Parade All-American basketball team for four consecutive years. She played in the 1984 Olympics in Los Angeles when the Americans won their first gold medal in women's basketball.

## 1984   PIONEERING HARLEM GLOBETROTTER

*LYNETTE WOODARD (1959–)* of the University of Kansas was the first woman to become a member of the Harlem Globetrotters. She had earlier been the first woman chosen for the NCAA Top Five award.

## DETERMINED WORLD TEAM ICE SKATER                                            1984

*DEBI (DEBRA) THOMAS (1967–)* was the first black skater on a World Team in 1984, and in 1986 she was the first black woman to hold United States and world figure skating championships. She first made history in France in 1983 at the Criterium International du Sucre, where she was the first black person to win an international senior-level singles competition. Thomas was the first black woman to make the U.S. Olympic figure-skating team. Her 1988 bronze medal was the first medal won by a black athlete in any Winter Olympics sport.

## 1984              OLYMPIC GOLD MEDAL WINNER

*VALERIE (ANN) BRISCO-HOOKS (1960–)* won a gold medal and set world records at the 1984 Olympics in Los Angeles for both the 200-meter run and the 400-meter run and became the first athlete to win at both distances.

Valerie Brisco-Hooks

## OLYMPIC GAMES REFEREE/JUDGE                          1984

The first black referee and judge for the Olympic Games, one of four Americans, was *CARMEN WILLIAMSON (1925–2020)*.

## 1986      PIONEERING ATHLETIC DIRECTOR

**HARRIET HAMILTON** of Fisk University became the first black woman athletic director in the Southern Intercollegiate Athletic Conference.

## PIONEERING COACH FOR MEN          1987
## AND WOMEN'S

**KAREN C. KEITH (1957–)** of Boston College was the first woman of any race to coach men's and women's teams at a major institution.

## 1988      "FLO-JO" OLYMPIC MEDALIST

**FLORENCE DELOREZ GRIFFITH-JOYNER (1959–1998)** was the first American woman to win four medals in track and field at a single Olympics, in Seoul, South Korea. She won gold in the 100- and 200-meter dashes and the 400-meter relays. She also won silver in the 1600-meter relay. Known affectionately by her fans as Flo-Jo, she made her first U.S. Olympic team in 1984 and finished second in the 200-meter sprint. By this time, she had begun growing the long fingernails that became one of her trademarks; the fingernails cost her a place on the 1984 sprint relay team.

## LONG JUMPER WINS IN OLYMPICS          1988

**JACQUELINE "JACKIE" JOYNER-KERSEE (1962–)** was the first U.S. woman to win the Olympic long jump and the first athlete in 64 years to win both a multievent competition and an individual event in one Olympics. She won a silver medal for the heptathlon at the 1984 Olympics and a gold medal in 1988 for the heptathlon, setting an Olympic and world record. This year she became the only woman to gain more than 7,000 points in the heptathlon. She became the first woman ever to repeat as Olympic heptathlon champion in 1992 when she won the two-day, seven-event marathon.

Jackie Joyner-Keress

Originals! Black Women Breaking Barriers

# 1988    FIRST BLACK OLYMPIC MEDALIST
# IN TENNIS

Zina Garrison

**ZINA (LYNNA) GARRISON (JACKSON) (1963–)** won a gold medal in doubles and a bronze in the singles in the Olympics held in Seoul, South Korea, becoming the first black Olympic winner in tennis. She was also the first black to rank in the top ten on the women's professional tour. She has been victorious in singles, doubles, and mixed doubles both in the United States and abroad. In 1990 Garrison was the first black woman to reach the finals in Wimbledon (or any other tennis Grand Slam competition) since Althea Gibson won the championship in 1957.

# BASEBALL'S WOMAN EXECUTIVE    1990

The first black woman assistant general manager of the Boston Red Sox was **ELAINE C. WEDDINGTON (1963–)**, on January 26, 1990. She also became the first black woman executive in a professional baseball organization.

# 1990    PIONEERING EQUESTRIAN
# TEAM MEMBER

**DONNA MARIE CHEEK (1963–)** became the first black member of the U.S. equestrian team. In the same year, she was the first and only equestrian to be inducted into the Women's Sports Hall of Fame.

# PIONEERING ATHLETIC DIRECTOR    1992

**VIVIAN L. FULLER (1954–)** was named athletic director at Northeastern Illinois University, becoming the first black woman to hold that post in Division I of the National Collegiate Athletic Association.

# 1992 GYMNAST OLYMPIC TEAM CONTESTANTS

The first black women gymnasts to compete on a U.S. Olympic team were **DOMINIQUE MARGAUX DAWES (1976–)** and **ELIZABETH ANNA (BETTY) OKINO (1975–)**, who were in the games in Barcelona, Spain.

## OLYMPIC COMMITTEE BOARD MEMBER 1992

**ANITA LUCETTE DeFRANTZ (1952–)**, president of the Athletic Foundation of Los Angeles and elected to the International Olympic Committee (IOC) in 1987, was the first black elected to the IOC executive board. She served as vice president of the board in 1997, the first woman accorded this honor. In 2001 she became the first woman and the first black to run for the presidency of the IOC. DeFrantz won a bronze medal for rowing eights in the Montreal Olympics in 1976, where she was the first black American to compete for the United States in Olympic rowing.

## 1993 RECORD-SETTING BASKETBALL COACH

**C. VIVIAN STRINGER (1948–)** became the first woman's basketball coach to advance to the Final Four from two different colleges. In 1982 she led Cheyney State College to the NCAA tournament, and in 1993 she led the University of Iowa Hawkeyes. Cheyney State made it to the final game, but it lost to Louisiana Tech; Iowa lost to Vanderbilt in the semifinals.

C. Vivian Stringer

## WORLD CUP TEAM MEMBER 1993

**CHERIE GREER (1972?–)** was named to her first World Cup team in 1993, becoming the first black and the youngest player named to a women's World Cup team. The team won the title that year. Greer was named to her second World Cup team in 1997 and led the U.S. women's team to its third straight World Cup title.

## 1994      GAME-WINNER IN LADIES SINGLES

Lori McNeil

**LORI MICHELLE McNEIL (1963–)** defeated five-time Wimbledon champion and number-one-ranked Steffi Graf in the first round of the Ladies' Singles held on the Centre Court. Until then, no reigning woman champion had lost in the first round to an unseeded opponent, making McNeil the first woman to accomplish this feat. It was McNeil's second straight victory over Graf. McNeil turned professional in 1986 and was primarily known as a doubles player until she reached the Wimbledon quarterfinals in singles in 1986 and later defeated Chris Evert in the U.S. Open singles quarterfinals in 1987.

## GYMNASTICS CHAMPIONSHIP           1994
## WINNER

**DOMINIQUE DAWES (1976–)** became the first black gymnast to sweep all five events in the National Gymnastics Championships held in Nashville, Tennessee, in August. She was the first black woman gymnast to win a national championship and the first woman to win a sweep since 1969, when Joyce Schroeder claimed the honor. She won four individual gold medals and a fifth for the All-Around title. Dawes returned to the Olympic Games in Atlanta in 1996, where she helped the U.S. women's team win its first Olympic gold medal.

Dominique Dawes

## 1995      WOMEN'S BASKETBALL COACH

**BERNADETTE LOCKE-MATTOX (1958–)** was named head coach of the women's basketball team at the University of Kentucky, the first black woman to hold that post.

## WOMEN'S SPORTS COMMISSION PRESIDENT                    1995

*WENDY HILLIARD (1960–)*, director of amateur sports for the New York City Sports Commission, became the first black elected president of the Women's Sports Foundation in that city.

## 1996          OLYMPIC GOLD–WINNING TEAM

Sheryl Swoopes

The first sportswoman to get her own signature line of athletic footwear was *SHERYL (DENISE) SWOOPES (1971–)*, when Nike introduced "Air Swoopes" for women. She also tried out and earned a place on the U.S. women's national basketball team; she was with the team when it won a gold medal in the 1996 Olympic Games. Swoopes joined the Houston Comets in the newly organized Women's National Basketball Association in 1997. She was the first woman in WNBA history to record a triple-double.

## FOUR-TIME OLYMPIAN IN BASKETBALL 1996

*TERESA EDWARDS (1964–)* became America's only four-time Olympian in basketball—in 1984, 1988, 1992, and 1996. She has won 12 international medals, including nine golds. USA Basketball named her the Female Athlete of the Year in 1996 for the third time. She was at the time the only three-time winner, male or female, of this award.

## 1996          AWARD-WINNING BASKETBALL PLAYER

The first woman to receive the Most Courageous Award from the United States Basketball Writers Association was *CORI CARSON (1971–)*, a junior guard for Marymount University and a Division III All-American. She had overcome a serious liver ailment.

# BOLD BLACK WOMAN REFEREE                         1997

The first black woman to serve as referee in the NBA was **VIOLET PALMER (1964–)**. The only other woman official in the league at this time was Dee Kanter; together they were the first two women officials in any men's professional sports league.

# 1997    JUNIOR FIGURE SKATING CHAMPION

**ANDREA GARDINER (1981–)** won the junior women's title at the U.S. Figure Skating Championships on February 13, becoming the first black to hold that title. Her performance included four triple jumps.

# SULLIVAN AWARD WINNER                         1998

**CHAMIQUE HOLDSCLAW (1977–)**, a member of the University of Tennessee–Knoxville Lady Vols, became the first women's basketball player to win the Sullivan Award, given annually to the top amateur athlete in the nation. She was named Associated Press Player of the Year for 1998 and 1999, becoming the first to repeat the title. She was also the first three-time All-American.

Chamique Holdsclaw

# 1999    AWARD-WINNING WNBA PLAYER

The Women's National Basketball Association's first All-Star Game was held at Madison Square Garden before a sell-out crowd. **LISA DESHAUN LESLIE (1972–)** led the Western Conference to victory over the East and was named the first Most Valuable Player in WNBA All-Star history.

# HISTORY-MAKING TENNIS SISTERS     1999

**SERENA WILLIAMS (1981–)** and her sister **VENUS EBONY STARR WILLIAMS (1980–)** became the first black women's team to succeed at the U.S. Open on September 12 in New York City. They won the doubles title 4–6, 6–1, 6–4, defeating Chandra Rubin of America and Sandrine Testud of France. The Williams sisters had won the French Open championship in June and the Wimbledon women's doubles title in July, making this their third Grand Slam doubles title. They took the gold medal in doubles at the 2000 Olympic Games in Sydney, Australia, winning 6–1, 6–1 in straight sets. They were the first sisters to win Olympic gold in doubles, and they extended their doubles winning streak to 22 matches. Inevitably, the time came when the sisters would have to play each other for a title. Several months prior to the Open, Venus defeated Serena in the WTA Lipton Championships match. It was the first time in 115 years that sisters had played each other for the title. In 2001 Venus defeated Serena again in the U.S. Open women's finals match. It was the first time two black players had faced each other in a Grand Slam singles match. The Williams sisters repeated their finals match for the 2002 U.S. Open; this time, Serena won. They are the first sister duo in which each has won a Grand Slam championship. To date, no player has ever beaten both sisters in the same Grand Slam match. In 2000 Venus won the Wimbledon 2000

Serena (left) and Venus Williams

Tennis Championship to become the first black woman winner since Althea Gibson in 1957 and 1958. She also won the U.S. Open Championship. Venus won Olympic gold medals in singles and doubles in the summer Olympic Games held in Sydney, Australia, in 1999, becoming the first black woman to achieve this honor. Serena was her doubles partner. She also signed a multiyear, $40 million contract with Reebok in what is believed to be the most lucrative deal for a woman athlete. In 2001 she won both the Wimbledon title and the U.S. Open title, giving her back-to-back titles in two of tennis's most prestigious events.

## 1999     NATIONAL BASKETBALL CHAMPIONSHIP WINNER

**CAROLYN PECK (1966–)** became the first black woman to coach a team to the women's NCAA national championship. She coached the Purdue Boilermakers to a 62–45 win over Duke University and to its first NCAA championship this year. As Purdue's women's basketball coach, she was the first woman to receive the New York Athletic Club's Winged Foot Award.

## TIMELY U.S. OPEN WINNER     1999

The first black woman to win the U.S. Open since 1958, when tennis pioneer Althea Gibson won, was **SERENA WILLIAMS (1981–)**. She beat number-one-ranked Martina Hingis of Switzerland 6–3, 7–6. Playing at first somewhat in the shadow of older sister Venus, Serena was the first sister to win a major championship. She was ranked number 4 in the world after her victory. She had won three titles earlier in the year. In 1998 she had won the mixed doubles title at Wimbledon. In 2012 she became a four-time winner of the U.S. Open and won gold in women's singles at the London Olympics.

## 2000     LPGA HONORARY MEMBER

**RENEE POWELL (1946–)** was the first black woman elected as an honorary member of the Ladies' Professional Golf Association. She is the only black woman to hold Class A membership in both the LPGA and PGA of America. Powell became the only club professional at Clearview Golf Club, at the course designed, built, and owned by her father, William Powell, in 1946.

## PIONEERING TRACK AND FIELD COACH

**2000**

*MARCIA FLETCHER* became the first black head coach of the women's track and field programs at Clemson University in South Carolina. She was Clemson's first black head coach in any sport.

**2000**

## RECORD-SETTING BASKETBALL COACH

*C. VIVIAN STRINGER (1948–)* became the first black woman and the third woman's basketball coach in Division I history to record 600 victories.

## WORLD'S FASTEST WOMAN

**2000**

Called the "fastest woman in the world," *MARION (LOIS) JONES (1975–)* won three gold medals and two bronze medals at the Sydney, Australia, Olympics and became the first woman to win five track medals in one Olympiad. The Associated Press named her Female Athlete of the Year for 2000. In 1998 she became the first woman since 1948 to win the 100-meter, 200-meter, and long jump, when she participated in the USA Outdoor Championships.

Marion Jones

**2000**

## GOAL-KEEPING SOCCER TEAM MEMBER

*BRIANA SCURRY (1971–)*, the only African American starter for the 1999 champion U.S. women's soccer team, became the first goalkeeper of any race or gender to play in 100 international games.

## BLACK BELT WORLD TITLE-WINNER

**2001**

*LAUREN BANKS (1990–)*, a second-degree black belt, became the youngest and the only black belt in the American Taekwondo

## LAILA ALI

## (1977–)

**"Madam Butterfly" Boxer Stings**

Laila Ali, also known as "Madame Butterfly," and "Laila 'She Bee Stingin' Ali," scored a majority decision in a 2001 fight with Jacqui Frazier-Lyde on June 8 at the Turning Stone Casino in Verona, New York. This was the first pay-for-view boxing match between two black women. By all accounts, the fight lived up to hopes and expectations, with both women slugging it out. Although both women were considered highly talented boxers, the pre-fight publicity and anticipation probably was due as much to their lineage as to their talent. Each is the daughter of a legendary boxer— Muhammad Ali and Joe Frazier—and the fathers had their own rivalry and contests.

Association (ATA), across all black belt girls divisions 8 through 16, to win a world title, which she did in 1999, 2000, and 2001.

## 2001        BASKETBALL COACH FOR MEN AND WOMEN

The first woman to coach a men's professional basketball team was **STEPHANIE READY (1975–)**. She helped break ground as an assistant for Coppin State's men's team for the previous two years and later left to become assistant coach of the Greenville Groove of the National Basketball Development League.

## HBCU GOLF TEAM                                2001

The **JACKSON STATE UNIVERSITY** women's golf team became the first women's golf team from a historically black college to receive an invitation to the NCAA regional championship. They played in the 21-team NCAA East Regional in Chapel Hill, North Carolina, in March.

## 2002                    FATHER-DAUGHTER BOXING CHAMPIONS

**JACQUI FRAZIER-LYDE (1961–)** beat Suzette Taylor at the Pennsylvania Convention Center in Philadelphia and won the Women's International Boxing Association (WIBA) light heavyweight belt. Her father, Joe Frazier, also won the bout during his career; thus, Frazier-Lyde's win marked the first time a father and daughter held boxing championships.

## OLYMPICS BOBSLED BRAKEMAN          2002
## WINNER

Bobsled brakeman **VONETTA FLOWERS (1973–)** became the first black American athlete to win a gold medal in a Winter Olympics, on February 19. She was also the first Alabamian to win a medal at the Winter Olympics. Held in Park City, Utah, this was a double-barrel historic event in that it was also the inaugural women's Olympic competition in the bobsled race. The medal was the first for the United States in the sport since 1948.

## 2002                    WTA TOP SPOT WINNER

**VENUS (EBONE STARR) WILLIAMS (1980–)** achieved the top spot in the Women's Tennis Association's (WTA) world ranking, becoming the first black player with a number-one rating since 1975, when Arthur Ashe held that honor. In June 2002 Serena Williams was ranked number two in the WTA Tour rankings, making the sisters the first siblings to reach a career high of 1-2. Playing in her third career Grand Slam, Serena defeated Venus Williams in the French Open women's singles finals on Saturday, June 8, 7–5, 6–3, to win the French Open.

Venus Williams

## CANCER SURVIVOR SKIS         2007
## TO NORTH POLE

**BARBARA HILLARY (1931–2019)**, then 75 years old and a cancer survivor, completed a trek to the North Pole on skis and was believed to be the first black woman to accomplish this feat. She was one of the oldest people to reach the world's northernmost point.

## 2007      PIONEERING COACH AT HARVARD

Tennis coach **TRACI GREEN (1979–)** became the first black woman to head any coaching staff for any Harvard University sport.

## KIDS WORLD CHAMPIONSHIP    2008
## MEMBER

**NAOMI MITCHELL (2000–)** became the youngest black golfer to win the U.S. Kids World Championship. This golf tournament is the largest competition for young golfers, ages 4 through 12.

## 2012      "FLYING SQUIRREL" GLIDES
## INTO OLYMPIC GOLD

Gabby Douglas

**GABRIELLE "GABBY" CHRISTINA VICTORIA DOUGLAS (1995–)**, 16-year-old gymnastic phenomenon and a member of the U.S. Women's Gymnastics team at the 2012 Summer Olympics held in London, became the first African American to win a gold medal in the women's all-around final competition. She was also the third straight American to win gymnastics' biggest prize at the Olympics. Douglas came away with two gold medals as she and her "Fierce Five" teammates won team gold two nights earlier. She became known as the "Flying Squirrel."

## BARRIER-BREAKING NASCAR DRIVER    2012

**SHAUNTIA LATRICE "TIA" NORFLEET (1986–)** was licensed as NASCAR's first black female driver. In August she made her NASCAR racing debut, racing as number 34. She achieved fame as a drag racing and stock car racing driver.

## 2015  BASKETBALL ASSOCIATION DIRECTOR

**MICHELE A. ROBERTS (1956–)** was elected executive director of the National Basketball Players Association, which made her the first woman to head a major professional sports union in North America.

## GOLD-WINNING OLYMPIC BOXER    2016

**CLARESSA SHIELDS (1995–)**, a middleweight boxing competitor, became the first black woman to win Olympic gold in boxing. She previously won gold in the 2015 Pan American Games in Toronto. In 2017 she became the WBC and IBF female super-weight champion, and in June 2018 she became the IBF female middleweight champion.

Claressa Shields

## 2016        SWIMMER GOES FOR GOLD

**SIMONE MANUEL (1996–)** was the first black woman to win an Olympic gold medal in the 100-meter freestyle individual swimming event in Rio de Janeiro, Brazil. She tied with Canadian Penny Oleksiak. She followed up with a silver medal in the 50-meter.

Simone Manuel

## OLYMPIC MEDAL SWEEP                                    2016

In a U.S. sweep during the Rio Olympics in 2016, **BRIANNA ROLLINS-McNEAL (1991–)** won the first gold for the United States in the 100-meter hurdle. Nia Ali won silver, and Kristi Castlin won the bronze.

## 2016        TRACK AND FIELD GOLD MEDALIST

**ALLYSON FELIX (1985–)** became the first American woman to win five gold medals in track and field competition. She won three golds at the 2012 Olympics in London and two more golds at the Rio Olympic Games in 2016.

Allyson Felix

## TREND-SETTING MUSLIM                           2016
## OLYMPIC ATHLETE

**IBTIHAJ MUHAMMAD (1985–)** changed the face of competitive fencing at the Olympics in Rio de Janeiro when she wore a hijab under her protective mask, becoming the first female athlete to wear the traditional Muslim covering at the Olympic Games.

## 2017     RECORD-SETTING PIT CREW MEMBER

**BREHANNA DAVIS (1994?–)** is said to have broken barriers when she became the first black woman pit crew member. In February 2018, she became a tire changer for Stephen Leicht's No. 55 Toyota in the Xfinity Series at Daytona Beach, hoping that one day she would become a member of a Cup team.

# SIMONE BILES

## (1997–)

### Olympic Gold Medalist

In 2016 gymnast **SIMONE BILES** was the first American woman to win gold in the vault competition, becoming the first American gymnast, male or female, to do so and the first to win four golds in a single Olympics. The diminutive Biles, who stands 4' 9" tall, made her first international appearance in 2013. In that year she became the first woman to hold a world title and win Olympic gold simultaneously. In August 2018 she won all four events at the U.S. Gymnastics Championship and four All-Around World titles, becoming the first woman of any race to win five national all-around titles. Biles won her 24th and 25th world championship medals in beam and floor during the October 2019 gymnastic world championship held in Stuttgart, Germany, which put her at the top of the all-time medal charts for the championship. She won five gold medals in one week during the competition. Earlier in the competition, she performed two signature moves now named after her: a simple dismount called the double-double (also known as "The Biles I") and the triple-double (or triple-twisting double, also known as "The Biles II"). Her earlier success at the competition enabled her to become the world's greatest gymnast ever, having won more gold medals than any male or female gymnast.

# HIGH-GOAL POLO RIDER                    2017

***SHARIAH HARRIS (1998?–)*** became the first black American woman to play high-goal polo, the top tier of polo in the United States. She was only 19 years old. Harris broke barriers in the wealthy, white, male-dominated sport that is often called "the sport of kings."

## 2017                 OLYMPIC SPEEDSKATING TEAM MEMBER

**MAAME BINEY (2000–)** became the first black woman to make the U.S. Olympic speedskating team. She cruised to victory in the first 500 final at the short track trials.

## FIRST SPORTS REPORTER                                          2017

**MARIA TAYLOR (1987–)**, often known as Maria Taylor Hyatt, became the first black female reporter for ESPN's College GameDay and ABC's Saturday Night Football. Due to her depth of knowledge, she has covered college football, college volleyball, and college baseball.

Maria Taylor

## 2017          PIONEERING SPORTS REPORTER

**KARA LAWSON (1981–)** became the first female analyst for a nationally televised NBA game. She spent the last two years as the primary television analyst for the NBA's Washington Wizards and has covered games on ESPN Radio.

## HBCU ATHLETIC DIRECTOR                              2018

**ETIENNE M. THOMAS** became the new director of athletics at Kentucky State University. She left her post at Kansas University to take over the Thoroughbreds' athletic program, and in doing so she became the first female from Power Five to lead athletics at a historically black college or university. "Power Five" is an economic term coined to refer to conferences approved by the National Collegiate Athletic Association in August 2014.

# 2018                        HALL OF FAME HONOREE

The first black woman inducted into the Athletic Trainers' Hall of Fame was **RENÉ REVIS SHINGLES**; it is an honor bestowed on only 317 of the 45,000 members. The Hall of Fame honors those who exemplify the mission of the National Athletic Trainers Association (NATA). In 1987 she became one of only 13 black women certified as an athletic trainer.

# HBCU TRIATHALON TEAM                        2018

**HAMPTON UNIVERSITY** added a varsity women's triathalon team to its athletic program to become the first historically black college or university (HBCU) to do so.

# 2019      CELTICS HISTORY–MAKING COACH

**KARA LAWSON (1981–)** became an assistant coach for the Boston Celtics, the team's first female to hold that post in its 73-year history.

# WIMBLEDON'S GRAND SLAM               2019
# SINGLES WINNER

Fifteen-year-old **CORI "COCO" GAUFF (2004–)** became the youngest competitor to qualify at the All England Club in the professional era. She seized the moment in her first Grand Slam singles match at Wimbledon and upset the five-time Wimbledon singles champion and her idol since childhood, Venus Williams, 6–4, 6–4. The Delray Beach, Florida, native was also the youngest U.S. Open junior girls finalist at age 13 and the second youngest French Open junior girls champion at age 14.

Cori "Coco" Gauff

Originals! Black Women Breaking Barriers

**2021**

# MOST DECORATED TRACK & FIELD SPRINTER

**ALLYSON FELIX (1985–)** became the most decorated athlete in track and field in Olympic history. Competing in the 2021 Olympics held in Tokyo, she crossed the finish line and won a gold in the $4 \times 400$-meter relay, bringing the total medals that she holds in track and field to 11. Felix made her Olympic debut in the 2004 Summer Games. She won three golds at the 2012 London Summer Olympics. In the Rio Olympic Games held in 2016, she became the first American woman to win five gold medals in the track and field competition. During her career, she has been honored with the Jesse Owens Award and the track and field ESPY Award.

# BARRIER-BREAKING GOALKEEPER          2021

**ASHLEIGH JOHNSON (1994–)**, goalkeeper, was the first black woman to win gold in water polo at the Summer Olympics held in Tokyo in 2021. Selected in 2016, she was the first black woman to join a U.S. Olympic water polo team. Johnson is regarded as the world's best athlete in this category.

**2021**

# RECORD-BREAKING HURDLER AND SPRINTER

When she completed in the 2020 Olympics, **SYDNEY McLAUGHLIN (1999–)** won a gold medal in the 400-meter relay and became the only woman of any race to break 52 seconds in hurdling and sprinting. She had a time of 51.46 seconds.

# PIONEERING OLYMPIC WRESTLER          2021

**TAMYRA MENSAH-STOCK (1992–)** became the first black female wrestler to win Olympic gold. She won in the women's 58-kilogram freestyle.

# FURTHER READING

Aasang, Nathan. *African-American Athletes.* Rev. ed. New York: Facts on File, 2010.

Abramson, Doris E. *Negro Playwrights in the American Theatre, 1925–1959.* New York: Columbia University Press, 1969.

Alford, Sterling G. *Famous First Blacks.* New York: Vantage, 1974.

Beasley, Delilah L. *The Negro Trailblazers in California.* Los Angeles: Times Mirror Printing and Binding House, 1919.

Bell, Janet Dewart. *Lighting the Fires of Freedom: African American Women in the Civil Rights Movement.* New York: The New Press, 2018.

Bontemps, Arna. *The Harlem Renaissance Remembered.* New York: Dodd, Mead, 1972.

Chalk, Oceania. *Pioneers of Black Sport.* New York: Dodd, Mead, 1975.

Clark, Patrick. *Sports Firsts.* New York: Facts on File, 1981.

*Contemporary Black Biography.* Vols. 1–149. Detroit: Cengage Learning, 2018.

Dates, Jannette L., and William Barlow, eds. *Split Image: African Americans in the Mass Media.* Washington: Howard University Press, 1990.

Finkelman, Paul, ed. *Encyclopedia of African American History 1896 to the Present.* 2 vols. New York: Oxford University Press, 2009.

Franklin, John Hope, and Evelyn Brooks Higginbotham. *From Slavery to Freedom.* 9th ed. New York: McGraw-Hill, 2011.

Gates, Henry Louis, and Evelyn Brooks Higginbotham, eds. *African American National Biography.* 8 vols. New York: Oxford University Press, 2008.

Haber, Louis. *Black Pioneers of Science and Invention.* New York: Harcourt, Brace and World, 1970.

Higginbotham, Evelyn Brooks. *Righteous Discontent: The Women's Movement in the Black Baptist Church 1880–1920.* Cambridge: Harvard University Press, 1993.

Hine, Darlene Clark., ed. *Black Women in America.* 2nd ed. 3 vols. New York: Oxford University Press, 2005.

Ifill, Gwen. *The Breakthrough: Politics and Race in the Age of Obama.* New York: Doubleday, 2009.

Johnson, James Weldon. *Black Manhattan.* New York: Knopf, 1981.

Kane, Joseph Nathan. *Famous First Facts.* New York: H. W. Wilson, 1981.

Lewis, David Levering. *When Harlem Was in Vogue.* New York: Knopf, 1981.

Lincoln, C. Eric, and Lawrence H. Mamiya. *The Black Church in the African American Experience.* Durham, NC: Duke University Press, 1990.

Logan, Rayford W., and Michael R. Winston, eds. *Dictionary of American Negro Biography.* New York: Norton, 1982.

Lowery, Charles D., and John F. Marszalek, eds. *Greenwood Encyclopedia of African American Civil Rights.* 2 vols. Westport, CT: Greenwood Press, 2003.

*The Negro Yearbook.* Various editions. Tuskegee, AL: Tuskegee Institute, 1913–1952.

*Notable American Women.* 3 vols. Cambridge: Belknap Press of Harvard University Press, 1971–1980.

Sadie, Stanley, ed. *The New Grove Dictionary of Music and Musicians.* 2nd ed. New York: Grove, 2001.

Shockley, Ann Allen. *Afro-American Women Writers 1746–1933.* Boston: G. K. Hall, 1988.

Smith, Jessie Carney. *Black Firsts.* 4th ed. Detroit: Visible Ink Press, 2021.

Smith, Jessie Carney, ed. *Encyclopedia of African American Business.* Updated and rev. ed. 2 vols. Santa Barbara, CA: Greenwood, 2018.

Smith, Jessie Carney, ed. *Notable Black American Women.* Detroit: Gale, 1992.

Smith, Jessie Carney, ed. *Notable Black American Women, Book II.* Detroit: Gale, 1996.

Smith, Jessie Carney, ed. *Notable Black American Women, Book III.* Detroit: Gale Research, 2003.

Walker, Juliet E. K. *Encyclopedia of African American Business History.* Westport, CT: Greenwood Press, 1999.

Warren, Wini. *Black Women Scientists in the United States.* Bloomington: Indiana University Press, 1999.

*Who's Who among African Americans.* Various editions. Detroit: Gale, 1998–2019.

# INDEX

Note: (ill.) indicates photos and illustrations.